AF426181

A COMPREHENSIVE GUIDE FOR MICROPROCESSOR AND MICROCONTROLLER

ELDHOSE P SIM

Copyright © Eldhose P Sim
All Rights Reserved.

This book has been self-published with all reasonable efforts taken to make the material error-free by the author. No part of this book shall be used, reproduced in any manner whatsoever without written permission from the author, except in the case of brief quotations embodied in critical articles and reviews.

The Author of this book is solely responsible and liable for its content including but not limited to the views, representations, descriptions, statements, information, opinions and references ["Content"]. The Content of this book shall not constitute or be construed or deemed to reflect the opinion or expression of the Publisher or Editor. Neither the Publisher nor Editor endorse or approve the Content of this book or guarantee the reliability, accuracy or completeness of the Content published herein and do not make any representations or warranties of any kind, express or implied, including but not limited to the implied warranties of merchantability, fitness for a particular purpose. The Publisher and Editor shall not be liable whatsoever for any errors, omissions, whether such errors or omissions result from negligence, accident, or any other cause or claims for loss or damages of any kind, including without limitation, indirect or consequential loss or damage arising out of use, inability to use, or about the reliability, accuracy or sufficiency of the information contained in this book.

Made with ❤ on the Notion Press Platform
www.notionpress.com

To My Family Members

Whose guidance, encouragement, and unwavering support have been instrumental in bringing this work to fruition. Your passion for knowledge and your belief in the power of education have been a constant source of inspiration. Thank you for being a mentor, a friend, and a source of strength throughout this journey.

With deep gratitude,

Authors

Contents

CHAPTER ONE

OVERVIEW OF MICROPROCESSORS

Microprocessor

A microprocessor is an electronic component that is used by a computer to do its work.

It is a central processing unit on a single integrated circuit chip containing millions of very small components including transistors, resistors, and diodes that work together.

A Microprocessor is a versatile chip, that is combined with memory and special-purpose chips and preprogrammed by a software.

It accepts digital data as i/p and processes it according to the instructions stored in the memory.

The microprocessor is a multipurpose, clock-driven, register-based, digital integrated circuit that accepts binary data as input, processes it according to instructions stored in its memory, and provides results (also in binary form) as output.

Intel® Core™ X-series Processors		Intel® Core™ X-series processors support powerful, high end desktops for amazing gaming and enthusiast performance.
Intel® Core™ i9 Processors		Delivering up to 10 unlocked cores for seamless 4K Ultra HD and 360 video, robust gameplay, and multitasking performance.
Intel® Core™ i7 Processors		This CPU packs the power of up to 8 cores for accelerated computing supporting high-end gaming, connectivity, and security.
Intel® Core™ i5 Processors		Experience exceptional performance for home and business PCs, with up to 6 cores for gaming, creativity and multitasking.
Intel® Core™ i3 Processors		These value-packed processors deliver outstanding performance for everyday tasks.

12th Generation Intel® Core™ i9 Processors

Product brief: 12th Gen Intel® Core™ desktop processors →

Product brief: Intel® Z690 Chipset →

2 Products   COMPARE ALL

Compare	Product Name	Status	Launch Date	# of Cores	Max Turbo Frequency	Cache	Processor Graphics ‡
	Intel® Core™ i9-12900KF Processor (30M Cache, up to 5.20 GHz)	Launched	Q4'21	16	5.20 GHz	30 MB Intel® Smart Cache	
	Intel® Core™ i9-12900K Processor (30M Cache, up to 5.20 GHz)	Launched	Q4'21	16	5.20 GHz	30 MB Intel® Smart Cache	Intel® UHD Graphics 770

Evolution of Microprocessor

Intel 4-bit microprocessor 4004 in 1971
8 bit microprocessor 8008 in 1972.
(These two couldn't survive due to the limitations in design and performance)
first general purpose 8 bit microprocessor 8080 in 1974.
Functionally complete 8 bit microprocessor-8085
Limitations -low speed, low memory addressing capability, limited number of general purpose registers and a less powerful instruction set.
16- bit microprocessor 8086.

NAME	YEAR	TRANSISTORS	DATA WIDTH	CLOCK SPEED
8080	1974	6,000	8 bits	2 MHz
8085	1976	6,500	8 bits	5 MHz
8086	1978	29,000	16 bits	5 MHz
8088	1979	29,000	8 bits	5 MHz
80286	1982	134,000	16 bits	6 MHz
80386	1985	275,000	32 bits	16 MHz
80486	1989	1,200,000	32 bits	25 MHz
PENTIUM	1993	3,100,000	32/64 bits	60 MHz
PENTIUM II	1997	7,500,000	64 bits	233 MHz
PENTIUM III	1999	9,500,000	64 bits	450 MHz
PENTIUM IV	2000	42,000,000	64 bits	1.5 GHz

8085 Microprocessor Arch

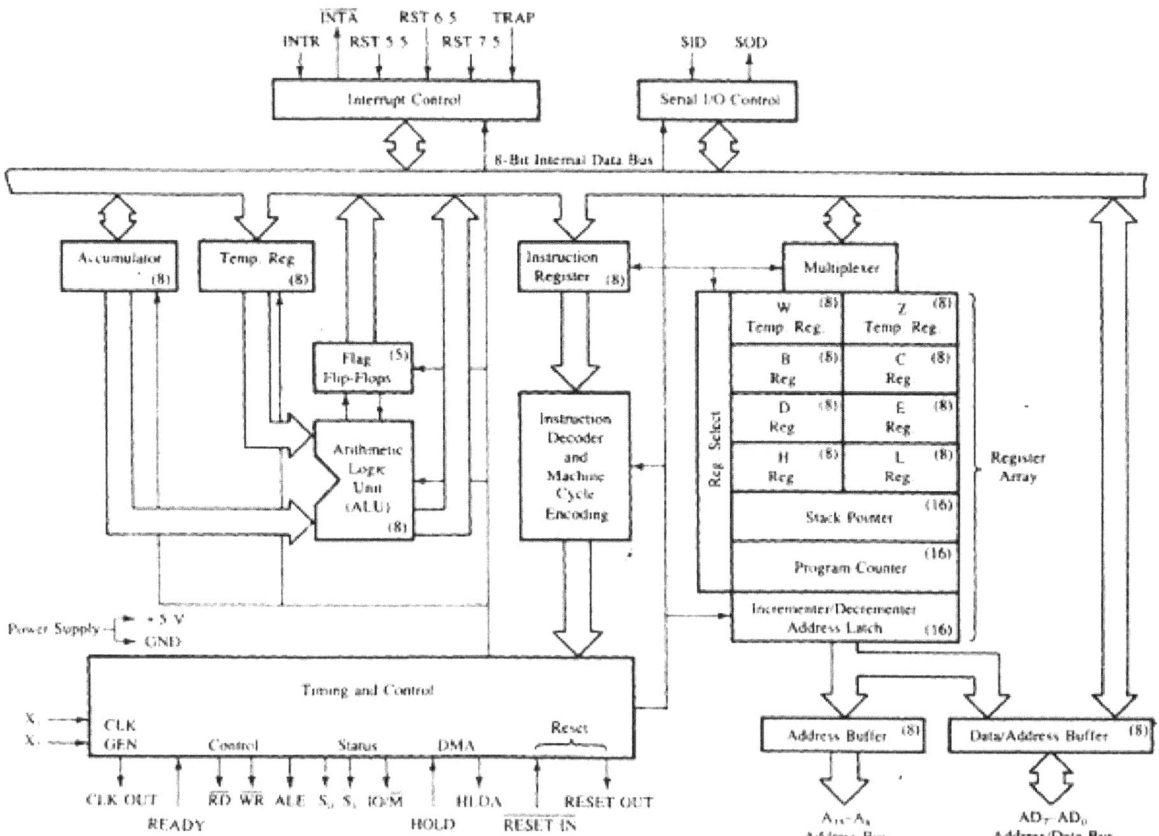

The 8085 Arch Includes

1. ALU
2. Timing & Control Unit
3. Instruction Register & Decoder
4. Register Array
5. Interrupt Control
6. Serial I/O Control

ALU

The ALU Preforms Arithmetic and Logic Operations, the operations performed by ALU of 8085 Includes Addition, Subtraction, Increment, Decrement ,Logical AND,OR, Exclusive OR, Compare, Complement, Left/Right Shift

The **accumulator and temporary registers** are used to hold the data during arithmetic/ logical operation

After the operation the result is stored in the accumulator and flags are set or reset according to the result of operation

After arithmetic or logical operation , if the result have even no, the parity flag is set, if operation carries any carry the CY Flag is set

Timing & Control Unit

It synchronizes all the Microprocessor operations with the clock and generate control signals for communication between MP and peripherals

Instruction Register and Decoder

When the instruction is fetched from the memory and its placed in instruction register

The instruction decoder , decodes the instruction and encode in to various machine cycles

Register Array

Apart from the accumulator , they are 6 general purpose registers (8bit) are (B,C,D,E,H) 8 BIT Registers used to store 16 bit data, they allow pairs are BC,DE,HL

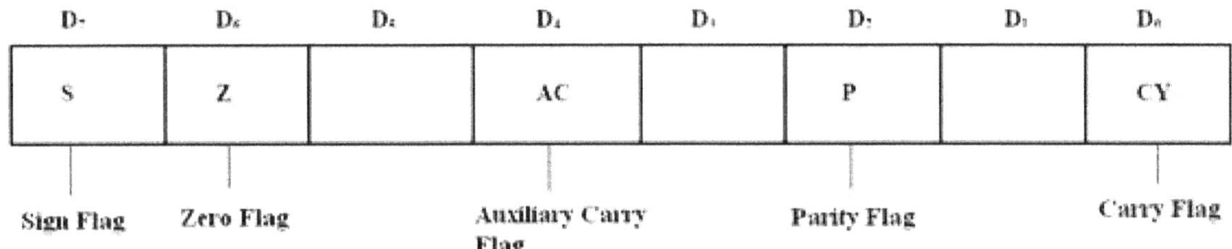

Five flags in 8085, they

1. Sign Flag (S)

2.Zero Flag (Z)

3. Auxiliary Carry Flag (AC)

4. Parity Flag (P)

5. Carry Flag (CY)

After ALU Operation, if Most significant bit (MSB) of result is 1, sign flag is set

After ALU Operation, if Result is zero the zero flag is set

Stack Pointer

It Holds the address of Stack Top

Stack is used to save the content of registers during the execution of the program

In an Arithmetic operation , when carry is generated by lower nibble, then AC Flag is set, its used for BCD Arithmetic

The temporary registers, TMP, W,Z cant be used by the programmer

Program Counter (PC)

It keep track of Program Execution

To execute the program , the starting address of program is loaded in to PC

The PC Send out address to fetch cycle and increment its content automatically , hence PC Holds the address of next byte instruction

8086 Architecture

The 8086 architecture supports

16-bit ALU.

Set of 16 bit registers

Provides segmented memory addressing scheme a rich instruction set.

Powerful interrupt structure

Fetched instruction queue for overlapped fetching and execution step.

The 8086 CPU is divided into two independent functional units

Bus Interface Unit (BIU)

Execution Unit (EU)

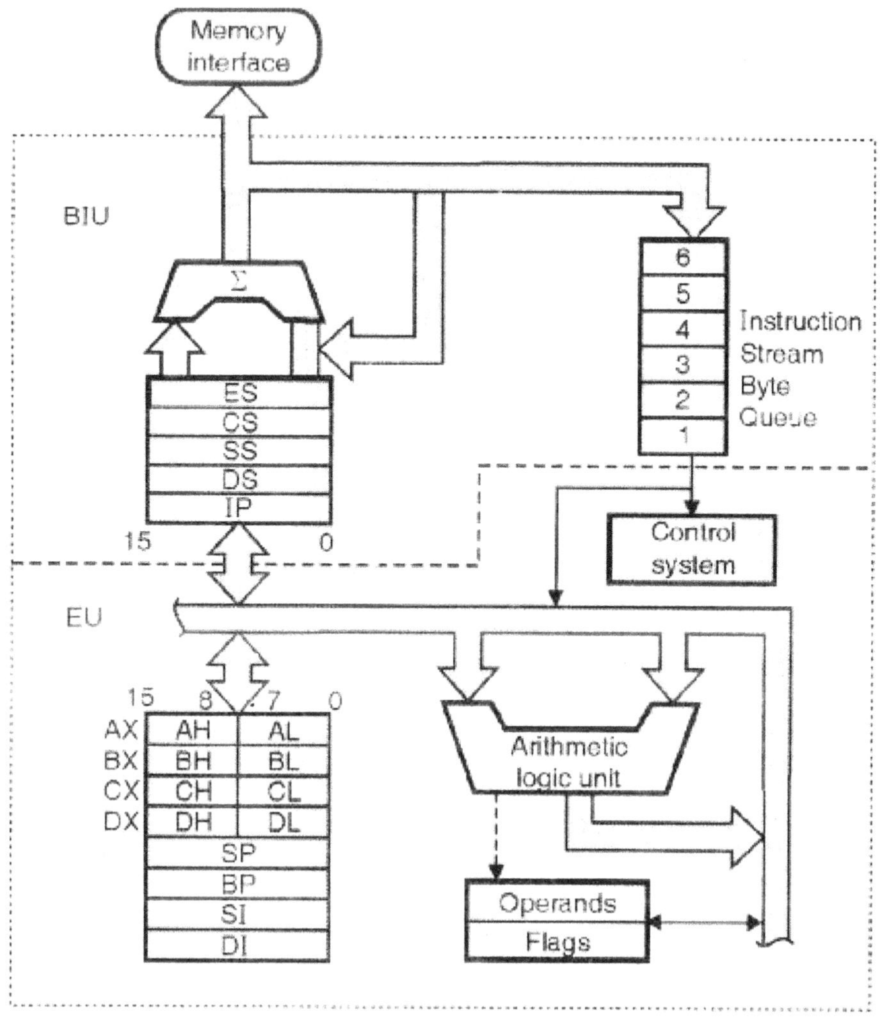

8086 internal architecture

<u>Bus Interface Unit (BIU)</u>

The function of BIU is to

Fetch the instruction or data from memory.

Write the data to memory.

Write the data to the port.

Read data from the port.

It contains a circuit for physical address calculation and preordering instruction byte queue

Its responsible for establishing communications with external devices and peripherals including memory via bus

To complete 1Mbyte memory is divided into 16 logical segments.

In the complete 1Mbyte memory segmentation, Each segment contains 64Kbyte of memory.

There are four segment registers.

Code segment (CS)

It is a 16-bit register containing address of 64 KB segment with processor instructions.

Segment registers:

The processor uses CS segment for all accesses to instructions referenced by instruction pointer (IP) register.

The CS register is automatically updated during far jump, far call and far return instructions.

Stack segment (SS)

Itis a 16-bit register containing address of 64KB segment with program stack.

By default, the processor assumes that all data referenced by the stack pointer (SP) and base pointer (BP) registers is located in the stack segment.

SS register can be changed directly using POP instruction.

It is used for addressing stack segment of memory.

The stack segment is that segment of memory, which is used to store stack data.

Data segment (DS)

Itis a 16-bit register containing address of 64KB segment with program data.

By default, the processor assumes that all data referenced by general

registers (AX, BX, CX, DX) and index register (SI, DI) is located in the data segment.

DS register can be changed directly using POP and LDS instructions.

It points to the data segment memory where the data is resided.

Extra segment (ES)

It is a 16-bit register containing address of 64KB segment, usually with program data.

By default, the processor assumes that the DI register references the ES segment in string manipulation instructions.

ES register can be changed directly using POP and LES instructions.

It also refers to segment which essentially is another data segment of the memory. It also contains data.

SPECIAL PURPOSE REGISTERS

IP - the instruction pointer:

1. Always points to next instruction to be executed

2. Offset address relative to CS

IP register always works together with **CS** segment register and it points to currently Executing instruction.

Instruction Byte Queue

In Case of 8085 after the instruction fetch and decode the external bus will be free for some amount of time, while the processor execute the initial instruction.

This time slot is used in 8086 by lapped fetch and execution cycles

While fetch instruction is executed internally, the external bus is fetch the machine code of next instruction and arrange in a queue is known as Instruction Byte Queue

Its 6 byte long, FIFO structure

Execution Unit (EU)

The functions of execution unit are:

To tell BIU where to fetch the instructions or data from.

To decode the instructions.

To execute the instructions.

The EU contains the control circuitry to perform various internal operations.

A decoder in EU decodes the instruction fetched memory to generate different internal or external control signals required to perform the operation.

EU has 16-bit ALU, which can perform arithmetic and logical operations on 8-bit as well as 16-bit.

General Purpose Registers of 8086

These registers can be used as 8-bit registers individually or can be used as 16-bit in pair to have AX, BX, CX, and DX.

AX Register: AX register is also known as accumulator register that stores operands for arithmetic operation like divided, rotate.

BX Register: This register is mainly used as a base register. It holds the starting base location of a memory region within a data segment.

CX Register: It is defined as a counter. It is primarily used in loop instruction to store loop counter.

DX Register: DX register is used to contain I/O port address for I/O instruction.

Pointer & Index registers

Stack Pointer (SP) is a 16-bit register pointing to program stack.

Base Pointer (BP) is a 16-bit register pointing to data in stack segment.

BP register is usually used for based, based indexed or register indirect addressing.

Source Index (SI) is a 16-bit register. SI is used for indexed, based indexed and register indirect addressing, as well as a source data address in string manipulation instructions.

Destination Index (DI) is a 16-bit register.

DI is used for indexed, based indexed and register indirect addressing, as well as a destination data address in string manipulation instructions.

Flags in 8086

Flags Register determines the current state of the processor.

They are modified automatically by CPU after mathematical operations, this allows to determine the type of the result, and to determine conditions to transfer control to other parts of the program.

The 8086 flag register as shown in the fig. 8086 has 9 active flags and they are divided into two categories:

The flags in 8086 are

Carry Flag (CY):

This flag is set to 1 if result of a arithmetic(Addition or Subtraction) operation carries a carry at MSB otherwise it will set to 0

It is also used in multiple-precision arithmetic.

Auxiliary Flag (AC):

If an operation performed in ALU generates a carry/barrow from lower nibble (i.e. D0 – D3) to upper nibble (i.e. D4 – D7), the AC flag is set i.e. carry given by D3 bit to D4 is AC flag.

This is not a general-purpose flag, it is used internally by the Processor to perform Binary to BCD conversion.

Parity Flag (PF):

This flag is set to 1 if the lower byte of result contain even number of Ones.

Zero Flag (ZF):

It is set; if the result of arithmetic or logical operation is zero else it is reset.

Sign Flag (SF):

In sign magnitude format the sign of number is indicated by MSB bit.

If the result of operation is negative, sign flag is set.to 1

Trap Flag (TF):

It is used for single step control.

It allows user to execute one instruction of a program at a time for debugging. When trap flag is set, program can be run in single step mode.

Interrupt Flag (IF):

It is an interrupt enable/disable flag. If it is set, the maskable interrupt of 8086 is enabled and if it is reset, the interrupt is disabled.

It can be set by executing instruction sit and can be cleared by executing CLI instruction.

Direction Flag (DF):

It is used in string operation. If it is set, string bytes are accessed from higher memory address to lower memory address.

When it is reset, the string bytes are accessed from lower memory address to higher memory address.

Overflow Flag:

The flag is set if overflow occurs

If the result of Signed operation is not enough to store the registers

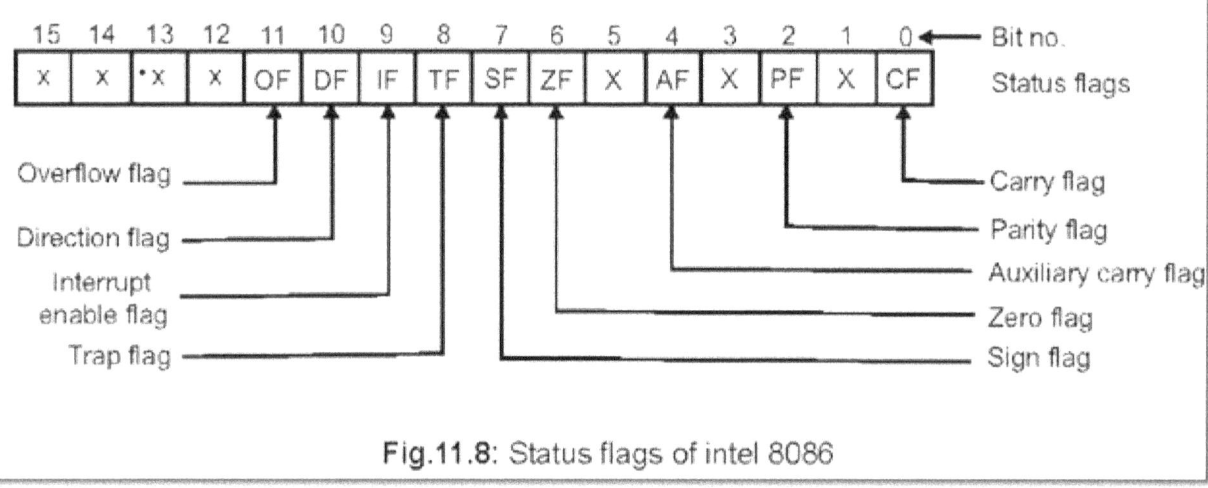

Fig.11.8: Status flags of intel 8086

Signal Descriptions of 8086

Pin Diagram of 8086

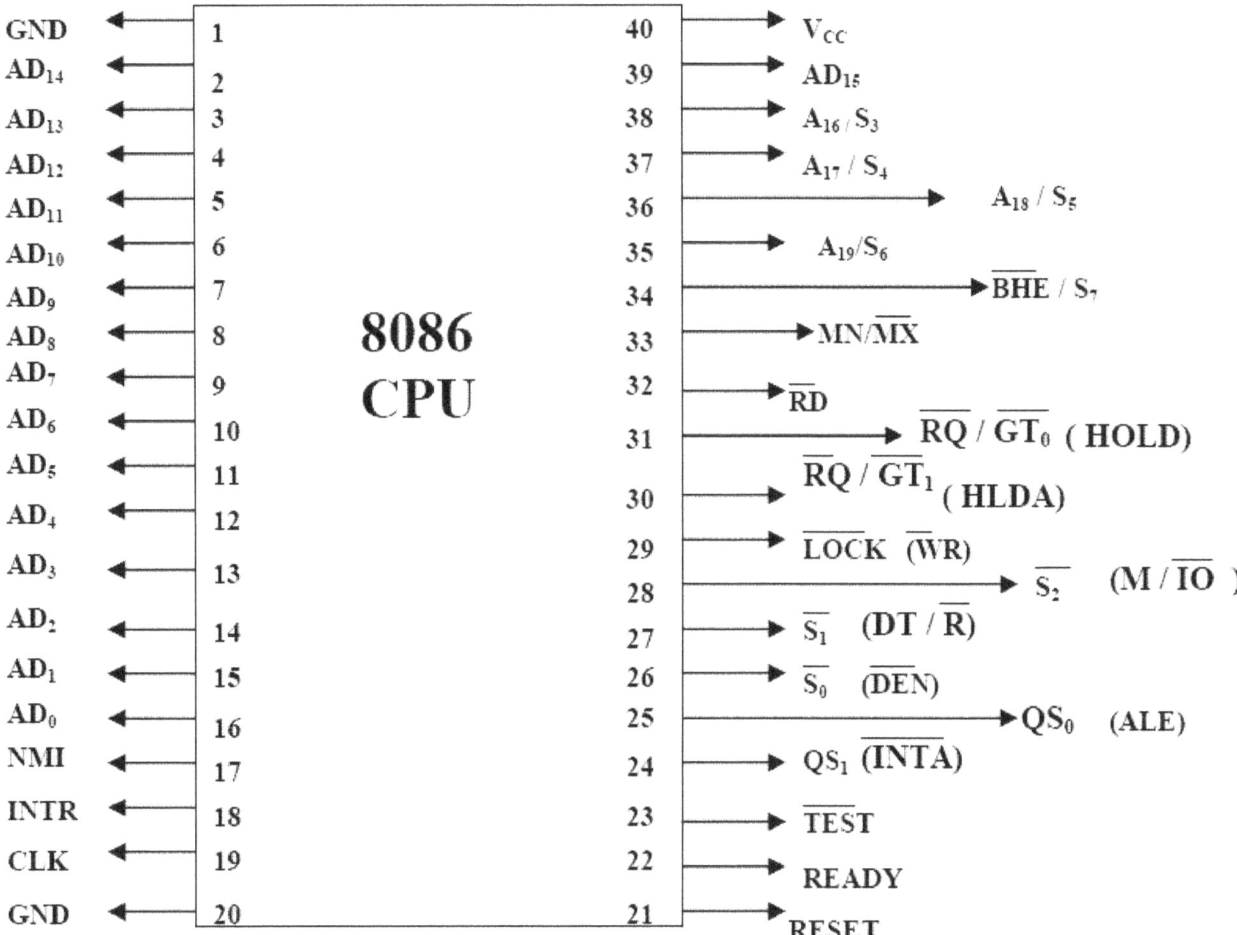

8086 is a 40 pin IC.

Its operating voltage is 5 volts.

Its operating frequency is 5 MHz.

It has 16-bit data bus and 20-bit address bus.

AD15-AD0:

These are the time multiplexed memory I/O address and data lines.

Address remains on the lines during T1 state

While the data is available on the data bus during T2, T3, TW and T4.

Here T1, T2, T3, T4 and TW are the clock states of a machine cycle. TW is a wait state.

These lines are active high

A19/S6, A18/S5, A17/S4, A16/S3:

These are the time multiplexed address and status lines.

During T1, these are the most significant address lines or memory operations. During I/O operations, these lines are low.

During memory or I/O operations, status information is available on those lines for T2, T3, TW and T4 .The status of the interrupt enable flag bit(displayed on S5) is updated at the beginning of each clock cycle. The S4 and S3 combinedly indicate which segment register is presently being used for memory accesses as shown in Table

The address bits are separated from the status bits using latches controlled by the ALE signal.

S4	S3	Indication
O	O	Alternate Data
O	1	Stack
1	O	Code or none
1	1	Data

-

BHE/S7-Bus High Enable/Status:

The bus high enable signal is used to indicate the transfer of data over the higher order (D15-D8) data bus as shown in below table

It goes low for the data transfers over D15-D8 and is used to derive chip selects of odd address memory bank or peripherals.

BHE is low during T1 for read, write and interrupt acknowledge cycles, when- ever a byte is to be transferred on the higher byte of the data bus.

The status information is available during T2, T3 and T4. The signal is active low and is tristated during 'hold'. It is low during T1 for the first pulse of the interrupt acknowledge cycle.

$\overline{BHE}$	A_0	Indication
O	O	Whole Word
O	1	Upper byte from or to odd address
1	O	Upper byte from or to even address
1	1	None

-

RD-Read:

Read signal, when low, indicates the peripherals that the processor is performing a memory or I/O read operation. RD is active low and shows the state for T2, T3, TW of any read cycle.

The signal remains tristated during the 'hold acknowledge'.

READY:

This is the acknowledgement from the slow devices or memory that they have completed the data transfer.

The signal made available by the devices is synchronized by the 8284A clock generator to provide ready input to the 8086. The signal is active high.

INTR- lnterrupt Request:

This is a level triggered input. This is sampled during the last clock cycle of each instruction to determine the availability of the request.

If any interrupt request is pending, the processor enters the interrupt acknowledge cycle. This can be internally masked by resetting the interrupt enable flag.

This signal is active high and internally synchronized.

TEST:

This input is examined by a 'WAIT' instruction.

If the TEST input goes low, execution will continue, else, the processor remains in an idle state. The input is synchronized internally during each clock cycle on leading edge of clock.

NMI-Non-mask able Interrupt:

This is an edge-triggered input which causes a Type2 interrupt. The NMI is not maskable internally by software.

A transition from low to high initiates the interrupt response at the end of the current instruction. This input is internally synchronized.

RESET:

This input causes the processor to terminate the current activity and start execution from FFFF0H. The signal is active high and must be active for at least four clock cycles. It restarts execution when the RESET returns low. RESET is also internally synchronized.

CLK-Clock Input:

The clock input provides the basic timing for processor operation and bus control activity. Its an asymmetric square wave with 33% duty cycle. The range of frequency for different 8086 versions is from 5MHz to 10MHz.

VCC:

+5V power supply for the operation of the internal circuit.

GND

ground for the internal circuit.

MN/MX: The logic level at this pin decides whether the processor is to operate in either minimum (single processor) or maximum (multiprocessor) mode.

The following pin functions are for the minimum mode operation of 8086.

M/IO -Memory/IO: This is a status line logically equivalent to S2 in maximum mode. When it is low, it indicates the CPU is having an I/O operation, and when it is high, it indicates that the CPU is having a memory operation. This line becomes active in the previous T4 and remains active till final T4 of the current cycle. It is tristated during local bus "hold acknowledge".

INTA -Interrupt Acknowledge:

This signal is used as a read strobe for interrupt acknowledge cycles. In other words, when it goes low, it means that the processor has accepted the interrupt. It is active low during T2, T3 and TW of each interrupt acknowledge cycle.

ALE-Address latch Enable:

This output signal indicates the availability of the valid address on the address/data lines, and is connected to latch enable input of latches. This signal is active high and is never tristated.

DT /R -Data Transmit/Receive: This output is used to decide the direction of data flow through the transreceivers (bidirectional buffers). When the processor sends out data, this signal is high and when the processor is receiving data, this signal is low. Logically, this is equivalent to S1 in maximum mode. Its timing is the same as M/I/O. This is tristated during 'hold acknowledge'.

DEN-Data Enable This signal indicates the availability of valid data over the address/data lines. It is used to enable the transreceivers (bidirectional buffers) to separate the data from the multiplexed address/data signal. It is active from the middle ofT2 until the middle of T4 DEN is tristated during 'hold acknowledge' cycle.

HOLD, HLDA-Hold/Hold Acknowledge:

When the HOLD line goes high, it indicates to the processor that another master is requesting the bus access. The processor, after receiving the HOLD request, issues the hold acknowledge signal on HLDA pin, in the middle of the next clock cycle after completing the current bus (instruction) cycle. At the same time, the processor floats the local bus and control lines.

When the processor detects the HOLD line low, it lowers the HLDA signal. HOLD is an asynchronous input and it should be externally synchronized.

If the DMA request is made while the CPU is performing a memory or I/O cycle, it will release the local bus during T 4 provided:

1. The request occurs on or before T 2 state of the current cycle.

2. The current cycle is not operating over the lower byte of a word (or operating on an odd address).

3. The current cycle is not the first acknowledge of an interrupt acknowledge sequence.

4. A Lock instruction is not being executed.

So far we have presented the pin descriptions of 8086 in minimum mode.

The following pin functions are applicable for maximum mode operation of 8086.

S2, S1, S0 -Status Lines:

These are the status lines which reflect the type of operation, being carried out by the processor.

These become active during T4 of the previous cycle and remain active during T1 and T2 of the current bus cycle.

The status lines return to passive state during T3 of the current bus cycle so that they may again become active for the next bus cycle during T4.

Any change in these lines during T3 indicates the starting of a new cycle, and return to passive state indicates end of the bus cycle. These status lines are encoded in table

$\overline{S_2}$	$\overline{S_1}$	$\overline{S_0}$	Indication
0	0	0	Interrupt Acknowledge
0	0	1	Read I/O Port
0	1	0	Write I/O Port
0	1	1	Halt
1	0	0	Code Access
1	0	1	Read memory
1	1	0	Write memory
1	1	1	Passive

-

LOCK:

This output pin indicates that other system bus masters will be prevented from gaining the system bus, while the LOCK signal is low.

The LOCK signal is activated by the 'LOCK' prefix instruction and remains active until the completion of the next instruction.

This floats to tri-state off during "hold acknowledge". When the CPU is executing a critical instruction which requires the system bus, the LOCK prefix instruction ensures that other processors connected in the system will not gain the control of the bus.

QS1, QS0-Queue Status:

These lines give information about the status of the code prefetch queue. These are active during the CLK cycle after which the queue operation is performed. These are encoded as shown in Table

QS_1.	QS_0	Indication
0	0	No operation
0	1	First byte of opcode from the queue
1	0	Empty queue
1	1	Subsequent byte from the queue

•

RQ/GT0, RQ/GT1-ReQuest/Grant:

These pins are used by other local bus masters, in maximum mode, to force the processor to release the local bus at the end of the processor's current bus cycle.

Each of the pins is bidirectional with RQ/GT0 having higher priority than RQ/ GT1, RQ/GT pins have internal pull-up resistors and may be left unconnected. The request! grant sequence is as follows:

1. A pulse one clock wide from another bus master requests the bus access to 8086.

2. During T4 (current) or T1 (next) clock cycle, a pulse one clock wide from 8086 to the requesting master, indicates that the 8086 has allowed the local bus to float and that it will enter the "hold acknowledge" state at next clock cycle. The CPU's bus interface unit is likely to be disconnected from the local bus of the system.

3. A one clock wide pulse from another master indicates to 8086 that the 'hold' request is about to end and the 8086 may regain control of the local bus at the next clock cycle. Thus each master to master exchange of the local bus is a sequence of 3 pulses. There must be at least one dead clock cycle after each bus exchange. The request and grant pulses are active low. For the bus requests those are received while 8086 is performing memory or I/O cycle, the granting of the bus is governed by the rules as discussed in case of HOLD, and HLDA in minimum mode

Minimum mode 8086 system and timings

In a minimum mode 8086 system, the microprocessor 8086 is operated in minimum mode by strapping its MN/MX* pin to logic1.

In this mode, all the control signals are given out by the microprocessor chip itself. There is a single microprocessor in the minimum mode system.

The remaining components in the system are latches, transreceivers, clock generator, memory and I/O devices. The opcode fetch and read cycles are similar.

Hence the timing diagram can be categorized in two parts, the first is the timing diagram for read cycle and the second is the timing diagram for write cycle.

Fig shows the read cycle timing diagram. The read cycle begins in T1 with the assertion of the address latch enable (ALE) signal and also M/IO* signal. During the negative going edge of this signal, the valid address is latched on the local bus. The BHE* and A0 signals address low, high or both bytes. From Tl to T4, the M/IO* signal indicates a memory or I/O operation. At T2 the address is removed from the local bus and is sent to the output. The bus is then tristated. The read (RD*) control signal is also activated in T2 .The read (RD) signal causes the addressed device to enable its data bus drivers. After RD* goes low, the valid data is available on the data bus. The addressed device will drive the READY line high, when the processor returns the read signal to high level, the addressed device will again tristate its bus drivers.

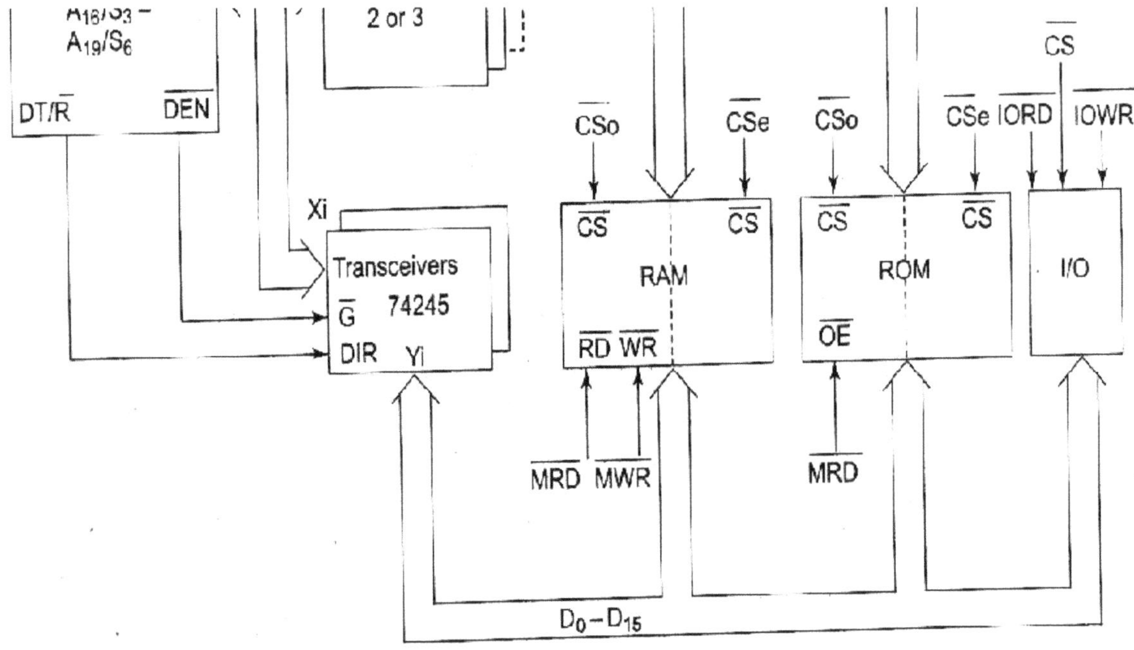

A write cycle also begins with the assertion of ALE and the emission of the address. The M/IO* signal is again asserted to indicate a memory or I/O operation. In T2 after sending the address in Tl the processor sends the data to be written to the addressed location. The data remains on the bus until middle of T4 state. The WR* becomes active at the beginning ofT2 (unlike RD* is somewhat delayed in T2 to provide time for floating). The BHE* and A0 signals are used to select the proper byte or bytes of memory or I/O word to be read or written. The M/IO*, RD* and WR* signals indicate the types of data transfer as specified in Table

M/IO	RD	WR	Transfer Type
0	0	1	I/O read
0	1	0	I/O write
1	0	1	Memory read
1	1	0	Memory write

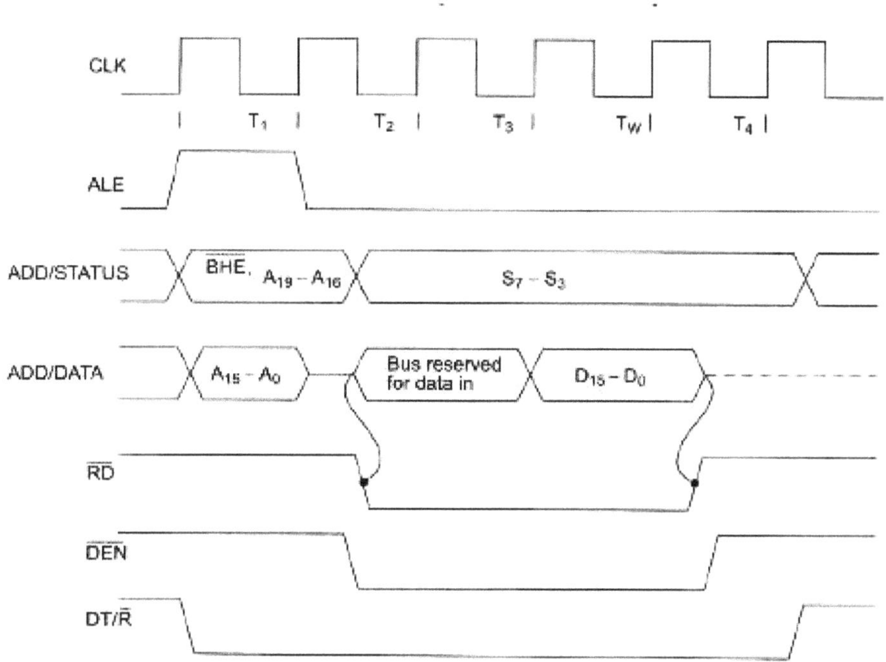

HOLD Response Sequence

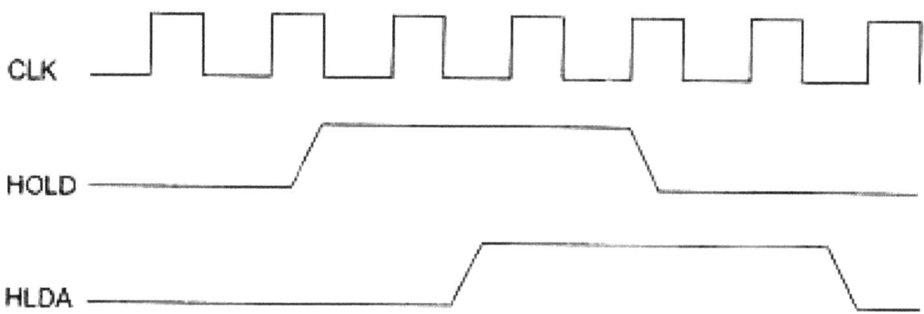

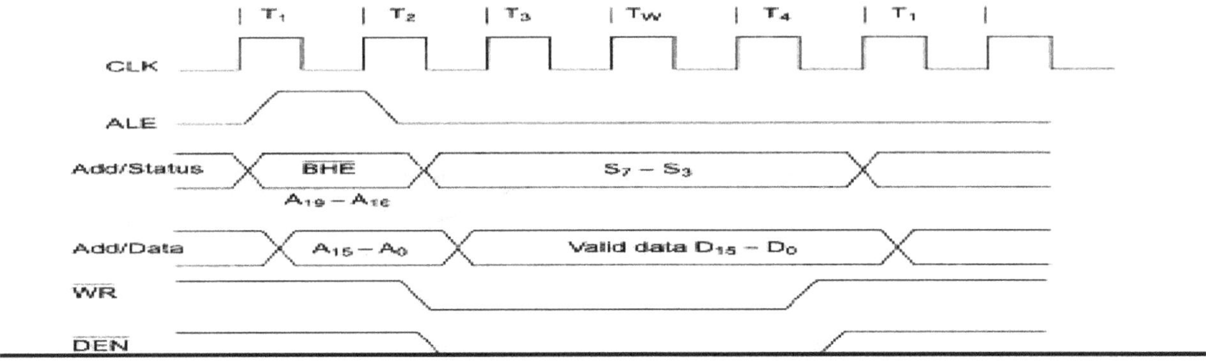

•

Maximum mode 8086 system and timings

In the maximum mode, the 8086 is operated by strapping the MN/MX* pin to ground. In this mode, the processor derives the status signals S2*, S1* and S0*. Another chip called bus controller derives the control signals using this status information. In the maximum mode, there may be more than one microprocessor in the system configuration. The basic functions of the bus controller chip IC8288, is to derive control signals like RD* and WR* (for memory and I/O devices), DEN*, DT/R*, ALE, etc. using the information made available by the processor on the status lines. The bus controller chip has input lines S2*, S1* and S0* and CLK. These inputs to 8288 are driven by the CPU. It derives the outputs ALE, DEN*, DT/R*, MWTC*, AMWC*, IORC*, IOWC* and AIOWC*. The AEN*, IOB and CEN pins are especially useful for multiprocessor systems. AEN* and IOB are generally grounded. CEN pin is usually tied to +5V.

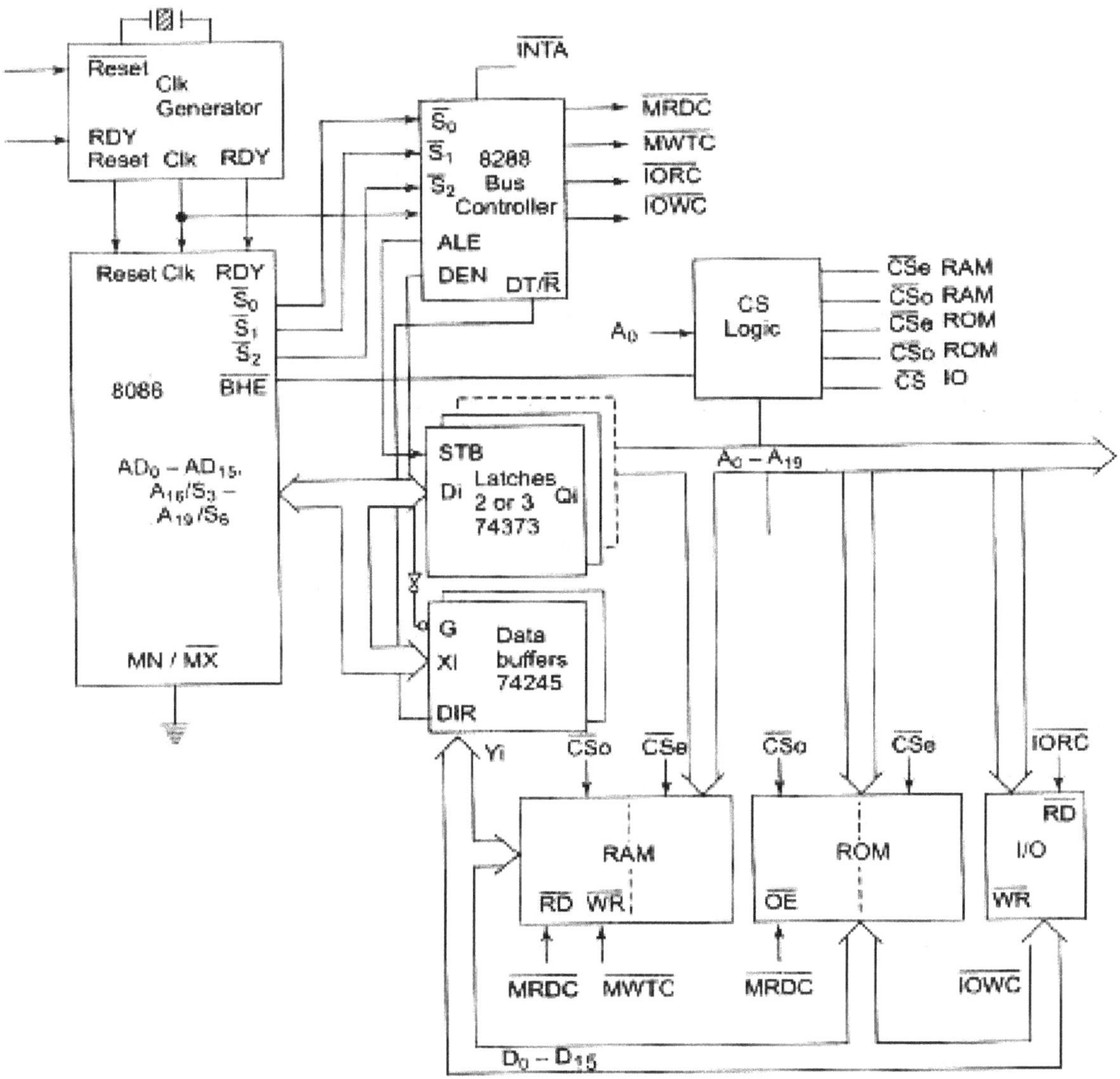

The significance of the MCE/PDEN* output depends upon the status of the IOB pin. If IOB is grounded, it acts as master cascade enable to control cascaded 8259A; else peripheral data enable used in the multiple bus configurations. it acts as INTA* pin is used to issue two interrupt acknowledge pulses to the interrupt controller or to an interrupting device. IORC*, IOWC* are I/O read command and I/O write command signals respectively. These signals enable an IO interface to read or write the data from or to the addressed port. The MRDC*, MWTC* are memory read command and memory write command signals respectively and may be used as memory read and write signals. All these command signals instruct the memory to accept or send data from or to the bus.

For both of these write command signals, the advanced signals namely AIOWC* and AMWTC* are available. They also serve the same purpose, but are activated one clock cycle earlier than the IOWC* and MWTC* signals, respectively. The maximum mode system is shown in fig. 2.1.

The maximum mode system timing diagrams are also divided in two portions as read (input) and write (output) timing diagrams. The address/data and address/status timings are similar to the minimum mode. ALE is asserted in T1, just like minimum mode. The only difference lies in the status signals used and the available control and advanced command signals. The fig. 1.2 shows the maximum mode timings for the same for the write operation.

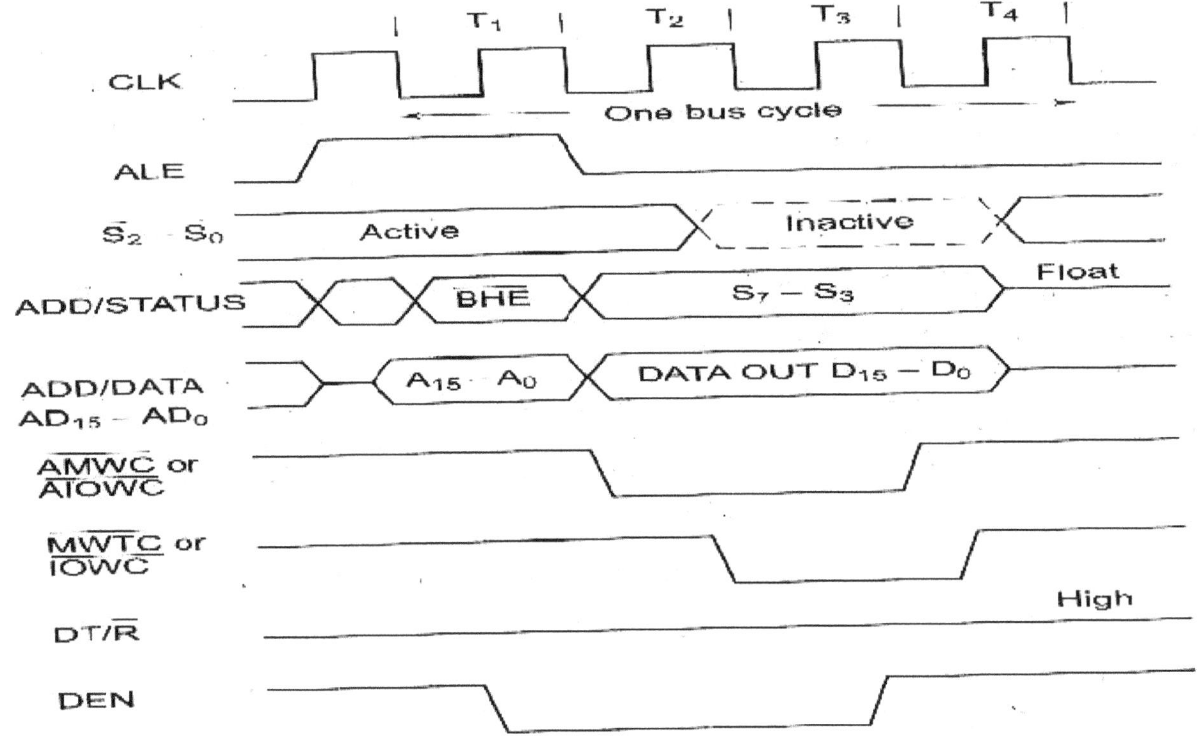

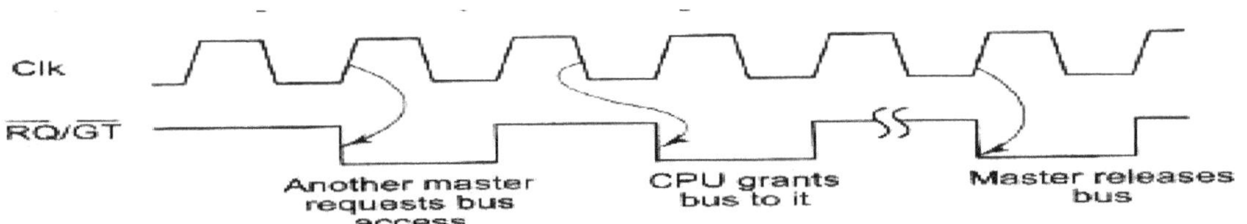

- Fig RG*/GT* Timings in maximum mode

<u>Comparison of 8086 and 8088 Microprocessor</u>

8086	8088
The instruction Queue is 6 byte long.	The instruction Queue is 4 byte long.
In 8086, memory divides into two banks -even or lower bank -odd or higher bank	The memory in 8088 does not divide into two banks.
The data bus of 8086 is 16-bit wide	The data bus of 8088 is 8-bit wide.
It has BHE (bar) signal on pin no. 34 & there is no SSO (bar) signal.	It does not have BHE (bar) signal on pin no. 34 & has only SSO (bar) signal. It has no S7 pin.
Control pin in 8086 is M/IO (bar).	Control pin in 8088 is IO/M (bar).
It needs one machine cycle to R/W signal if it is at even location otherwise it needs two.	It needs one machine cycle to R/W signal if it is at even location otherwise it needs two.
In 8086, all address & data Buses are multiplexed.	In 8088, address bus; AD7- AD0 buses are multiplexed.
It needs two IC 74343 for de-multiplexing AD_0-AD_{19}.	It needs one IC 74343 for de-multiplexing AD0-AD7.
Maximum supply current 360mA.	Maximum supply current 340mA.
Three clock speed: 5, 8, 10 MHz	Two clock speed: 5, 8 MHz

CHAPTER TWO

8086 ASSEMBELY LANGUAGE PROGRAMMING

ADDRESSING MODES OF 8086

Q.what do you mean by addressing modes? What are the different addressing modes supported by 8086? Explain each one of them with suitable examples?

Q.Explain physical address formation in different addressing modes?

Q. Compare indexed, based indexed, based indexed with displacement addressing mode?

Addressing mode indicate a way of locating data or operands. According to the flow of instruction execution, the instruction may be categorized as

1.Sequential control flow instructions

2.Control transfer instructions

Classification of addressing modes

1.Immediate

2.Direct

3.Register

4.Register Indirect

5.Indexed

6.Register Relative

7.Based Indexed

8.Relative Based Indexed

9.Intrasegment Direct

10.Intrasegment Indirect

11.Intersegment Direct

12.Intersegment Indirect

<u>1.Immediate</u>

In this type of addressing, immediate data is a part of instruction and appears in the form of successive byte or bytes.

Eg: MOV AX, 0005H

Here 0005H is the immediate data.

<u>2.Direct</u>

Here 16-bit memory address (offset) is directly specified in the instruction.

Eg: MOV AX, [5000H]

Here, data resides in a memory location in the data segment, whose effective address may be computed using 5000H as the offset address and content of DS as segment address. Thus the effective address is 10H*DS+5000H

<u>3.Register</u>

Here the data is stored in a register and it is referred using the particular register. All the registers, except IP, may be used in this mode.

Eg: MOV BX, AX

<u>4.Register Indirect</u>

In this mode, the offset address of data is in either BX or SI or DI register. The default segment is either DS or ES.

Eg: MOV AX, [BX]

Here data is present in a memory location in DS whose offset address is in BX. The effective address of the data is given as 10H*DS+[BX]

<u>5.Indexed</u>

In this addressing mode, offset of the operand is stored in one of the index registers. DS is the default segment for index registers SI and DI.

Eg: MOV AX, [SI]

Here data is available at an offset address stored in SI in DS. The effective address is computed as 10H*DS+[SI]

<u>6.Register Relative</u>

In this mode, the data is available at an effective address formed by adding an 8-bit or 16-bit displacement with the content of any one of the registers BX, BP, SI and DI in the default (either DS or ES) segment.

Eg: MOV AX, 50H[BX]

Here the effective address is given as 10H*DS+50H+[BX]

<u>7.Based Indexed</u>

In this mode, the effective address is formed by adding content of a base register (any one of BX or BP) to the content of an index register (any one of SI or DI). The default segment register may be ES or DS.

Eg: MOV AX, [BX][SI]

Here, BX is the base register and SI is the index register. The effective address is 10H*DS+[BX]+[SI]

<u>8.Relative Based Indexed</u>

The effective address is formed by adding an 8 or 16 bit displacement with the sum of contents of any one of the base registers (BX or BP) and any one of the index registers, in a default segment.

Eg: MOV AX, 50H[BX][SI]

Here 50H is an immediate displacement, BX is a base register and SI is an index register. The effective address of data is computed as 10H*DS+[BX]+[SI]+50H

Q.Explain addressing modes for control transfer instructions?

There are two addressing modes for control transfer instructions

1. intrasegment mode: If the destination location lies in the same segment

2. intersegment mode: If the location to which the control is to be transferred lies in a different segment other than the current one.

<u>9.Intrasegment direct mode:</u>

In this mode, the address to which the control is to be transferred lies in the same segment in which the control transfer instruction lies and appears directly in the instruction as an immediate displacement value. In this mode, the displacement is computed relative to the content of the IP.

The effective address to which the control will be transferred is given by the sum of 8 or 16 bit displacement and current content of IP. In case of jump instruction, if the signed displacement(d) is of 8 bits (i.e, -128<d<+127), then it is short jump and if it is of 16 bits(i.e.-32768<d<+32767), it is long jump.

Eg: JMP SHORT LABEL

<u>10.Intrasegment Indirect mode</u>

In this mode, the displacement to which the control is to be transferred, is in the same segment in which the control transfer instruction lies, but it is passed to the instruction indirectly. Here the branch address is found as the content of a register or a memory location.

Eg: JMP [BX]

<u>11.Intersegment Direct</u>

In this mode, the address to which the control is to be transferred is in a different segment. This addressing mode provides a means of branching from one code segment to another code segment. Here, the CS and IP of the destination address are specified directly in the instruction.

Eg: JMP 5000H:2000H

<u>12.Intersegment Indirect</u>

In this mode, the address to which the control is to be transferred lies in a different segment and it is passed to the instruction indirectly. i.e contents of a memory block containing four bytes, i.e. IP(LSB), IP(MSB), CS(LSB) and CS(MSB) sequentially.

Eg: JMP [2000H]

Forming the Effective Addresses   The following examples explain forming of the effective addresses in the different modes.

Example 2.13

The contents of different registers are given below. Form effective addresses for different addressing modes.

Offset (displacement) = 5000H

[AX]-1000H, [BX]-2000H, [SI]-3000H, [DI]-4000H, [BP]-5000H,

[SP]-6000H, [CS]-0000H, [DS]-1000H, [SS]-2000H, [IP]-7000H.

Shifting a number four times is equivalent to multiplying it by 16_D or 10_H.

(i) Direct addressing mode

```
                        MOV AX, [5000H]
```

$$
\begin{aligned}
\text{DS:OFFSET} &\Leftrightarrow \quad 1000H{:}\,5000H \\
10H^{*}\,DS &\Leftrightarrow \quad 10000 \\
\text{Offset} &\Leftrightarrow \quad +\,5000 \\
\hline
&\quad\ 15000H \text{ - Effective address}
\end{aligned}
$$

(ii) Register indirect

```
                        MOV AX, [BX]
```

$$
\begin{aligned}
\text{DS:BX} &\Leftrightarrow \quad 1000H{:}2000H \\
10H^{*}DS &\Leftrightarrow \quad 10000 \\
[BX] &\Leftrightarrow \quad +\,2000 \\
\hline
&\quad\ 12000H \text{ - Effective address}
\end{aligned}
$$

(iii) Register relative

```
                        MOV AX, 5000 [BX]
```

$$
\begin{aligned}
\text{DS: } & [5000 + BX] \\
10H^{*}DS &\Leftrightarrow \quad 10000
\end{aligned}
$$

$$\begin{aligned}
\text{Offset} &\Leftrightarrow +5000 \\
[BX] &\Leftrightarrow +2000 \\
\hline
\end{aligned}$$

17000H - Effective address

(iv) Based indexed

                    MOV AX, [BX] [SI]

DS:[BX + SI]
$$\begin{aligned}
10H^*DS &\Leftrightarrow 10000 \\
[BX] &\Leftrightarrow +2000 \\
[SI] &\Leftrightarrow +3000 \\
\hline
\end{aligned}$$

15000H - Effective address

(v) Relative based indexed

                    MOV AX, 5000 [BX] [SI]

DS: [BX + SI + 5000]
$$\begin{aligned}
10H^*DS &\Leftrightarrow 10000 \\
[BX] &\Leftrightarrow +2000 \\
[SI] &\Leftrightarrow +3000 \\
\text{Offset} &\Leftrightarrow +5000 \\
\hline
\end{aligned}$$

1A000 - effective address

Below, we present examples of address formation in control transfer instructions.

Example 2.14

Suppose our main program resides in the code segment where CS = 1000H. The main program calls a subroutine which resides in the same code segment. The base register contains offset of the subroutine, i.e. BX = 0050H. Since the offset is specified indirectly, as the content of BX, this is indirect addressing. The instruction CALL [BX] calls the subroutine located at an address 10H*CS + [BX] = 10050H, i.e. in the same code segment. Since the control goes to the subroutine which resides in the same segment, this is an example of intrasegment indirect addressing mode.

Example 2.15

Let us now assume that the subroutine resides in another code segment, where CS = 2000H. Now CALL 2000H:0050H is an example of intersegment direct addressing mode, since the control now goes to different segment and the address is directly specified in the instruction. In this case, the address of the subroutine is 20050H.

Q.write the name of the addressing mode, effective address and operand value in each of the addressing mode
i)MOV AX, [BX]
ii)MOV AX, BX
iii)MOV AX, [6002]
iv)MOV AX,6001H
v)Call 500H

Register	Memory Content	Memory Address
DS 6000H	10	66000
CS 6001H	11	66001
BX 6005H	12	66002
SI 6001H	13	66003
IP 0001H	14	66004
BP 6002H	15	66005
DI 6007H	16	66006
	17	66007
	18	66008
	19	66009
	20	66010

•

Addressing mode- Register indirect mode.,
EA= 10H*DS+[BX]=60000+6005=66005H(Content of 66005=15 will be moved to AX
Addressing mode-Register mode
Addressing mode-Direct mode,
EA=10H*DS+6002=66002(Content of 66002=12 will be moved to AX
Addressing mode- Immediate, Immedite data 6001H moved to AX
Addressing mode- Intrasegment direct mode,
Effective ddress =Displcement+Content of IP=500+0001H=0501H,

INSTRUCTION SET OF 8086/8088

Q.What are different instruction types of 8086?

Q. Explain classification of instructions of 8086 with examples.?

An instruction is a binary pattern designed inside a microprocessor to perform a specific function. The entire group of instructions that a microprocessor supports is called Instruction Set. 8086 has more than 20,000 instructions.

Opcode:- It stands for operational code. It specifies the type of operation to be performed by CPU. It is the first field in the machine language instruction format. E.g. 08 is the opcode for instruction "MOV X,Y".

Operand:- We can also say it as data on which operation should act. operands may be register values or memory values. The CPU executes the instructions using information present in this field. It may be 8-bit data or 16-bit data.

Assembler:- it converts the instruction into sequence of binary bits, so that this bits can be read by the processor.

Mnemonics:- these are the symbolic codes for either instructions or commands to perform a particular function. E.g. MOV, ADD, SUB etc.

The instruction set of 8086 is classified into:

(1). Data Copy/Transfer instructions.
(2). Arithmetic & Logical instructions.
(3). Branch instructions.
(4). Loop instructions.
(5). Machine Control instructions.
(6). Flag Manipulation instructions.
(7). Shift & Rotate instructions.
(8). String instructions.

(1). Data copy/transfer instructions.

MOV Destination, Source;

There will be transfer of data from source to destination.

Source can be register, memory location or immediate data.

Destination can be register or memory operand.

Both Source and Destination cannot be memory location or segment registers at the same time.

E.g.

(1). MOV CX, 037A H

(2). MOV AL, BL

(3). MOV BX, [0301 H]

PUSH Source

Source can be register, segment register or memory.

This instruction pushes the contents of specified source on to the stack.

In this stack pointer is decremented by 2.

The higher byte data is pushed first (SP-1).

Then lower byte data is pushed (SP-2).

E.g.:

(1). PUSH AX

(2). PUSH DS

(3). PUSH [5000H]

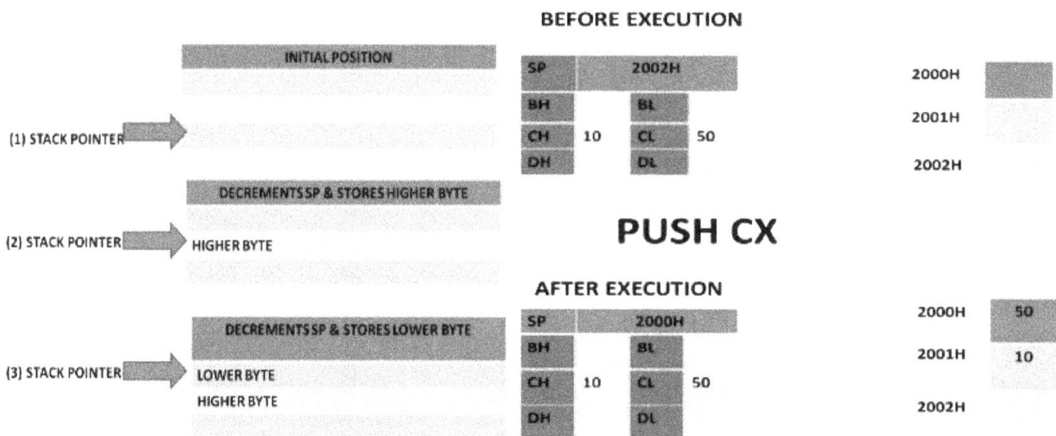

POP Destination

Destination can be register, segment register or memory.

This instruction pops (takes) the contents of specified destination.

In this stack pointer is incremented by 2.

The lower byte data is popped first (SP+1).

Then higher byte data is popped (SP+2).

E.g.

(1). POP AX

(2). POP DS

(3). POP [5000H]

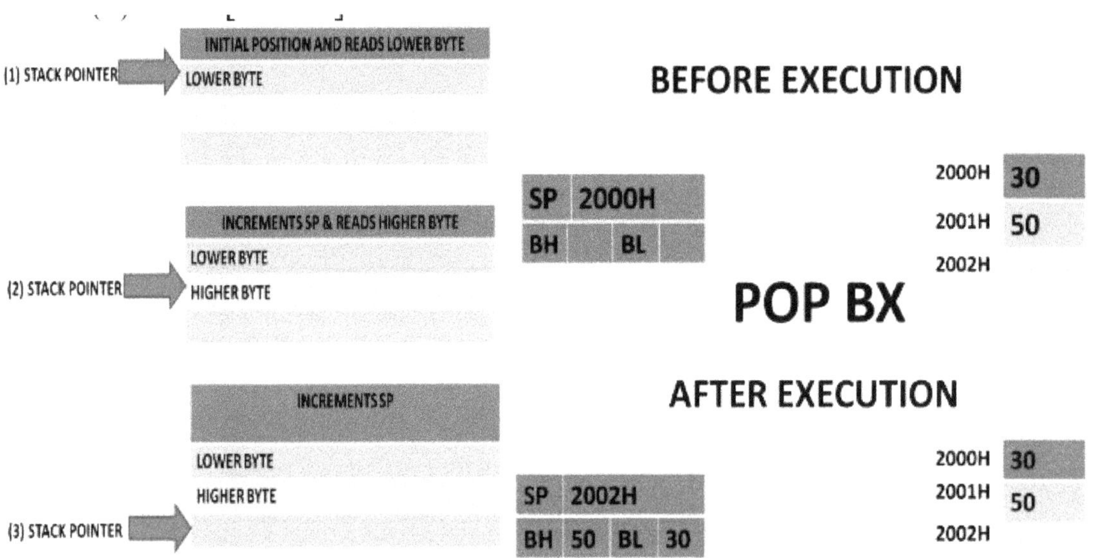

XCHG Destination, source

This instruction exchanges contents of Source with destination.

It cannot exchange two memory locations directly.

The contents of AL are exchanged with BL.

The contents of AH are exchanged with BH.

E.g. (1). XCHG BX, AX

(2). XCHG [5000H],AX

BEFORE EXECUTION **AFTER EXECUTION**

| AH | 20 | AL | 40 |

| BH | 70 | BL | 80 |

| AH | 70 | AL | 80 |

| BH | 20 | BL | 40 |

XCHG AX,BX;

-

IN AL/AX, 8-bit/16-bit port address

It reads from the specified port address.

It copies data to accumulator from a port with 8-bit or 16-bit address.

DX is the only register is allowed to carry port address.

E.g.

(1). IN AL, 80H;

(2). IN AX,DX; //DX contains address of 16-bit port.

BEFORE EXECUTION

PORT 80H 10 AL

IN AL,80H;

AFTER EXECUTION

PORT 80H 10 AL 10

OUT 8-bit/16-bit port address, AL/AX

It writes to the specified port address.

It copies contents of accumulator to the port with 8-bit or 16-bit address.

DX is the only register is allowed to carry port address.

E.g.

(1). OUT 80H,AL;

(2). OUT DX,AX; //DX contains address of 16-bit port

BEFORE EXECUTION

OUT 50H,AL;

AFTER EXECUTION

OUT 8-bit/16-bit port address, AL/AX

It writes to the specified port address.

It copies contents of accumulator to the port with 8-bit or 16-bit address.

DX is the only register is allowed to carry port address.

E.g.

(1). OUT 80H,AL;

(2). OUT DX,AX; //DX contains address of 16-bit port

Q.Which instruction of 8086 used for look up table manipulation?
Ans:XLAT

XLAT

Also known as translate instruction.

It is used to find out codes in case of code conversion.

i.e. it translates code of the key pressed to the corresponding 7-segment code.

After execution this instruction contents of AL register always gets replaced.

E.g. XLAT

LEA 16-bit register (source), address (dest.)

LEA Also known as Load Effective Address (**LEA**).

It loads effective address formed by the destination into the source register.

E.g.

(1). LEA BX,Address

(2). LEA SI,Address[BX]

LDS 16-bit register (source), address (dest.) & LES 16-bit register (source), address (dest.)

LDS Also known as Load Data Segment (**LDS**).

LES Also known as Load Extra Segment (**LES**).

It loads the contents of DS (Data Segment) or ES (Extra Segment) & contents of the destination to the contents of source register.

E.g.(1). LDS BX,5000H (2). LES BX,5000H

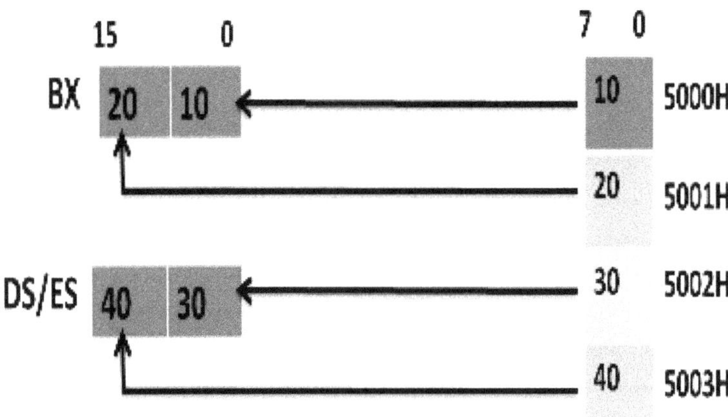

LAHF

This instruction loads the AH register from the contents of lower byte of the flag register.

This command is used to observe the status of the all conditional flags of flag register.

E.g. LAHF

SAHF

This instruction sets or resets all conditional flags of flag register with respect to the corresponding bit positions.

If bit position in AH is 1 then related flag is set otherwise flag will be reset.

E.g. SAHF

PUSH F

This instruction decrements the stack pointer by 2.

It copies contents of flag register to the memory location pointed by stack pointer.

E.g. PUSH F;

POP F

This instruction increments the stack pointer by 2.

It copies contents of memory location pointed by stack pointer to the flag register.

E.g. POP F;

(2). Arithematic Instructions

Q. Exemplify the following arithmetic instructions of 8086 1)AAA 2)AAS 3) AAM and 4)DAA ?

Q.Write the usage of DIV and MUL instructions with an example.?

Q.describe the difference between ADD and ADDC instruction?

These instructions perform the operations like:

Addition,

Subtraction,

Increment,

Decrement

ADD destination, source

This instruction adds the contents of source operand with the contents of destination operand.

The source may be immediate data, memory location or register.

The destination may be memory location or register.

The result is stored in destination operand.

AX is the default destination register.

E.g. (1). ADD AX,2020H;

(2). ADD AX,BX;

ADC destination, source

This instruction adds the contents of source operand with the contents of destination operand with carry flag bit.

The source may be immediate data, memory location or register.

The destination may be memory location or register.

The result is stored in destination operand.

AX is the default destination register.

E.g. (1). ADC AX,2020H;

(2). ADC AX,BX

INC source

This instruction increases the contents of source operand by 1.

The source may be memory location or register.

The source can not be immediate data.

The result is stored in the same place.

E.g. (1). INC AX;

(2). INC [5000H];

DEC source;

This instruction decreases the contents of source operand by 1.

The source may be memory location or register.

The source can not be immediate data.

The result is stored in the same place.

E.g. (1). DEC AX;

(2). DEC [5000H];

SUB destination, source;

This instruction subtracts the contents of source operand from contents of destination.

The source may be immediate data, memory location or register.

The destination may be memory location or register.

The result is stored in the destination place.

E.g. (1). SUB AX,1000H;

(2). SUB AX,BX;

SBB destination, source;

Also known as Subtract with Borrow.

This instruction subtracts the contents of source operand & borrow from contents of destination operand.

The source may be immediate data, memory location or register.

The destination may be memory location or register.

The result is stored in the destination place.

E.g. (1). SBB AX,1000H;

(2). SBB AX,BX;

CMP destination, source

Also known as Compare.

This instruction compares the contents of source operand with the contents of destination operands.

For comparison it subtracts the source operand from the destination operand but does not store the result

The source may be immediate data, memory location or register.

The destination may be memory location or register.

Then resulting carry & zero flag will be set or reset.

E.g. (1). CMP AX,1000H;

(2). CMP AX,BX;

AAA

Also known as ASCII Adjust After Addition.

This instruction is executed after ADD instruction.

AAA converts the resulting contents of AL to unpacked decimal digits.(

In the case of unpacked BCD numbers, each four-bit BCD group corresponding to a decimal digit is stored in a separate register inside the machine)

After addition AAA examines the contents of AL

(1). IF lower bits of AL<=09 and AF=0 then,

Higher bits of AL should loaded with zeroes.

There should be no change in lower bits of AL.

AH also must be cleared (AH=0000 0000).

(2). IF lower bits of AL<=09 and AF=1 then,

.Al=AL+06

Higher bits of AL should loaded with zeroes

Bits of AH must be incremented by 01 (i.e. AH+0001).

(3)IF lower bits of AL>09 then,

Bits of AL must be incremented by 06 (i.e. AL+0110).

Bits of AH must be incremented by 01 (i.e. AH+0001).

Then higher bits of AL should be loaded with 0000.

E.g. (1). AAA;

AAS

Also known as ASCII Adjust After Subtraction.

This instruction is executed after SUB instruction.

(1). IF lower bits of AL<=09 then,

Higher bits of AL should loaded with zeroes.

There should be no change in lower bits of AL.

AH also must be cleared (AH=0000 0000).

(2). IF lower bits of AL>09 then,

Bits of AL must be decremented by 06 (i.e. AL-0110).

Bits of AH must be decremented by 01 (i.e. AH-0001).

Then higher bits of AL should be loaded with 0000.

E.g. (1). AAS;

AAM

Also known as ASCII Adjust After Multiplication.

This instruction is executed after MUL instruction.

Then AH=AL/10 & AL=Remainder.

E.g. MOV AL,04 // AL=04

MOV BL,09 // BL=09

MUL BL // 04*09=36 (i.e. BL*AL)

AAM // AH=03 & AL=06

E.g. (1). AAM;

AAD

AAD instruction converts two unpacked BCD digits in AH and AL to the equivalent binary number in AL
Also known as ASCII Adjust before Division.

Then AL=AH*10 +AL & AH=0.

E.g. MOV AX, 0105 // AH=01, AL=05

AAD // AL=15 (i.e.0FH) & AH=00

E.g. (1). AAD;

DAA

Decimal Adjust Accumulator.

Used to convert the result of addition of two unpacked BCD numbers to a valid BCD number.

IF lower bits of AL>09.

Then AL=AL+06.

If now upper nibble 0f AL >9,DAA adds 60 H to AL

E.g. MOV AL,53H //AL=53H

MOV CL,29H //CL=29H

ADD AL,CL // AL=7CH (i.e. 12=C) & C>9.

DAA // AL=7C+06=82H. (i.e. 0111 1100 + 0000 0110)=1000 0010

Example 2.33

```
(i)   AL = 53          CL = 29
      ADD AL, CL       ; AL ← (AL) + (CL)
                       ; AL ← 53 + 29
                       ; AL ← 7C
      DAA              ; AL ← 7C + 06  (as C>9)
                       ; AL ← 82

(ii)  AL = 73          CL = 29
      ADD AL, CL       ; AL ← AL + CL
                       ; AL ← 73 + 29
                       ; AL ← 9C
      DAA              ; AL ← 02 and CF = 1
                          AL = 7 3
                              +
                          CL = 2 9
                          ─────────
                               9 C
                             + 6
                          ─────────
                               A 2
                           + 6 0
                          ─────────
                      CF = 1  0 2   in AL
```

DAS

Decimal Adjust after Subtraction.

IF lower bits of AL>09.

Then AL=AL-06.

E.g. MOV AL,30H // AL=30H

MOV CL,20H // CL=20H

SUB AL,CL // AL=0AH (i.e. A=10) & C=10>9.

DAS // AL=0A-06=04H. (i.e. 0000 1010 - 0000 0110)=0000 0100

E.g. (1). DAS

MUL operand

Unsigned Multiplication.

Operand contents are positively signed.

Operand may be general purpose register or memory location.

If operand is of 8-bit then multiply it with contents of AL.

If operand is of 16-bit then multiply it with contents of AX. And MSB bit of result is stored in DX and LSB stored in AX

Result is stored in accumulator (AX).

E.g.(1). MUL BH // (AX)= AL*BH; // (+3) * (+4) = +12.

(2). MUL CX //(DX) (AX)=AX*CX;

IMUL operand

Signed Multiplication.

Operand contents are negatively signed.

Operand may be general purpose register, memory location or index register.

If operand is of 8-bit then multiply it with contents of AL.

If operand is of 16-bit then multiply it with contents of AX.

Result is stored in accumulator (AX). And LSB in DX

E.g. (1). IMUL BH // AX= AL*BH; // (-3) * (-4) = 12.

(2). IMUL CX // AX=AX*CX;

DIV operand

Unsigned Division.

Operand may be register or memory.

Operand contents are positively signed.

Operand may be general purpose register or memory location.

For 16 bit dividend: AL-Quotient,AH-Reminder

For 32 bit dividend: higher order bits in DX and lower order bits in AX: Quotient in AX and reminder in DX

AL=AX/Operand (8-bit/16-bit) & AH=Remainder.

E.g. MOV AX, 0203 // AX=0203

MOV BL, 04 // BL=04

DIV BL // AL=0203/04=50 (i.e. AL=50 & AH=03)

IDIV operand

Signed Division.

Operand may be register or memory.

Operand contents are negatively signed.

Operand may be general purpose register or memory location.

AL=AX/Operand (8-bit/16-bit) & AH=Remainder.

E.g. MOV AX, -0203 // AX=-0203

MOV BL, 04 // BL=04

DIV BL // AL=-0203/04=-50 (i.e. AL=-50 & AH=03)

NEG Src:

—It creates 2's complement of a given number.

—That means, it changes the sign of a number.

CBW (Convert Byte to Word):

This instruction converts byte in AL to word in AX.

The conversion is done by extending the sign bit of AL throughout AH.

CWD (Convert Word to Double Word):

This instruction converts word in AX to double word in DX : AX.

The conversion is done by extending the sign bit of AX throughout DX.

(3). Logical Instructions

AND destination,source

Destination operand may be register, memory location.

Source operand may be register, immediate data or memory location.

Result is stored in destination operand.

E.g. MOV AX, 3F0FH // AX=3F0FH

MOV BX, 0008H // BX=0008H

AND AX,BX // AX=0008H

Follow the rules as given below:-

(1). 1 AND 1 = 1

(2). 1 AND 0 = 0

(3). 0 AND 1 = 0

(4). 0 AND 0 = 0

3F0FH= 0011 1111 0000 1111

0008H=0000 0000 0000 1000

0000 0000 0000 1000 = 0008H

OR destination,source

Destination operand may be register, memory location.

Source operand may be register, immediate data or memory location.

Result is stored in destination operand.

E.g. MOV AX, 3F0FH // AX=3F0FH

MOV BX, 0098H // BX=0098H

OR AX,BX // AX=3F9FH

Follow the rules as given below:-

(1). 1 OR 1 = 1

(2). 1 OR 0 = 1

(3). 0 OR 1 = 1

(4). 0 OR 0 = 0

3F0FH= 0011 1111 0000 1111

0098H=0000 0000 1001 1000

0011 1111 1001 1111 = 3F9FH

NOT operand;

Operand may be register, memory location.

This instruction inverts (complements) the contents of given operand.

Result is stored in Accumulator (AX).

E.g. MOV AX, 0200FH // AX=200FH

NOT AX // AX=DFF0H

Follow the rules as given below:-

(1). 1 NOT = 0

(2). 0 NOT = 1

200FH= 0010 0000 0000 1111

1101 1111 1111 0000 = DFF0H

XOR Des, Src:

It performs XOR operation of Des and Src.

Src can be immediate number, register or memory location.

Des can be register or memory location.

Both operands cannot be memory locations at the same time.

CF and OF become zero after the operation.

PF, SF and ZF are updated.

TEST destination,source

Both operands may be register, memory location or immediate data.

This instruction performs bit by bit logical AND operation for flags only (i.e. only flags will be affected).

If the corresponding 0th bit of result contains '1' then result will be non-zero & zero flag will be cleared/reset (i.e. ZF=0).

If the corresponding 0th bit of result contains '0' then result will be zero & zero flag will be set (i.e. ZF=1)..

E.g. (1). TEST AX,BX

(2). TEST [0500],06H

4)SHIFT AND ROTATE INSTRUCTIONS

Q.Describe the shift and rotate instruction of 8086?

RCR

Also known as Rotate Right through Carry.

Each binary bit of the operand is rotated towards right by one position through Carry flag.

Least Significant Bit (LSB) i.e. B0 is placed in the Carry flag.

Then carry flag bit is placed in the Most Significant Bit (MSB) position B15

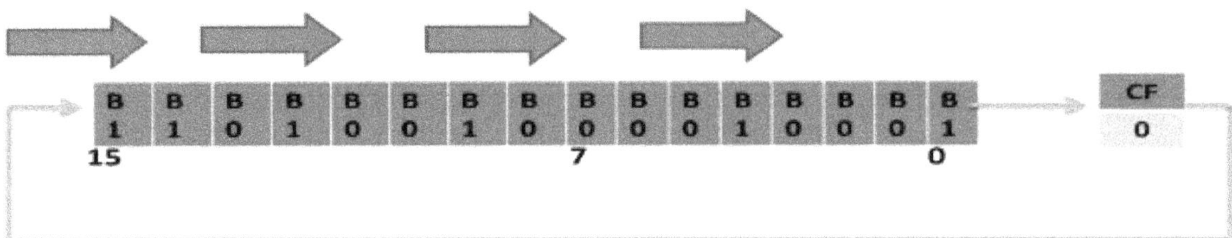

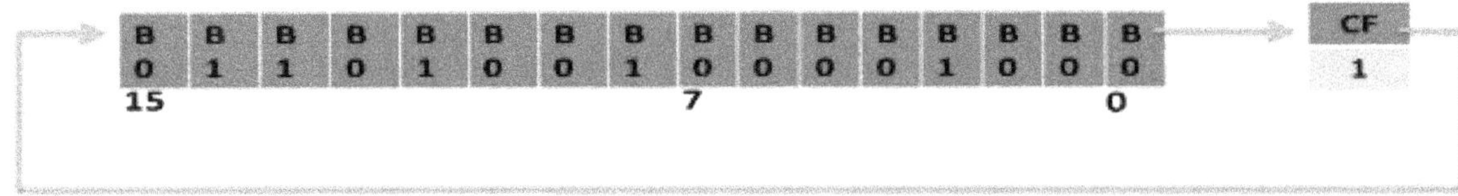

•

RCL

Also known as Rotate Left through Carry.

Each binary bit of the operand is rotated towards left by one position through Carry flag.

Least Significant Bit (LSB) of operand i.e. B0 is placed in the B1.

Then Most Significant Bit (MSB) of operand is placed in carry flag bit.

BEFORE EXECUTION

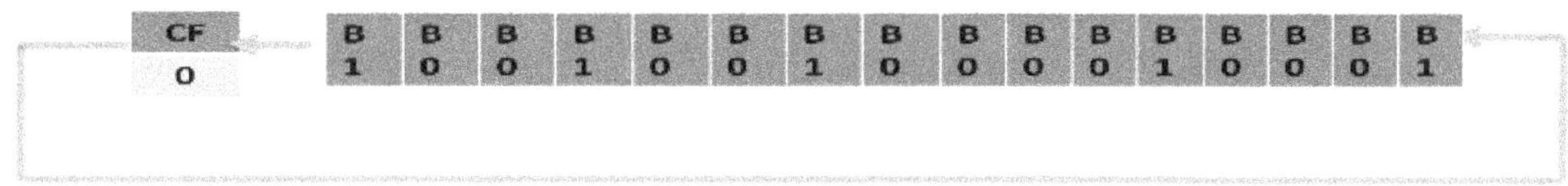

AFTER EXECUTION

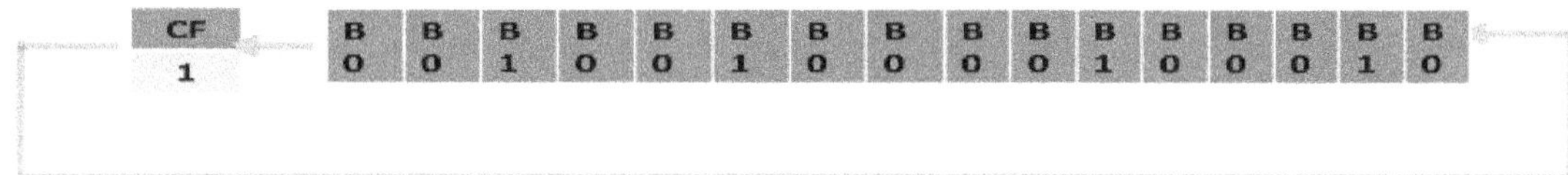

SHL/SAL

Shift logical/ arithmetic left

Shift operand word or byte bit by bit to left and insert zero in newly introduced LSB

The count is either 1 or specified in CL register

Operand may reside in register or memory location

Cannot be immediate data

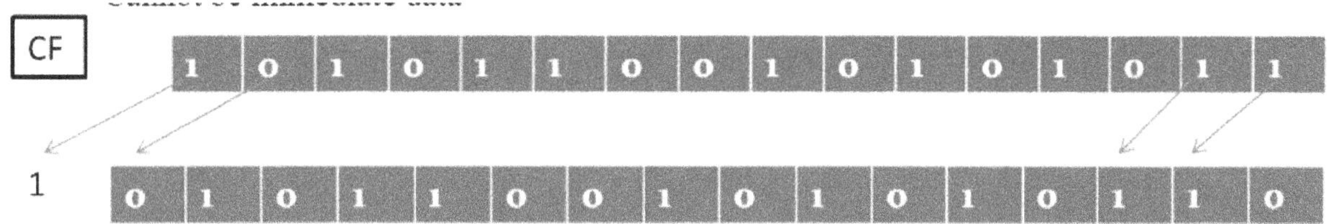

SHR

Shift logical right

Shift operand word or byte bit by bit to right and insert zero in newly introduced MSB

The count is either 1 or specified in CL register

Operand may reside in register or memory location

Instruction shifts data through carry flag

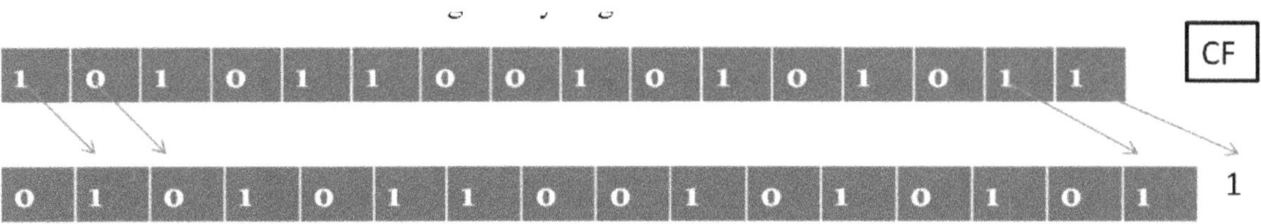

-

SAR

Performs right shift on operand
It inserts MSB of operand to newly inserted position
Shifts through carry flag

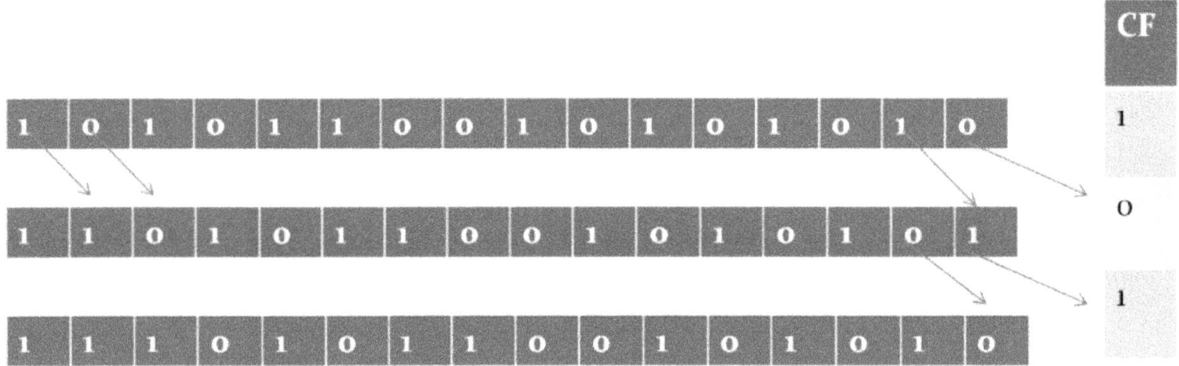

-

ROR

Rotate right without carry
Contents of destination operand is rotated to right bit wise either by one or count specified in CL register
LSB is shifted to carry flag and it is also transferred into MSB position

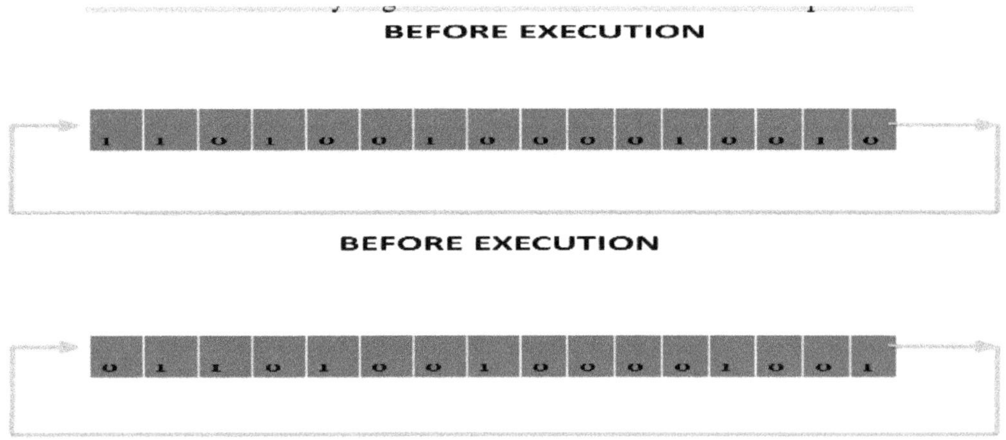

•

ROL

Rotate left without carry

Contents of destination operand is rotated to leftt bit wise either by one or count specified in CL register

MSB is shifted to carry flag and it is also transferred into LSB position

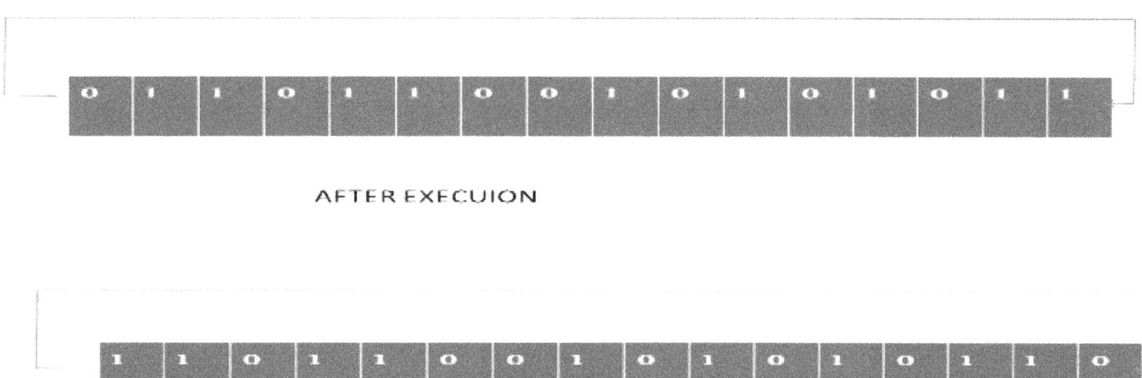

•

(4). String Manipulation Instructions

Q.Describe the string manipulation instructions of 8086?

REP

Also known as Repeat instruction prefix.

This instruction executed repeatedly until the 'CX' register becomes zero.

When 'CX' becomes zero then program control passes to next instruction.

There are following sub types of 'REP' instruction,

(i). REPE:- REPeat instruction while Equal.

(ii). REPZ:- REPeat instruction while Zero.

(iii). REPNE:- REPeat instruction while Not Equal.

(iv). REPNZ:- REPeat instruction while Not Zero.

CMPS

Also known as Compare String Byte or String Word.

The length of the string must be stored in register CX.

If both the byte or word are equal then zero flag will be set (i.e. ZF=1) otherwise it will be reset (i.e. ZF=0).

When zero flag will be set then 'CX'=0.

There are following sub types,

(i). CMPSB:- Compare String Byte.

(ii). CMPSW:- Compare String Word.

SCAS String:

It scans a string. It compares the String with byte in AL or with word in AX.

MOVS / MOVSB / MOVSW:

It causes moving of byte or word from one string to another.

In this instruction, the source string is in Data Segment and destination string is in Extra Segment.

SI and DI store the offset values for source and destination index.

(5). Branching Instructions (Control Insructions)

CALL

Also known as unconditional call.

Under unconditional call, the execution control is transferred to the specified location independent of any status or condition.(displacement is given along with instruction)

This instruction is used to call subroutine from a main program.

There are following sub types,

(i). NEAR CALL:- It pushes only IP into the stack.(Procedure and main program available in same segment

(ii). FAR CALL:- It pushes IP & CS into the stack. .(Procedure and main program available in Different segment

RET:

It returns the control from procedure to calling program.

Every CALL instruction should have a RET.

Q.What is the difference between JMP and LOOP instructions?

JMP

Also known as unconditional jump.

Under unconditional jump, the execution control is transferred to the specified location using 8-bit or 16-bit displacement.

There are following three formats of jump instruction,

(i). JMP

(ii). JMP

(iii). JMP

LOOP

This instruction executes the part of the program from the label or address specified in the instruction upto the loop instruction ,CX number of times.

Conditional jump instruction

Mnemonic	Operation	Flag tested
JC	Jump if carry	CF=1
JNC	Jump if no carry	CF=0
JZ/JE	Jump if zero	ZF=1
JNZ/JNE	Jump if not zero	ZF=0
JS	Jump if sign or negative	SF=1
JNS	Jump if positive	SF=0
JP/JPE	Jump if parity is even	PF=1
JNP/JPO	Jump if parity is odd	PF=0
JO	Jump if overflow	OF=1
JNO	Jump if no overflow	OF=0
JA/JNBE	Jump if above/if neither bellow nor equal	CF=0
JAE/JNB	Jump if above or equal/if not bellow	CF=0

JB/JNAE	Jump if bellow/if neither equal nor above	CF=1
Mnemonic	Operation	Flag tested
JC	Jump if carry	CF=1
JNC	Jump if no carry	CF=0
JZ/JE	Jump if zero	ZF=1
JNZ/JNE	Jump if not zero	ZF=0
JS	Jump if sign or negative	SF=1
JNS	Jump if positive	SF=0
JP/JPE	Jump if parity is even	PF=1
JNP/JPO	Jump if parity is odd	PF=0
JO	Jump if overflow	OF=1
JNO	Jump if no overflow	OF=0
JA/JNBE	Jump if above/if neither bellow nor equal	CF=0
JAE/JNB	Jump if above or equal/if not bellow	CF=0
JB/JNAE	Jump if bellow/if neither equal nor above	CF=1

•

(6). Flag Manipulation Instructions
Q.Exemplify flag manipulation instructions of 8086?
CMC
Also known as Complement Carry Flag.
It inverts contents of carry flag.
if CF = 1 then CF will be = 0.
if CF = 0 then CF will be = 1.
E.g. CMC
STC
Also known as Set Carry Flag.
It makes carry flag in set condition.
After execution CF = 1.
E.g. STC
CLI

Also known as Clear Interrupt Flag.
It makes interrupt flag in reset condition.
After execution IF = 0.
E.g. CLI
CLD
Also known as Clear Direction Flag.
It makes direction flag in reset condition.
After execution DF = 0.
E.g. CLD

Table 2.5 *Flag Manipulation Instructions*		
CLC	–	Clear carry flag
CMC	–	Complement carry flag
STC	–	Set carry flag
CLD	–	Clear direction flag
STD	–	Set direction flag
CLI	–	Clear interrupt flag
STI	–	Set interrupt flag

<u>(7). Machine Control Instructions</u>
HLT
Also known as Halt
It makes the processor to be in stable (do nothing) condition.
E.g. HLT
NOP
Also known as No Operation.
It tells about further there will be no operation to be performed.
E.g. NOP
<u>**ASSEMBLER DIRECTIVES AND OPERATORS**</u>
Q.What are assembler directives and pseudo-ops?
Q. Explain any five assembler directives of 8086?
Q. Write the usage of directives DUP and EVEN in 8086 assembly language programming.
Q. Explain the assembly process, assembler directives and operators in detail.?

The source program is composed of three types of lines: opcode, assemble directive(pseudo opcodes) & the comments. The opcode create the instruction for the CPU. Assembler directives give instruction to the assembler. Comments tells us what the program wants to tell us. Assembler directives are specific for a particular assembler. They are used only during the assembly of program & generate machine executable code.

An assembler is a program used to convert an assembly language program into the equivalent machine code modules which may further be converted to executable codes. The assembler decides the address of each label and substitutes the values for each of the constants and variables. It then forms the machine code for the mnemonics and data in the assembly language program. While doing these things, the assembler may find out syntax errors. The logical errors or other programming errors are not found out by the assembler. For completing all these tasks, an assembler needs some hints from the programmer, i.e. the required storage for a particular constant or a variable, logical names of the segments, types of the different routines and modules, end of file, etc. These, types of hints are given to the assembler using some predefined alphabetical strings called assembler directives. Assembler directives help the assembler to correctly understand the assembly language programs to prepare the codes.

Another type of hint which helps the assembler to assign a particular constant with a label or initialize particular memory locations or labels with constants is called an operator. Rather, the operators perform the arithmetic and logical tasks unlike directives that just direct the assembler to correctly interpret the program to code it appropriately. The following directives are commonly used in the assembly language programming practice using Microsoft Macro Assembler (MASM) or Turbo Assembler (TASM).

ASSUME: This directive tell the assembler the name of the logical segment it should use for a specified segment.

Assume logical segment name

This directive tell the assembler the name of the logical segment it should use for a specified segment.

Each segment is given a name in ALP

For eg, code segment is given name CODE

ASSUME CS:CODE à directs assembler that machine codes are available in segment CODE and CS register must loaded with that address

DB: This directive is used to declare a byte-type variable or to set aside one or more storage locations of type byte in memory (Define Byte).

Eg: RANKS DB 01 H, 02H, 03H,04H

VALUE DB 50H

DD: This directive is used to declare a variable of type double word or to reserve memory locations which can be accessed as type double word (Define Doubleword).

DW: This directive is used to tell the assembler to declare a variable of type word or to reserve storage locations of type word in memory.

EG: WORDS DW 1234H, 4567H

WDATA DW 5 DUP (6666H

DQ - Defined Quad Word. This directive is used to direct the assembler to reserve 4 words (8 bytes) of memory for the specified variable and may initialise it with the specified values.

DT - Define Ten Bytes. The DT directive directs the assembler to define the specified variable requiring la-bytes for its storage and initialise the 10bytes with the specified values. The directive may be used in case of variables facing heavy numerical calculations, generally processed by numerical processors.

ENDS: This directive is used with the name of a segment to indicate the end of that logical segment

```
DATA        SEGMENT
            :
            :
DATA        ENDS
ASSUME      CS : CODE, DS : DATA
CODE        SEGMENT
            :
            :
CODE        ENDS
END
```

EQU: It is used to give a name to some value or symbol

It is used assign label with a value or symbol

Used to reduce the recurrance of numerical values or constants in the program code.

LABEL EQU 0500H

END: This is put after the last statement of program. It tells the assembler this is the end of the program.

ENDP This directive is used with name procedure to indicate the end of a procedure to the assembler.

EVEN: This **EVEN** directive instructs the assembler to increment the location of the counter to the next even address if it is not already in the even address. If the word is at even address 8086 can read a memory in 1 bus cycle. If the word starts at an odd address, the 8086 will take 2 bus cycles to get the data. A series of words can be read much more quickly if they are at even address. When EVEN is used the location counter will simply incremented to next address and NOP instruction is inserted in that incremented location.

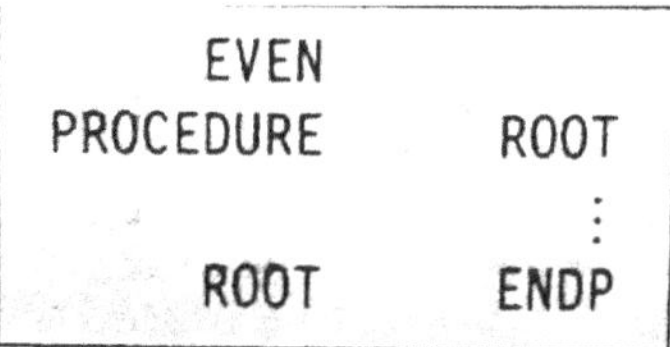

The above structure shows a procedure ROOT that is to be aligned at an even address. The assembler will start assembling the main program calling ROOT. When the assembler comes across the directive EVEN, it checks the contents of the location counter. If it is odd, it is updated to the next even value and then the ROOT procedure is assigned to that address, i.e. the updated contents of the location counter. If the content of the location counter is already even, then the ROOT procedure will be assigned with the same address.

GROUP - The **GROUP** directive is used to group the logical segments named after the directive into one logical group segment.

Eg:PROGRAM GROUP CODE, DATA, STACK

PROC: The **PROC** directive is used to identify the start of a procedure. The term near or far is used to specify the type of the procedure.

RESULT PROC NEAR *//marks the start of the procedure named result which is to be called by a program located in the same segment of the memory.*

ROUTINE PROC FAR

EXTRN: Tells the assembler that the name or labels following the directive are in some other assembly module.

Tells the assembler that the name or labels following the directive are in some other assembly module.

to call a procedure factorial in module 1 from module 2:-

In module 1 :declare Factorial as public.

In module 2 : it must be declared external

```
MODULE1        SEGMENT
PUBLIC         FACTORIAL  FAR
MODULE1        ENDS
MODULE2        SEGMENT
EXTRN          FACTORIAL  FAR
MODULE2        ENDS
```

•

ORG: Originate. The assembler uses a location counter to account for its relative position in data code segment.

Directs the assembler to start the memory allotment for a particular segment,block or code from the declared address in the ORG statement.

If ORG stmt is not present in the pgm,the LC is initialised to 0000.

If ORG 200H present at the starting of pgm,then the code will start from 200H address in the code segment.

Label:

Used to assign a name to the current content of the location counter.

During assembly process,whenever the assembler comes aross the LABEL directive,it assigns the declared label with the current contents of the location counter

Eg: DATA SEGMENT

DATAS DB 50H

DATA-LAST LABEL BYTE FAR

DATA ENDS

After reserving 50h locations for datas,the next location will be assigned a label DATA-LAST and its type will be byte and far.

MACRO: This directive defines the macros in the program.

ENDM is used along with MACRO. It defines the end of the macro.

OPERATORS

OFFSET: Offset of a Label When the assembler comes across the OFFSET operator along with a label, it first computes the 16-bit displacement (also called as offset interchangeably) of the particular label, and replaces the string 'OFFSET LABEL' by the computed displacement. This operator is used with arrays, strings, labels and procedures to decide their offsets in their default segments. The segment may also be decided by another operator of similar type, viz, SEG. Its most common use is in the case of the indirect, indexed, based indexed or other addressing techniques of similar types, used to refer to the memory indirectly. The examples of this operator are as follows:

Example:
CODE SEGMENT
MOV SI, OFFSET LIST
CODE ENDS
DATA SEGMENT
LIST DB 10H
DATA ENDS

PTR: Pointer The pointer operator is used to declare the type of a label, variable or memory operand. The operator PTR is prefixed by either BYTE or WORD. If the prefix is BYTE, then the particular label, variable or memory operand is treated as an 8-bit quantity, while if WORD is the prefix, then it is treated as a 16- 9 bit quantity. In other words, the PTR operator is used to specify the data type - byte or word. The examples of the PTR operator are as follows:

Example:
MOV AL, BYTE PTR [SI] //Moves content of memory location addressed by SI (8-bit) to AL

INC BYTE PTR [BX] //Increments byte contents of memory location addressed by BX

MOV BX, WORD PTR [2000H] //Moves 16-bit content of memory location 2000H to BX, i.e. [2000H] to BL [2001 H] to BH

INC WORD PTR [3000H] - Increments word contents of memory location 3000H considering contents of 3000H (lower byte) and 3001 H (higher byte) as a 16-bit number

SHORT The SHORT operator indicates to the assembler that only one byte is required to code the displacement for a jump (i.e. displacement is within -128 to +127 bytes from the address of the byte next to the jump opcode). This method of specifying the jump address saves the memory. Otherwise, the assembler may reserve two bytes for the displacement. The syntax of the statement is as given below.JMP SHORT LABEL

SEG: Segment of a Label The SEG operator is used to decide the segment address of the label, variable, or procedure and substitutes the segment base address in place of 'SEG label'. The example given below explain the use of SEG operator.

Example
MOV AX, SEG ARRAY //This statement moves the segment address
MOV DS, AX //of ARRAY in which it is appearing, to register AX and then to DS.

TYPE The TYPE operator directs the assembler to decide the data type of the specified label and replaces the 'TYPE label' by the decided data type. For the word type variable, the data type is 2, for double word type, it is 4, and for byte type, it is 1. Suppose, the STRING is a word array. The instruction MOV AX, TYPE STRING moves the value 0002H in AX.

'+' & '—' OPERATORS: These operators represent arithmetic addition and subtraction respectively and are typically used to add or subtract displacements(8 or 16 bit) to base or index registers or stack or base pointers.

Eg: MOV AL, [SI+2]
MOV DX, [BX – 5]
MOV BX, [OFFSET LABEL + 10H]

FAR PTR: This directive indicates the assembler that the label following FAR PTR is not available within the same segment and the address of the label is of 32 bits ie 2 bytes offset followed by 2 bytes segment address.

Eg:

JMP FAR PTR LABEL

CALL FAR PTR ROUTINE

NEAR PTR: This directive indicates that the label following NEAR PTR is in the same segment and needs only 16 bit ie 2 byte offset to address it

Eg:

JMP NEAR PTR LABEL

CALL NEAR PTR ROUTINE

Assembly Language programming

ASSEMBLY PROCESS

Microsoft assembler MASM is an easy to use and popular assembler. The MASM accepts the file names only with extension .ASM. Even if a filename without any extension is given as input, it provides an .ASM extension to it. The command for assembling the program is

C> MASM <filename.asm>

Eg:

C> MASM KMB.ASM

or

C> MASM KMB

After the cross reference file name is entered the assembly process starts. If the program contains syntax errors, they are displayed using error code number and the corresponding line number at which they appear. Once these syntax errors and warnings are taken care of by the programmer, the assembly process is completed successfully. The successful assembly process may generate the .OBJ,.LST and .CRF files, which may further be used by the linker program to link the object modules and generate an executable (.EXE) file from a .OBJ file.

LINKING AND RELOCATION

The DOS linking program LINK.EXE links the different object modules of a source program and function library routines to generate an integrated executable code of the source program. The main input to the linker is the .OBJ file that contains the object modules of the source programs. Other supporting information may be obtained from the files generated by the MASM. The linker program is invoked using the following options.

C> LINK

or

C>LINK <filename.OBJ>

The .OBJ extension is a must for a file to be accepted by the LINK as a valid object file. The first option may generate a display asking for the object file, list file and libraries as inputs and an expected name of the .EXE file to be generated. The output of the LINK program is an executable file with the entered filename and .EXE extension. This executable filename can further be entered at the DOS prompt to execute the file.

After linking, there has to be re-allocation of the sequences of placing the codes before actually placement of the codes in the memory. The loader program performs the task of reallocating the codes after finding the physical RAM addresses available at a given instant.

DEBUGGING

DEBUG.COM is a DOS utility that facilitates the debugging and trouble shooting of assembly language programs. The DEBUG utility enables you to have the control of resources.

The DEBUG command at DOS prompt invokes this facility. A '_' (dash) display signals the successful invoke operation of DEBUG.

DEBUG offers a good platform for trouble shooting, executing and observing the results of the assembly language programs. There are different debug commands for executing debug statement.

Write an assembly language program for addition of two numbers.

ASSUME CS:CODE, DS:DATA

DATA SEGMENT
OPR1 DW 1234H
OPR2 DW 0002H
RESULT DW O1 DUP(?)
DATA ENDS
CODE SEGMENT
START: MOV AX, DATA
MOV DS,AX
MOV AX,OPR1
MOV BX,OPR2
CLC
ADD AX,BX
MOV DI,OFFSET RESULT
MOV [DI],AX
MOV AH,4CH
INT 21H
CODE ENDS
END START

Write a program to find out the number of even and odd numbers from a given series of 16 bit hexadecimal numbers.

ASSUME CS:CODE, DS:DATA
DATA SEGMENT
LIST DW 2357H, 3456H, 1234H, 6754H
COUNT EQU O4H
DATA ENDS
CODE SEGMENT
START: XOR BX,BX
XOR DX,DX
MOV AX, DATA
MOV DS,AX
MOV CL, COUNT
MOV SI, OFFSET LIST
AGAIN: MOV AX, [SI]
ROR AX,01
JC ODD
INC BX
JMP NEXT
ODD : INC DX
NEXT: ADD SI, 02
DEC CL
JNZ AGAIN
MOV AH,4CH
INT 21H
CODE ENDS
END START

MACROS

Q.Differentiate macro and subroutine?

Q. What are macros.?

Q. Write short notes on a) assembler b)macros?

Macro is a segment of code that needs to be written only once but whose basic structure can be repeated with each reference. Suppose a number of instructions are repeating through in the main program, the listings become lengthy. So a macro definition, i.e. a label, is assigned with the repeatedly appearing string of instructions. The process of assigning a label or macroname to the string is called defining a macro.

A macro within a macro is called a nested macro. The macroname or macro definition is then used throughout the main program to refer to that string of instructions.

Differences between macro and subroutine

Macro	Subroutine
The complete code of the instructions string is inserted at each place where the macro-name appears. Hence the EXE file becomes lengthy.	The executable code in case of subroutines becomes smaller as the subroutine appears only once in the executable code. Hence, the EXE file is smaller.
Macro does not utilize the service of stack	The control is transferred to a subroutine whenever it is called, and thus utilizes the stack service.
Requires more memory space for execution	Requires less memory space for execution
Requires less time for execution	Requires more time for execution, as it contains CALL and RET instructions.

•

Defining a MACRO

A MACRO can be defined anywhere in a program using the directives MACRO and ENDM. The label prior to MACRO is the macro name which should be used in the actual program. The ENDM marks the end of the instructions or statements sequence assigned with the macro name.

The following macro DISPLAY displays the message MSG on the CRT. The syntax is as given:

DISPLAY MACRO

MOV AX, SEG MSG

MOV DS, AX

MOV DX, OFFSET MSG

MOV AH, 09H

INT 21H

ENDM

A macro may also be used to represent statements and directives. A macro may be called by quoting its name, along with any values to be passed to the macro.

Passing parameters to a MACRO

Using parameters in a definition, the programmer specifies the parameters of the macro those are likely to be changed each time the macro is called. For example, the DISPLAY macro written above can be made to display two different messages MSG1 and MSG2 as shown

DISPLAY MACRO MSG

MOV AX, SEG MSG

MOV DS, AX

MOV DX, OFFSET MSG

MOV AH, 09H

INT 21H

ENDM

The parameter MSG can be replaced by MSG1 or MSG2 while calling the macro as shown.

:

:

:

:DISPLAY MSG1

:

:

DISPLAY MSG2

:

:

MSG1 DB 0AH,0DH,"Program terminated normally:,0AH,0DH,"$"

MSG2 DB 0AH, 0DH, "Retry, Abort, Fail",0AH,0DH,"$"

<u>PROCEDURES</u>

Q.What are different ways of passing parameters to procedures?

A procedure is a set of code that can be branched to and returned from in such a way that the code is as if it were inserted at the point from which it is branched to. The branch to procedure is referred to as the *call,* and the corresponding branch back is known as the *return*. The return is always made to the instruction immediately following the call regardless of where the call is located.

The CALL instruction not only branches to the indicated address, but also pushes the return address onto the stack. The RET instruction simply pops the return address from the stack. The registers used by the procedure need to be stored before their contents are changed, and then restored just before their contents are changed, and then restored just before the procedure is excited.

A CALL may be direct or indirect and intrasegment or intersegment. If the CALL is intersegment, the return must be intersegment. Intersegment call must push both (IP) and (CS) onto the stack. The return must correspondingly pop two words from the stack. In the case of intrasegment call, only the contents of IP will be saved and retrieved when call and return instructions are used.

Procedures are used in the source code by placing a statement of the form at the beginning of the procedure.

Procedure name PROC Attribute and by terminating the procedure with a statement Procedure name ENDP

The attribute that can be used will be either **NEAR** or **FAR**. If the attribute is NEAR, the RET instruction will only pop a word into the IP register, but if it is FAR, it will also pop a word into the CS register.

A procedure may be in:

1. The same code segment as the statement that calls it.

2. A code segment that is different from the one containing the statement that calls it, but in the same source module as the calling statement..

3. A different source module and segment from the calling statement.

<u>Passing parameters to procedures</u>

Procedures or subroutines may require input data or constants for their execution. Their data or constants may be passed to the subroutine by the main program (host or calling program) or some subroutine may access readily available data of constants available in memory.

Generally, the following techniques are used to pass input data/parameter to procedures in assembly language programs.

1)Using global declared variable

2)Using registers of CPU architecture

3)Using memory locations(reserved)

4)using stack

5)Using PUBLIC & EXTRN

Besides these methods, if a procedure is interactive, it may directly accept inputs from input devices.

STACKS

Q.Describe the stack structure of 8086?

Stack is a block of memory that may be used for temporarily storing the contents of the registers inside the CPU. It is a top-down data structure whose elements are accessed using a pointer that is implemented using the Stack Pointer (SP)and Stack Segment (SS) registers.

The process of storing the data in the stack is called 'pushing into' the stack and the reverse process of transferring the data back from the stack to the CPU register is known as 'popping off' the stack. The stack is essentially *Last-In-First-Out* (LIFO) data segment. This means that the data which is pushed into the stack last will be on top of stack and will be popped off the stack first.

STACK STRUCTURE OF 8086/8088

The stack contains a set of sequentially arranged data bytes, with the last item appearing on top of the stack. This item will be popped off the stack first for use by the CPU. The Stack Pointer (SP) register is a 16-bit register that contains the offset address of the memory location in the stack segment. The stack segment, like any other segment, may have a memory block of a maximum of 64 Kbyte locations, and thus may overlap with any other segments. The Stack Segment register (SS) contains the base address of the stack segment in the memory. The Stack Segment register (SS) and Stack Pointer register (SP) together address the stack-top as explained below:

SS : 5000H

SP : 2050H

Physical address of Stack-top = 5000H * 10H + 2050H= 52050H

If the stack top points to a memory location 52050H, it means that the location 52050H is already occupied with the previously pushed data. The next 16 bit push operation will decrement the stack pointer by two, so that it will point to the new stack-top 5204EH and the decremented contents of SP will be 204EH. This location will now be occupied by the recently pushed data.

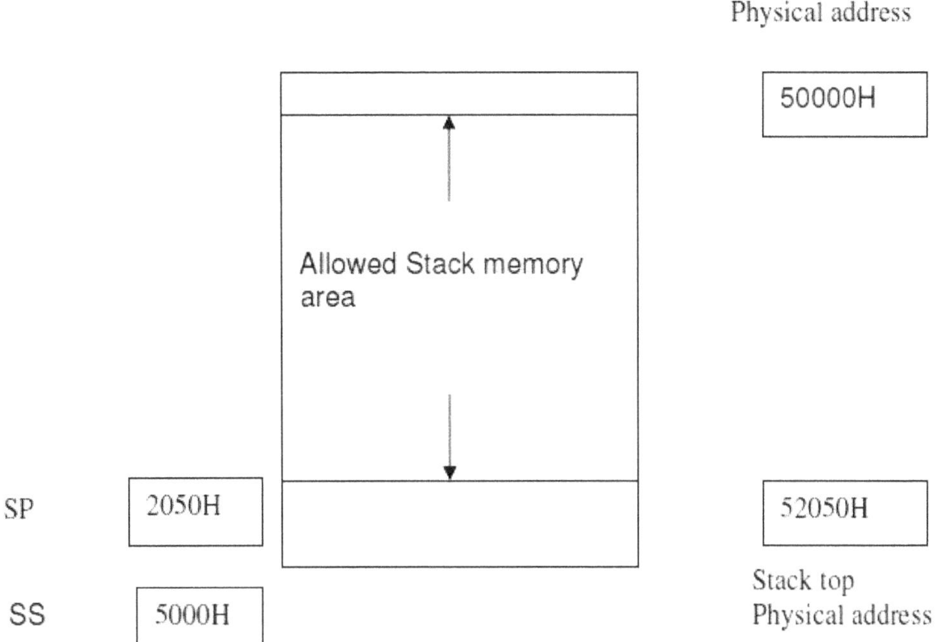

Fig. 4.4 Stack-top address calculation

•

Thus for a selected value of SS, the maximum value of SP=FFFFH and the segment can have maximum of 64K locations.

After a subroutine is called using the CALL instruction, the IP is incremented to the next instruction. Then the contents of IP,CS and flag register are pushed automatically to the stack. The control is then transferred to the specified address in the CALL instruction i.e. the starting address of the subroutine. Then the subroutine is executed.

****

More programming examples:-

```
ASSUME CS:CODE,DS:DATA
DATA SEGMENT
NUMLIST DB 52H,23H,-
COUNT EQU 100D
RESULT DW 01H DUP(?)
DATA ENDS
CODE SEGMENT
ORG 200H
START:          MOV AX,DATA
                MOV DS,AX
                MOV CX,COUNT
                XOR AX,AX
                XOR BX,BX
                MOV SI,OFFSET NUMLIST
AGAIN:          MOV BL,[SI]
                ADD AX,BX
                INC SI
                DEC CX
                JNZ AGAIN
                MOV DI,OFFSET RESULT
                MOV [DI],AX
                MOV AH,4CH
                INT 21H
                CODE ENDS
END             START
```

2.Largest number from a given unordered array of 8 bit numbers

```
                            ; ... been compared.
ASSUME CS:CODE,DS:DATA
DATA SEGMENT
LIST DB 52H,23H,56H,45H,--
COUNT EQU OF
LARGEST DB 01H DUP(?)
DATA ENDS
CODE SEGMENT
START:          MOV AX,DATA
                MOV DS,AX
                MOV SI,OFFSET LIST
                MOV CL,COUNT
                MOV AL,[SI]
AGAIN:          CMP AL,[SI+1]
                JL NEXT
                MOV AL,[SI+1]
NEXT:           INC SI
                DEC CL
                JNZ AGAIN
                MOV SI,OFFSET LARGEST
                MOV [SI],AL
                MOV AH,4CH
                INT 21H
                CODE ENDS
END             START
```

Above pgm for a series of words

```
ASSUME CS:CODE,DS:DATA
DATA SEGMENT
LIST DW 1234H,2354H,0056H,045AH,-
COUNT EQU OF
LARGEST DW 01H DUP(?)
DATA ENDS
CODE SEGMENT
START:              MOV AX,DATA

                    MOV DS,AX
                    MOV SI,OFFSET LIST
                    MOV CL,COUNT
                    MOV AX,[SI]
AGAIN:              CMP AX,[SI+2]
                    JNL NEXT
                    MOV AX,[SI+2]
NEXT:               INC SI
                    INC SI
                    DEC CL
                    JNZ AGAIN
                    MOV SI,OFFSET LARGEST
                    MOV [SI],AX
                    MOV AH,4CH
                    INT 21H
CODE                ENDS
                    END       START
```

Program 3.4 *Listings*

4. Pgm to find out the number of +ve and −ve numbers from a given list

```
ASSUME  CS:CODE,DS:DATA
DATA  SEGMENT
LIST  DW  2579H,0A500H,0C009H,0159H,0B900H
COUNT  EQU  05H
DATA  ENDS
CODE  SEGMENT
START:              XOR  BX,BX
                    XOR  DX,DX
                    MOV  AX,DATA
                    MOV  DS,AX
                    MOV  CL,COUNT
                    MOV  SI,OFFSET  LIST
AGAIN:              MOV  AX,[SI]
                    SHL  AX,01
                    JC  NEG
                    INC  BX
                    JMP  NEXT
NEG:                INC  DX
NEXT:               ADD  SI,02
                    DEC  CL
                    JNZ  AGAIN
                    MOV  AH,4CH
                    INT  21H
                    CODE  ENDS
                    END  START
```

5. Pgm to move a string of data words from offset 2000H to Offset 3000H .The length of string is 0FH

```
                        MOV     SI ,2000H
                        MOV     DI ,3000H
                        MOV     CX ,0FH
        AGAIN :         MOV     AX ,[SI]
                        MOV     [DI], AX
                        ADD     SI, 02H
                        ADD     DI, 02H
                        DEC     CX
                        JNZ     AGAIN
                        HLT
```

6. WAP to perform one byte BCDaddition

Solution It is assumed that the operands are in BCD form, but the CPU considers it hexadecimal and accordingly performs addition. Consider the following example for addition. Carry is set to be zero.

```
      92
   +  59
   ─────
      E B        Actual result after addition considering hex. operands

     1011
   + 0110        As 0BH (LSD of addition) > 09, add 06 to it.
   ──────
    10001        Least significant nibble of result (neglect the auxiliary
                 carry) → AF is set to 1
```

0110 is added to most significant nibble of the result if it is greater than 9 or AF is set.

```
                              1         Carry from previous digit (AF)
              E       →    1 1 1 0
                      +    0 1 1 0
                      ___________
CF is set to 1             0 1 0 1       next significant nibble of result
```

Result CF   Most significant   Least significant digit
     1   5   1

```
    ASSUME  CS:CODE,DS:DATA
    DATA SEGMENT
                    OPR1  EQU  92H
                    OPR2  EQU  52H
    RESULT DB 02 DUP(00)
    DATA ENDS
    CODE SEGMENT
    START:
                    MOV AX, DATA
                    MOV DS,AX
                    MOV BL,OPR1
                    XOR AL,AL
                    MOV AL,OPR2
                    ADD AL,BL
                    DAA
                    MOV RESULT,AL
                    JNC MSBO
                    INC [RESULT+1]
    MSBO:
                    MOV AH,4CH
                    INT 21H
    CODE ENDS
    END START
```

7.ALP to arrange a given series of hexadecimal bytes in ascending order

Program 3.8

Write an assembly language program to arrange a given series of hexadecimal bytes in ascending order.

Solution   There exist a large number of sorting algorithms. The algorithm used here is called *bubble sorting*. The method of sorting is explained as follows. To start with, the first number of the series is compared with the second one. If the first number is greater than second, exchange their positions in the series otherwise leave the positions unchanged. Then, compare the second number in the recent form of the series with third and repeat the exchange part that you have carried out for the first and the second number, and for all the remaining numbers of the series. Repeat this procedure for the complete series $(n-1)$ times. After $(n-1)$ iterations, you will get the largest number at the end of the series, where n is the length of the series. Again start from the first address of the series. Repeat the same procedure right from the first element to the last element. After $(n-2)$ iterations you will get the second highest number at the last but one place in the series. Continue this till the complete series is arranged in ascending order. Let the series be as given:

```
53 , 25 , 19, 02              n = 4
25 , 53 , 19, 02              1st operation
25 , 19 , 53 , 02             2nd operation
25 , 19 , 02 , 53             3rd operation
largest no.          ⇒       4 – 1 = 3 operations
19 , 25 , 02 , 53             1st operation
19 , 02 , 25 , 53             2nd operation
2nd largest number   ⇒       4 – 2 = 2 operations
02 , 19 , 25 , 53             1st operation
3rd largest number   ⇒       4 – 3 = 1 operations
```

Instead of taking a variable count for the external loop in the program like $(n-1)$, $(n-2)$, $(n-3)$, ..., etc. It is better to take the count $(n-1)$ all the time for simplicity. The resulting program is given as shown.

```
        ASSUME CS:CODE,DS:DATA
        DATA SEGMENT
        LIST DW 53H,25H,19H,02H
        COUNT EQU 04
        DATA ENDS
        CODE SEGMENT
        START:          MOV AX,DATA
                        MOV DS,AX
                        MOV DX,COUNT-1
        AGAIN0:         MOV CX,DX
                        MOV SI,OFFSET LIST
        AGAIN1:         MOV AX,[SI]
                        CMP AX,[SI+2]
                        JL PR1              Jump on Less
                        XCHG [SI+2],AX
                        XCHG [SI],AX
        PR1:            ADD SI,02
                        LOOP AGAIN1
                        DEC DX
                        JNZ AGAIN0
                        MOV AH,4CH
                        INT 21H
        CODE            ENDS
                        END START
```

ALP to find the Factorial of a given number

```
DATA SEGMENT
A EQU 5
DATA ENDS
CODE SEGMENT
ASSUME DS:DATA,CS:CODE
START:
MOV AX,DATA
MOV DS,AX
MOV AH,00
MOV AL,A
L1: DEC A
MUL A
MOV CL,A
CMP CL,01
```

```
JNZ L1
MOV AH,4CH
INT 21H
CODE ENDS
END START
```
****

CHAPTER THREE

INTERRUPTS IN 8086

INTERRUPTS AND INTERRUPT SERVICE ROUTINE

The meaning of 'interrupts' is to break the sequence of operation.

While the Microprocessor is executing a program, an 'interrupt' breaks the normal sequence of execution of instructions, diverts its execution to some other program called Interrupt Service Routine (ISR).

After executing, control returns the back again to the main program. Nested Interrupt:- interrupt within interrupt

Whenever a number of devices interrupt a CPU at a time, and if the processor is able to handle them them properly, it is said to have <u>multiple interrupt processing capability</u>.

In the case of 8086 there are two interrupt pins: INTR, NMI

The NMI is a non maskable interrupt input pin which means that any interrupt request at NMI pin cannot be masked or disabled by any means.

The INTR pin may be masked using IF(Interrupt Flag).. If more than one INTR interrupt occurs at a time, then an external chip called programmable interrupt controller is required to handle them.

The <u>Interrupt Service Routines</u> are the programs to be executed by interrupting the main program execution of the CPU, after an interrupt request appears.

After the execution of ISR, the main program continues its execution further from the point at which it was interrupted.

INTERRUPT CYCLE OF 8086/8088

There are two types of interrupts.

External Interrupt: An external device or signal interrupts the processor from outside or the interrupt is generated outside the processor.Eg: Keyboard Interrupt

Internal interrupt: It is generated internally by the processor circuit, or by the execution of an interrupt instruction.Eg: Divide by zero interrupt, overflow interrupt, interrupts due to INT instructions etc.

When an external device interrupts the CPU at the interrupt pin, either NMI or INTR of the 8086, while the CPU is executing an instruction of the program. The CPU first completes the execution of current instruction and IP is incremented to point to next instruction.

The CPU then acknowledges the requesting device on its INTA pin immediately if it is a NMI, TRAP or DIVIDE BY ZERO interrupt.

If it is an INT request, CPU checks the IF flag. If the IF is set, the interrupt request is acknowledged using the INTA pin. If IF is not set, the request is not ignored.

After the interrupt is acknowledged, the CPU computes the vector address from the type of the interrupt that may be passed to the interrupt structure of the CPU internally(in case of software interrupts like NMI, TRAP or DIVIDE BY ZERO interrupt) or externally i.e. from an interrupt controller (The contents of IP and CS are pushed onto stack. The IP and CS now point to address of next instruction of main program from which the execution is to be continued after executing ISR. The PSW are pushed onto stack).

The interrupt flag (IF) is cleared.

The TF is also cleared after every response to the single step interrupt.

The control is then transferred to ISR for serving the interrupting device.

The new address of ISR is found out from the Interrupt vector table.

The execution of ISR starts.

If further interrupts are to be responded during the time the first interrupt is serviced, The IF should again be set to 1 by the ISR of the first interrupt.

If the interrupt flag is not set, the subsequent interrupt signals will not be acknowledged by the processor, till the current one is completed.

The programmable interrupt controller is used for managing the multiple interrupts based on their priorities.

And the end of ISR, the last instruction should be IRET.

When the CPU executes IRET, the contents of flags, IP and CS which were saved at the start by the CALL instruction are now retrieved to the respective registers.

The execution continues onwards from this address, received by IP and CS.

<u>HOW THE 8086/88 FINDS OUT THE ADDRESS OF AN ISR?</u>

Every external and internal interrupt is assigned with a type(N), that is either implicit(in case of NMI, TRAP or DIVIDE BY ZERO interrupt) or specified in the instruction INT N(in case of internal interrupts).

In case of external interrupts the type is passed to the processor by an external hardware like programmable interrupt controller.

In the zero[th] segment of physical address space i.e. CS=0000, Intel has reserved 1024 locations for storing the interrupt vector table.

The 8086 supports a total of 256 types of interrupts from 00 to FFH. Each interrupt requires four bytes, two bytes for IP and CS of its ISR.

Thus a total of 1024 bytes are required for 256 interrupt types, hence the interrupt vector table starts at location 0000:0000 and ends at 0000:03FFH.

The IVT contains IP and CS of all the interrupt types stored sequentially from address 0000:0000 to 0000:03FFH.

The interrupt type N is multiplied by 4 and the hexadecimal multiplication obtained gives the offset address in the zero[th] code segment at which the IP and CS addresses of the ISR are stored.

The execution automatically starts from the new CS:IP.

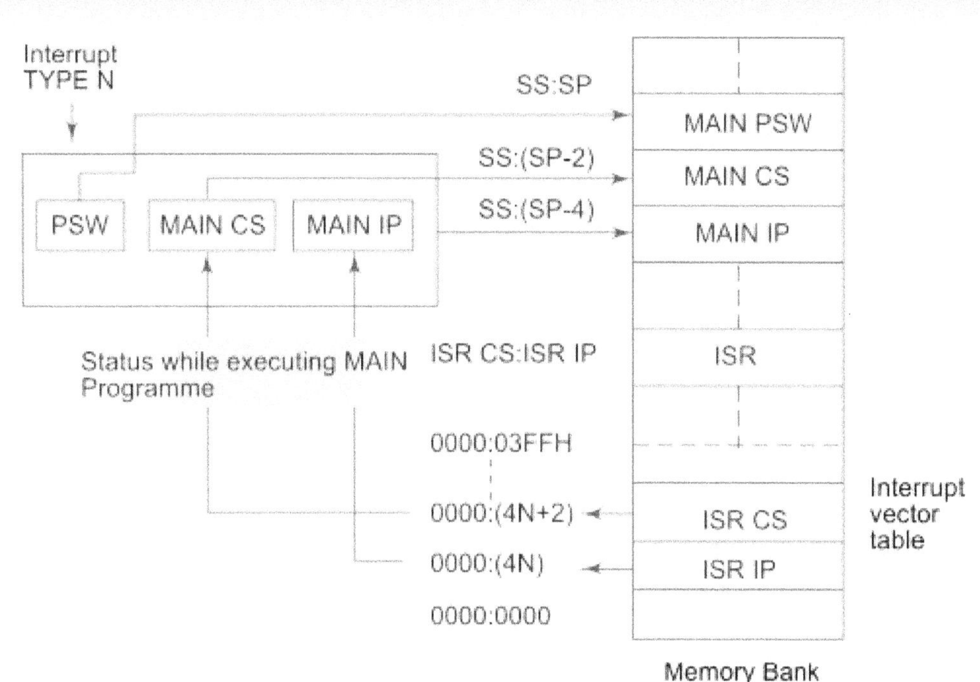

Fig. 4.4 *Interrupt Response Sequence*

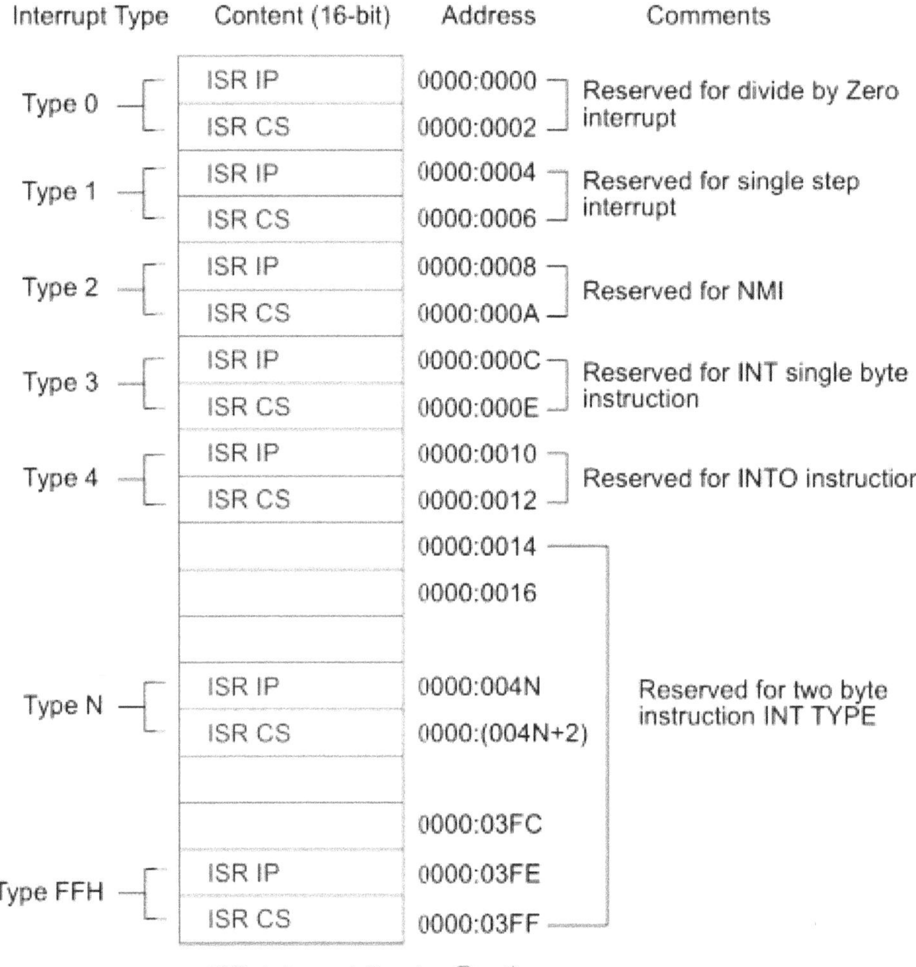

Fig. 4.5 *Structure of Interrupt Vector Table of 8086/88*

NON MASKABLE INTERRUPT

The pin for non maskable interrupt is NMI that has the highest priority among the external interrupts.

TRAP (Single Step-Type-1) is an internal interrupt having highest priority amongst all the interrupts except the Divide by Zero (Type0) exception.

The NMI pin should remain high for at least two clock cycles and need not synchronized with the clock being sensed.

When NMI is activated, the current instruction being executed is completed and then the NMI is served.

In case of string type instructions, this interrupt will serve only after the complete string has been manipulated.

MASKABLE INTERRUPT (INTR)

The processor 8086/88 provides a pin INTR, that has the lower priority compared to NMI.

The priorities within the INTR Types are decided by the type of the INTR signal that is to be passed to processor via data bus by some external programmable interrupt controller.

The INTR pin can be masked by resetting the interrupt flag.

It is internally synchronized with the high transition of the clock.

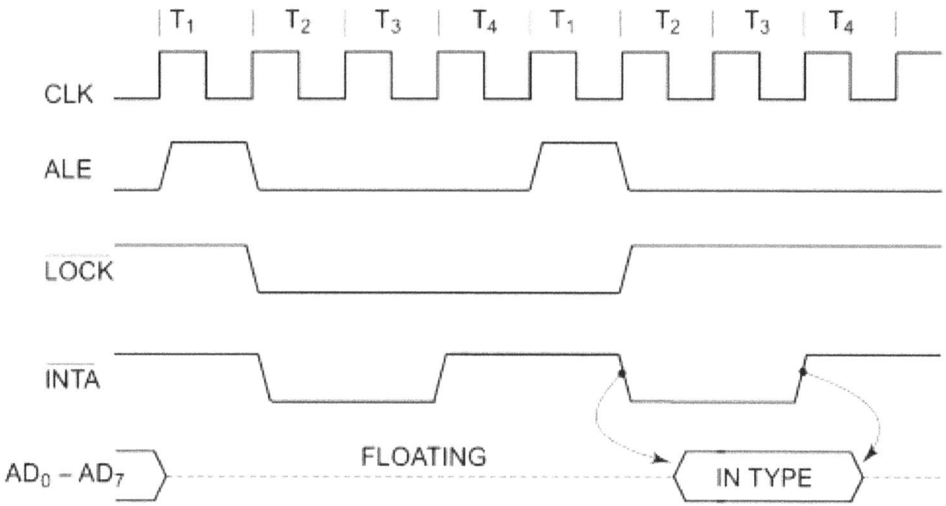

Fig. 4.6   *Interrupt Acknowledge Sequence of 8086*

Suppose an external signal interrupts the processor and the pin LOCK goes low at the trailing edge of first ALE pulse that appears after the interrupt signal preventing the use of bus for any other purpose.

The pin LOCK remains low till the start of the next machine cycle. With the trailing edge of LOCK, the INTA goes a low remains low for two clock states before returning back to the high state. It remains high till the start of the next machine cycle.

The INTA again goes low, remains low for the two states before running to high state.

The first trailing edge of ALE floats the bus AD0-AD7, while the second trailing edge prepares the bus to accept the type of interrupt.

The type of interrupt remains on the bus for a period of two cycles

For INTR signal, to be responded in the next instruction cycle, it must go high in the last clock cycle of the current instructions. The INTR requests appearing after the last clock cycle of the current instruction will be responded to after the execution of the next instruction.

The status of pending interrupts is checked at the end of each instruction cycle,

If the IF is set, the processor is ready to respond to INTR and if it is reset, the processor will be automatically reset. The interrupt acknowledge sequence is shown below:

Interrupt programming

Before programming any type of interrupt, the interrupt vector table must be set with the IP and CS address of the ISR. The interrupt vector table is initialized correctly to point to ISR.

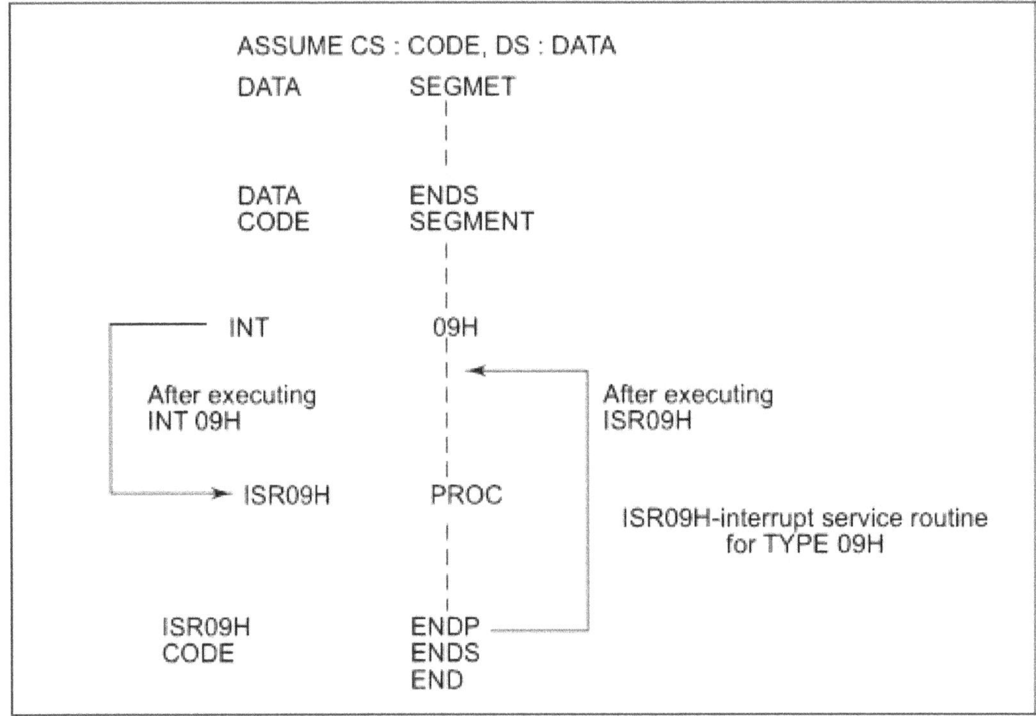

Fig. 4.7   *Transfer of Control during Execution of an Interrupt Service Routine*

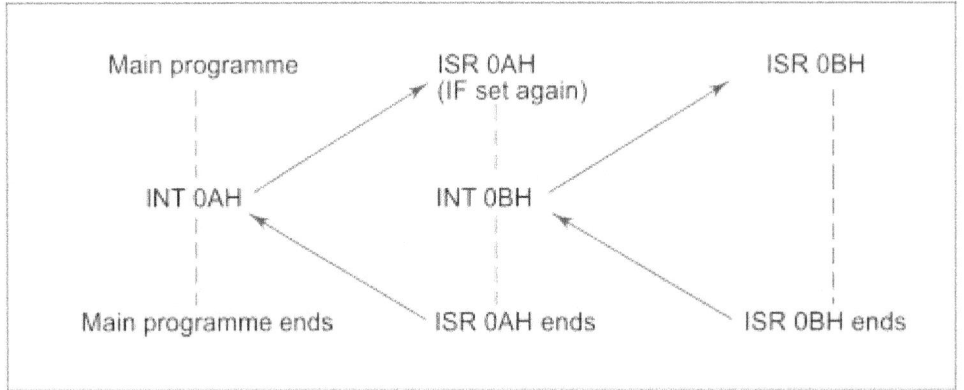

Fig. 4.8   *Transfer of Control for Nested Interrupts*

Write a program to create a file RESULT and store in it 500H bytes from the memory block starting at 1000:1000, if either an interrupt appears at INTR pin with Type 0AH or an instruction equivalent to the above interrupt is executed.

Note: Pin IRQ_2 available at IO channel of PC is equivalent to Type 0AH interrupt.

```
ASSSUME CS : CODE, DS : DATA
DATA        SEGMENT
    FILENAME      DB "RESULT", "$"
    MESSAGE DB "FILE WASN'T CREATED SUCCESSFULLY",0AH,0DH,"$"
DATA        ENDS
CODE        SEGMENT
START:      MOV AX, CODE
            MOV DS, AX              ; Set DS at CODE for setting IVT.
            MOV DX, OFFSET ISROA    ; Set DX at the offset of ISROA.
            MOV AX,250AH            ; Set IVT using function value 250AH
                                              in AX
            INT 21H                 ; under INT21H.
            MOV DX, OFFSET FILENAME ; Set pointer to Filename.
            MOV AX, DATA            ; Set the DS at DATA for Filename
            MOV DS, AX
            MOV CX, 00H
            MOV AH, 3CH             ; Create file with the File name
                                              'RESULT'.
            INT 21H
            JNC FURTHER             ; If no carry, create operation is
            MOV DX,OFFSET MESSAGE   ; successful else
            MOV AH,09H              ; display the MESSAGE.
            INT 21H
            JMP STOP
FURTHER :       INT 0AH            ; If the file is created



successfully,
STOP :          MOV AH,4CH         ; write into it and return
                INT 21H            ; to DOS prompt.
                                   ; This interrupt service routine
                                          writes 500 bytes into the
```

```
                                 ; file RESULT and returns to the mai
                                     program.

ISROA PROC NEAR
    MOV BX, AX                   ; Take file handle in BX,
    MOV CX, 500H                 ; byte count in CX,
    MOV DX, 1000H                ; offset of block in DX,
    MOV AX, 1000H                ; Segment value of block
    MOV DS, AX                   ; in DS.
    MOV AH, 40 H                 ; Write in the file and
    INT 21 H                     ; return.
    IRET                         ;
ISROA       ENDP
CODE        ENDS
    END START
```

Program 4.4

Write a program that gives display 'IRT2 is OK' if a hardware signal appears on IRQ$_2$ pin and 'IRT3 is OK' if it appears on IRQ$_3$ pin of PC IO Channel.

```
ASSUME      CS:CODE, DS:DATA
DATA        SEGMENT
MSG1        DB "IRT2 IS OK" ,0AH, 0DH, "$"
MSG2        DB "IRT3 IS OK",0AH,0DH, "$"
DATA        ENDS
CODE        ES

START:      MOV AX, CODE
            MOV DS, AX                  : Set IVT for Type 0AH
            MOV DX, OFFSET ISR1
            MOV AX,250AH                : IRQ2 is equivalent to Type 0AH
            INT 21H
            MOV DX, OFFSET ISR2         : Set IVT for Type 0BH
            MOV AX, 250BH               : IRQ3 is equivalent to TYPE 0BH
            INT 21H
HERE :      JUMP HERE
                                        : ISR1 and ISR2 dispaly the message
ISR1        PROC  LOCAL
            MOV AX, DATA
            MOV DS, AX


            MOV DX, OFFSET MSG1              : Display message MSG
            MOV AH, 09H
            INT 21 H
            IRET
ISR1        ENDP
ISR2        PROC LOCAL
            MOV AX, DATA
            MOV DS, AX
            MOV DX, OFFSET MSG2              : Display message MSG
            MOV AH,09H
            INT 21H
            IRET
ISR2        ENDP
CODE        ENDS
      END   START
```

Programmable Interrupt Controller - 8259

Consider an application in which a number of I/O devices connected with a CPU desire to transfer data using interrupt driven transfer mode. So more interrupt pins are required than available in a typical microprocessor. The processor also needs to take care of priorities of interrupts simultaneously occurring at the interrupt request pins.

To overcome these difficulties, a Programmable Interrupt Controller is required which will handle a number of interrupts at a time. <u>A programmable interrupt controller (PIC) is adevice that is used to combine several sources of interrupt onto one or more CPU lines, whileallowing priority levels to be assigned to its interrupt outputs</u>. When the device has multiple interrupt outputs to assert, it asserts them in the order of their relative priority. The controller takes care of number of simultaneously occurring interrupts requests along with their types and priorities. So processor is relieved from all these tasks. The Programmable Interrupt Controller - 8259 A from Intel is such kind of device. It is compatible with 8 bit as well as 16 bit processors.

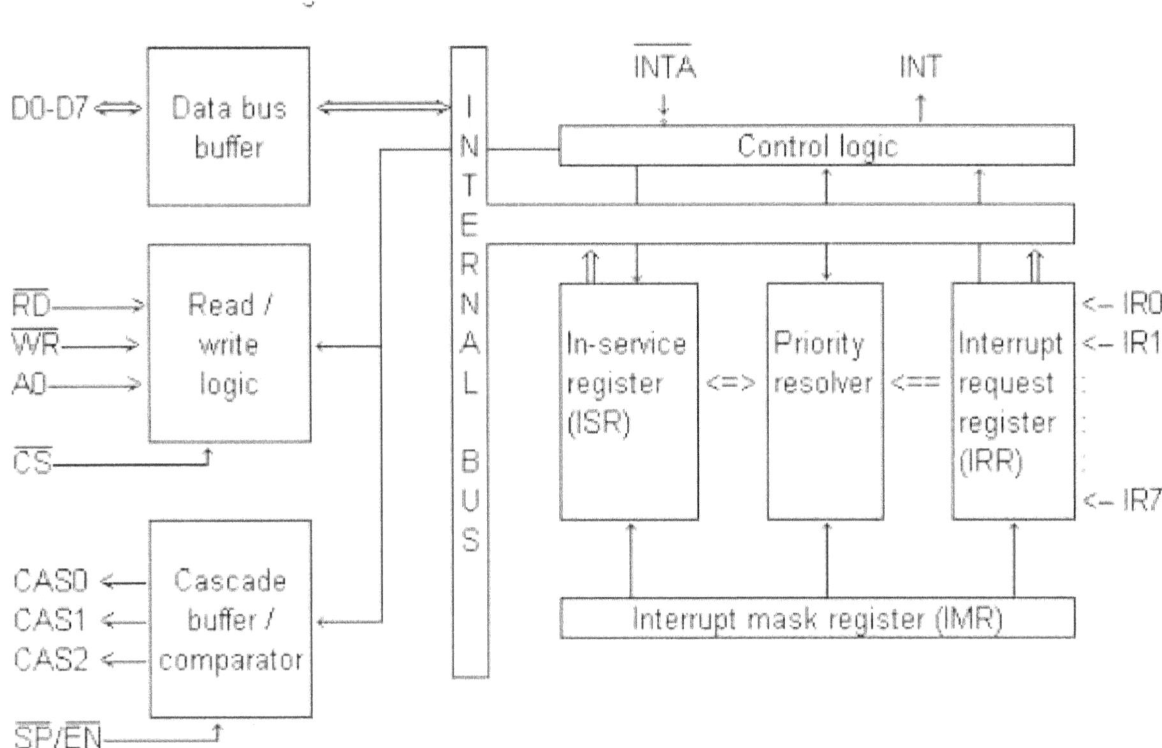

Interrupt Request Register (IRR):- The interrupts at IRQ input lines are handled by the Interrupt Request Register internally. The Interrupt Request Register stores the requests to save then based on priority.

In-Service Register (ISR):- This keeps track of the requests being served.

Priority Resolver: - This unit determines the priority of interrupts that occur simultaneously. The highest priority interrupt is selected and stored in the ISR during INTA pulse. The IR0 has the highest priority and IR7 has the lowest priority.

Interrupt Mask Register (IMR):-The IMR stores the bits which mask the interrupt lines to be masked. The IMR operates on the IRR.

Interrupt Control Logic: - This block manages the interrupt and interrupt acknowledge signals to be sent to CPU for serving one of the eight requests. This also accepts INTA signal from CPU that cause the 8259A to release the vector address on to the data bus.

Data Bus Buffer.-This tri-state, bidirectional 8-bit buffer is used to interface the 8259A to the system Data Bus. Control words and status information are transferred through the Data Bus Buffer.

Read/Write Control Logic: - This accepts and decoded the commands from CPU. This function block also allows the status of the 8259A to be transferred onto the Data Bus.

Cascade Buffer/Comparator: - This function block stores and compares the IDs of all 8259A's used in the system. The associated three I/O pins (CAS0-2) are outputs when the 8259A is used as a master and are inputs when the 8259A is used as a slave. As a master, the 8259A sends the ID of the interrupting slave device onto these lines. The slave thus selected will send its preprogrammed subroutine address onto the Data Bus during the next one or two consecutive INTA pulses.

CS (Chip Select):-A LOW on this input enables the 8259A. It enables the read and write operations (RD, WR) of 8259. No reading or writing of the chip will occur unless the device is selected.

WR (Write):- A LOW on this input enables the CPU to write control words (ICWs and OCWs) to the 8259A.

RD (READ):- A LOW on this input enables the 8259A to send the status of the Interrupt Request Register (IRR), In Service Register (ISR), the Interrupt Mask Register (IMR), or the Interrupt level onto the Data Bus.

A0:-This input signal is used in conjunction with WR and RD signals to write commands into the various command registers, as well as reading the various status registers of the chip. This line can be tied directly to one of the address lines.

D7-D0:- These pins form a bidirectional data bus that carries 8 bit data either to control word or from status word registers. This carries interrupt vector information.

SP/EN :- This is a dual purpose pin. When the chip is used in buffered mode, this pin can be used as a buffer enable to control buffer transceivers. If this is not used in buffered mode, the pin is used as input to designate whether the chip is used as a master(SP=1) or slave(EN=0).

INT: - This pin goes high when a valid interrupt request is asserted. This is used to interrupt the CPU and is connected to the interrupt input of CPU.

IR0-IR7:- These pins act as inputs to accept the interrupt requests to CPU. In the edge triggered mode, an interrupt service is requested by raising the IR pin from low to high state. It is held high until it is acknowledged.

INTA (Interrupt Acknowledge):- This pin is an input used to strobe-in 8259A interrupt vector data on to the data bus. In conjunction with CS, WR, RD pins, this selects different operations like writing command words, reading status word etc.

The 8259A can be interfaced with any CPU using 1. Polling 2. Interrupt

In**polling**, the CPU keeps on checking each peripheral device on sequence, to check if it requires a service from CPU. If any such service request is noted, CPU serves the request and goes to next device on sequence. After scanning all the peripheral devices, CPU starts again from first device.

Disadvantage: Reduction in processing speed (because most of the CPU time is consumed in polling)

In the **Interrupt driven Method**, CPU performs main processing till it is interrupted by a service requesting peripheral device.

Advantage: Processing speed is more (CPU serves the peripheral only if it receives an interrupt request)If more than one request is received, it is processed in priority basis.If the requests are more than the interrupt pins, then additional hardware is required for interfacing.

Interrupt Sequencing in 8086 System

The interrupt sequence is as described as follows:

One or more IRR bits are high that set corresponding IRR bits.

8259A resolves priority and sends an INT signal to CPU.

The CPU acknowledges with INTA pulse.

Upon receiving INTA signal, the highest priority ISR bit is set and corresponding IRR bit is reset. 8259A does not drive data bus at this time.

8086 initiate second INTA pulse. During this period 8259A releases an eight bit pointer on to data bus from where it is read by the CPU.

This completes the interrupt cycle. The ISR bit is reset at the end of second INTA pulse if automatic end of interrupt (AEOI) mode is programmed. ISR bits remains set until an appropriate EOI command is issued at the end of Interrupt Subroutine.

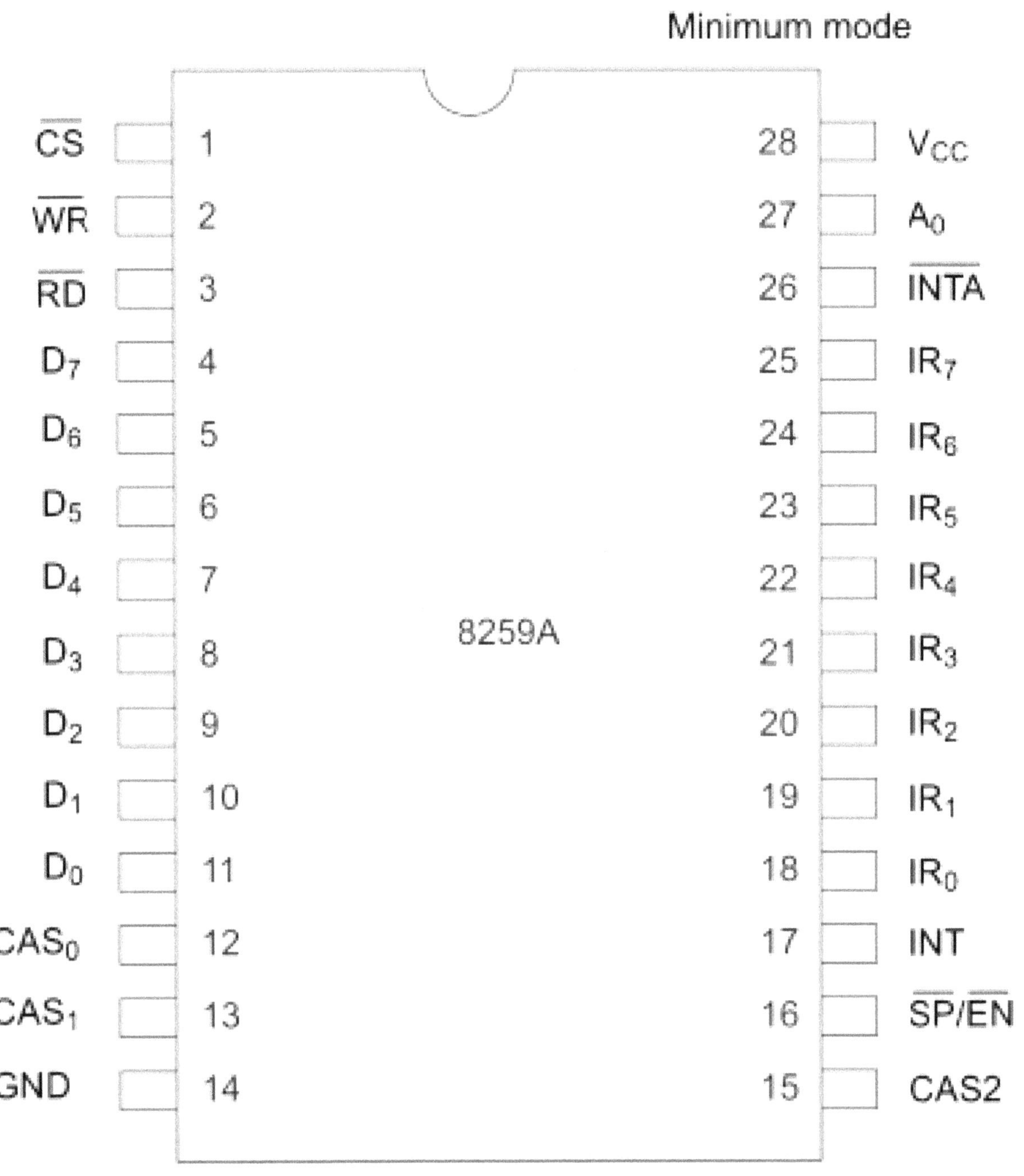

Fig. 6.13 *8259 Pin Diagram*

Command Words of 8259A

The command word is classified into two groups:

Initialization Command Words

Operation Command Words

Initialization Command Words: Before starting the processing, 8259A must be initialized by writing two or four command words into respective command word register. These are called Initialization Command Words (ICWs).

If A0=0 and D4=1: The control word recognized as ICW1 (It contains control bits for edge/level triggered mode, single/cascade mode, call address interval, whether ICW4 is required or not)

If A0=1: The control word recognized as ICW2 (ICW2 stores details of Interrupt vector address)

ICW1 and ICW2 are the compulsory command words while ICW3 and ICW4 are optional. The ICW3 is read only when there are more than one 8259A s in the system i.e. cascading is used. The SNGL bit in ICW1 Indicates whether the 8259A is in the cascade mode or not.

Intitialization sequence of 8259A

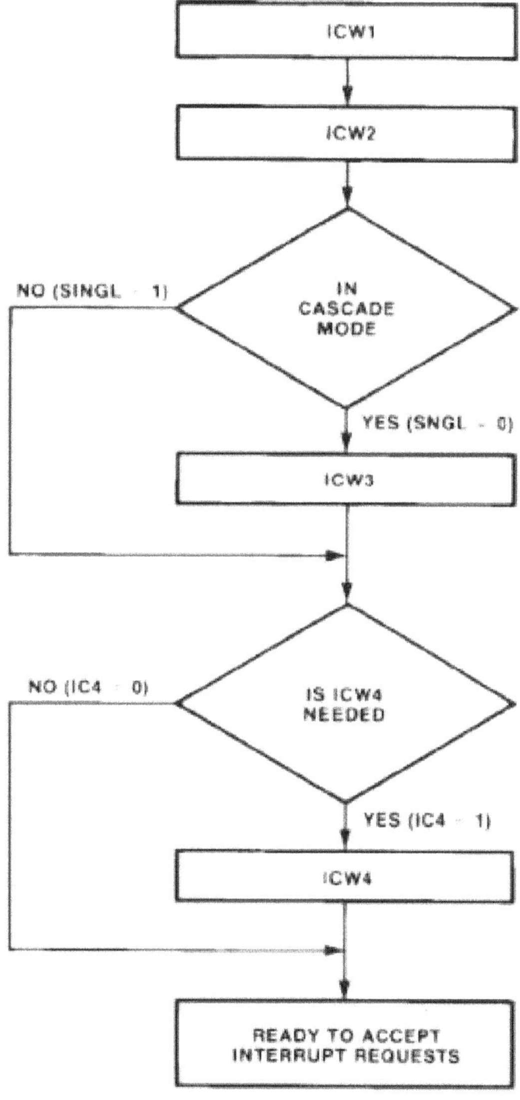

Bit functions of ICW1 and ICW2

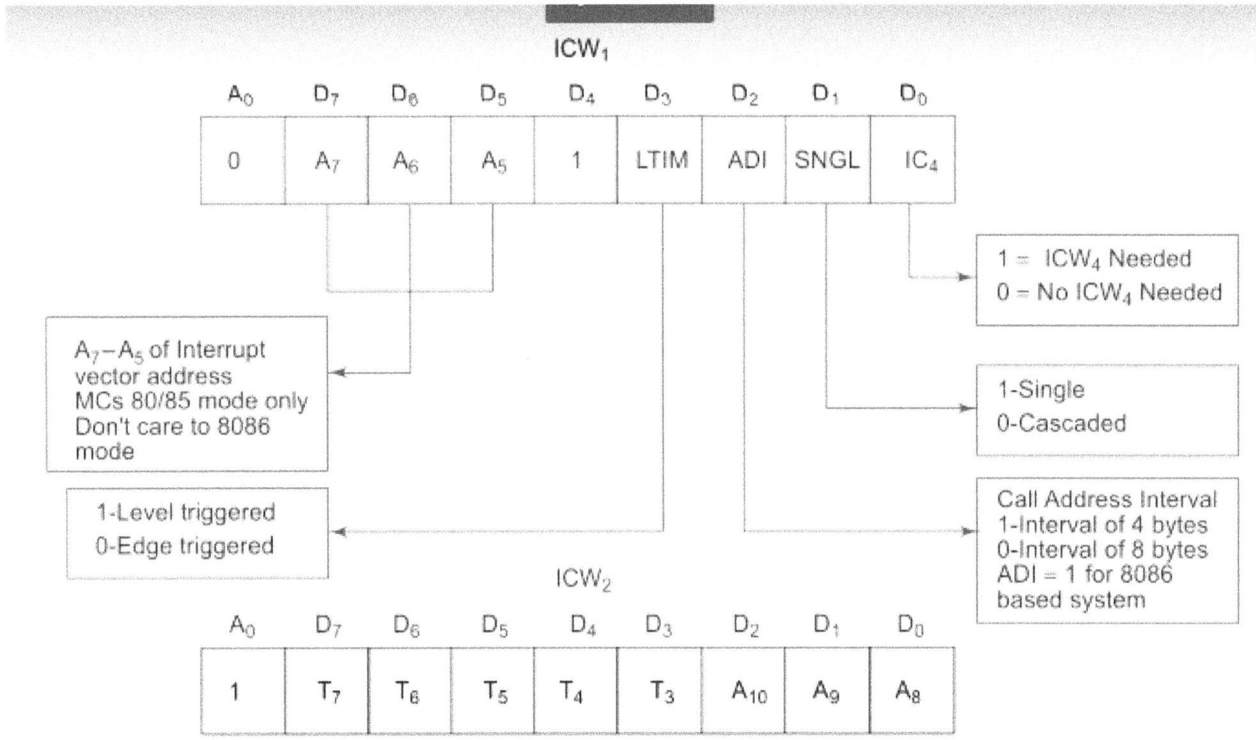

Fig. 6.15   *Initialization Command Words ICW₁ and ICW₂*

Once ICW1 is loaded, the following initialization procedure is carried out:

The edge sense circuit is reset

IMR is cleared

IR7 is assigned to lowest priority

Slave mode address is set to 7

Mask mode is cleared and status read is set to IRR

If IC4=0, all the functions of ICw4 are set to 0. Master/Slave bit in ICW4 is used in the buffered mode only

ICW2: In 8086 system, the five most significant bits of the interrupt type byte are inserted in place of T7-T3 respectively and remaining three bits are inserted internally as 000.

000: IR0

001: IR1....

The **ICW3** loads 8 bit slave register. In the Master mode, the 8 bit slave register will set bit wise to 1 for each slave in the system.

Master mode ICW$_3$

A$_0$	D$_7$	D$_6$	D$_5$	D$_4$	D$_3$	D$_2$	D$_1$	D$_0$
1	S$_7$	S$_6$	S$_5$	S$_4$	S$_3$	S$_2$	S$_1$	S$_0$

Sn = 1-IRn Input has a slave
= 0-IRn Input does not have a slave

Slave mode ICW$_3$

A$_0$	D$_7$	D$_6$	D$_5$	D$_4$	D$_3$	D$_2$	D$_1$	D$_0$
1	0	0	0	0	0	ID$_2$	ID$_1$	ID$_0$

D$_2$D$_1$D$_0$ - 000 to 111 for IR$_0$ to IR$_7$ or slave 1 to slave 8

Fig. 6.16   ICW$_3$ in Master and Slave Mode

ICW$_4$

A$_0$	D$_7$	D$_6$	D$_5$	D$_4$	D$_3$	D$_2$	D$_1$	D$_0$
1	0	0	0	SFNM	BUF	M/$\overline{\text{S}}$	AEOI	mPM

Fig. 6.17   ICW$_4$ Bit Functions

ICW4: The use of this command word depends on the IC4 bit of ICW1. If IC4=1 , ICW4 is used otherwise is neglected.

SFNM: Special fully nested mode is selected if SFNM=1.

BUF: If BUF=1, the buffered mode is selected. In the buffered mode, SP/EN act as the enable output and the master/slave is determined using M/S bit of ICW4.

M/S: if M/S=1, 8259 is a master otherwise slave. AEOI=1: Automatic End of Interrupt is selected.

mPM: if 0: Mcs-85 system operation is selected and 1 then 8086/88 operation is selected.

Operation command Words:

Operation Command Words: Once 8259A is initialized using the previously discussed command words for initialization, it is ready for its normal function, i.e. for accepting the interrupts but 8259A has its own way of handling the received interrupts called as modes of operation.

These modes of operations can be selected by programming, i.e. writing three internal registers called as operation command words.

In the three operation command words OCW1, OCW 2 and OCW 3 every bit corresponds to some operational feature of the mode selected, except for a few bits those are either 1 or 0.

The three operation command words are shown in fig with the bit selection details.

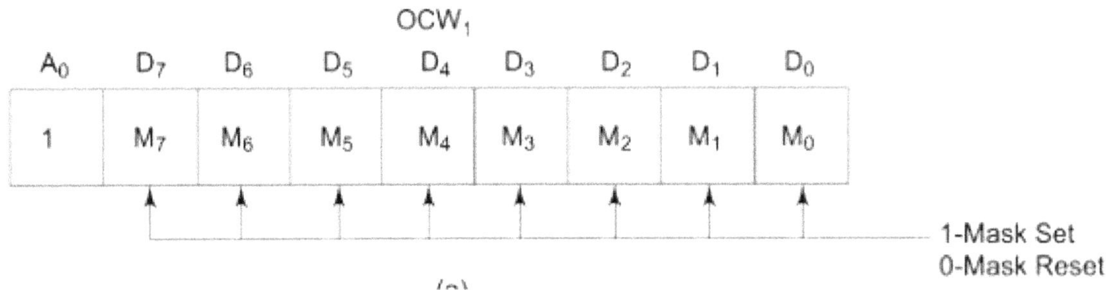

OCW1 is used to mask the masked and if it is 0 the request is enabled.

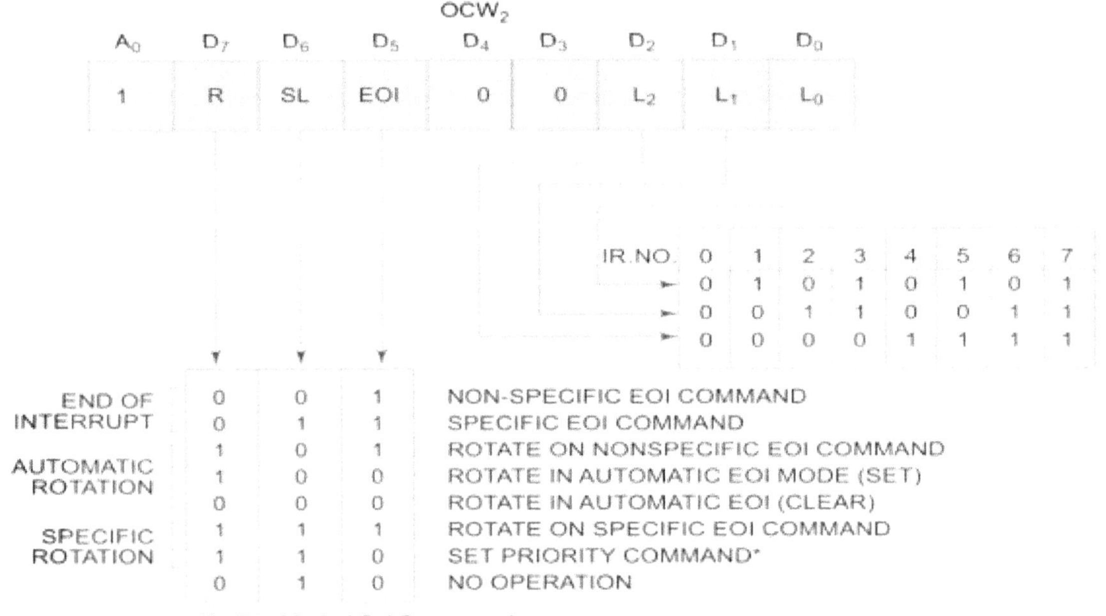

In OCW 2 the three bits, R, SL and EOI control the end of interrupt, the rotate mode and their combinations as shown in fig

The three bits L2, L1 and L0 in OCW 2 determine the interrupt level to be selected for operation, if SL bit is active i.e. 1.

In operation command word 3 (OCW 3), if the ESMM bit, i.e. enable special mask mode bit is set to 1, the SMM bit is neglected.

SMM is special mask mode. When ESMM bit is 0 the SMM bit is neglected.

If the SMM bit. I.e. special mask mode bit is 1, the 8259A will enter special mask mode provided ESMM=1.• If ESMM=1 and SMM=0, the 8259A will return to the normal mask mode.

Operating Modes of 8259

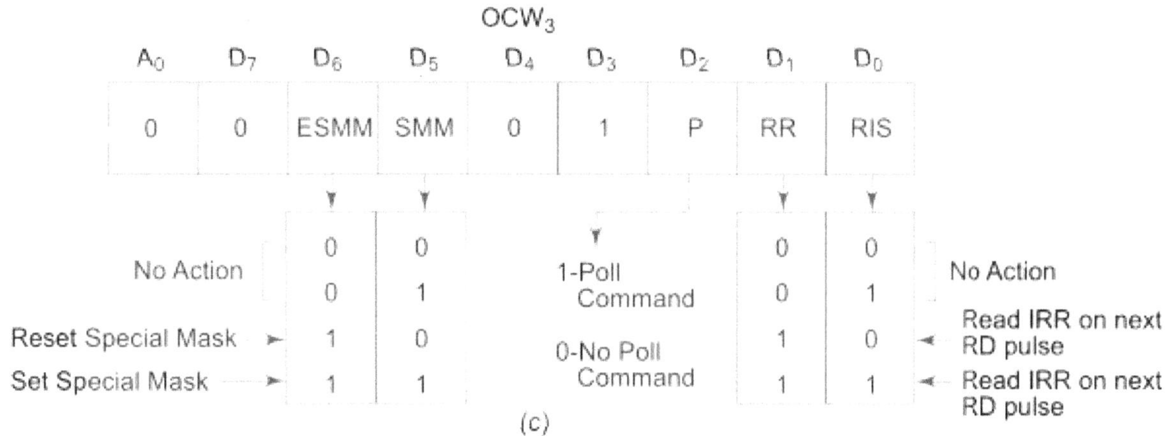

Fig. 6.18 *Operation Command Words*

The different modes of operation of 8259A can be programmed by setting or resetting the appropriate bits of the ICW or OCW as discussed previously. The different modes of operation of 8259A are explained in the following.

Fully Nested Mode: This is the default mode of operation of 8259A. IR0 has the highest priority and IR 7 has the lowest one. When interrupt request are noticed, the highest priority request amongst them is determined and the vector is placed on the data bus. The corresponding bit of ISR is set and remains set till the microprocessor issues an EOI command just before returning from the service routine or the AEOI bit is set.

If the ISR (in service) bit is set, all the same or lower priority interrupts are inhibited but higher levels will generate an interrupt, that will be acknowledge only if the microprocessor interrupt enable flag IF is set. The priorities can afterwards be changed by programming the rotating priority modes.

End of Interrupt (EOI): The ISR bit can be reset either with AEOI bit of ICW1 or by EOI command, issued before returning from the interrupt service routine. There are two types of EOI commands specific and non- specific. When 8259A is operated in the modes that preserve fully nested structure, it can determine which ISR bit is to be reset on EOI. When non-specific EOI command is issued to 8259A it will be automatically reset the highest ISR bit out of those already set.

When a mode that may disturb the fully nested structure is used, the 8259A is no longer able to determine the last level acknowledged. In this case a specific EOI command is issued to reset a particular ISR bit. An ISR bit that is masked by the corresponding IMR bit will not be cleared by non-specific EOI of 8259A, if it is in special mask mode.

Automatic Rotation: This is used in the applications where all the interrupting devices are of equal priority. In this mode, an interrupt request IR level receives priority after it is served while the next device to be served gets the highest priority in sequence. Once all the devices are served like this, the first device again receives highest priority.

Automatic EOI Mode: Till AEOI=1 in ICW 4, the 8259A operates in AEOI mode. In this mode, the 8259A performs a non-specific EOI operation at the trailing edge of the last INTA pulse automatically. This mode should be used only when a nested multilevel interrupt structure is not required with a single 8259A.

Specific Rotation: In this mode a bottom priority level can be selected, using L2, L1 and L0 in OCW 2 and R=1, SL=1, EOI=0. The selected bottom priority fixes other priorities. If IR 5 is selected as a bottom priority, then IR 5 will have least priority and IR4 will have a next higher priority. Thus IR 6 will have the highest priority. These priorities can be changed during an EOI command by programming the rotate on specific EOI command in OCW 2.

Specific Mask Mode: In specific mask mode, when a mask bit is set in OCW1, it inhibits further interrupts at that level and enables interrupt from other levels, which are not masked.

Edge and Level Triggered Mode: This mode decides whether the interrupt should be edge triggered or level triggered. If bit LTIM of ICW1 =0 they are edge triggered, otherwise the interrupts are level triggered.

Reading 8259 Status: The status of the internal registers of 8259A can be read using this mode. The OCW 3 is used to read IRR and ISR while OCW1 is used to read IMR. Reading is possible only in no polled mode.

Poll Command: In polled mode of operation, the INT output of 8259A is neglected, though it functions normally, by not connecting INT output or by masking INT input of the microprocessor. The poll mode is entered by setting P=1 in OCW 3.

The 8259A is polled by using software execution by microprocessor instead of the requests on INT input. The 8259A treats the next RD pulse to the 8259A as an interrupt acknowledge. An appropriate ISR bit is set, if there is a request. The priority level is read and a data word is placed on to data bus, after RD is activated. A poll command may give more than 64 priority levels.

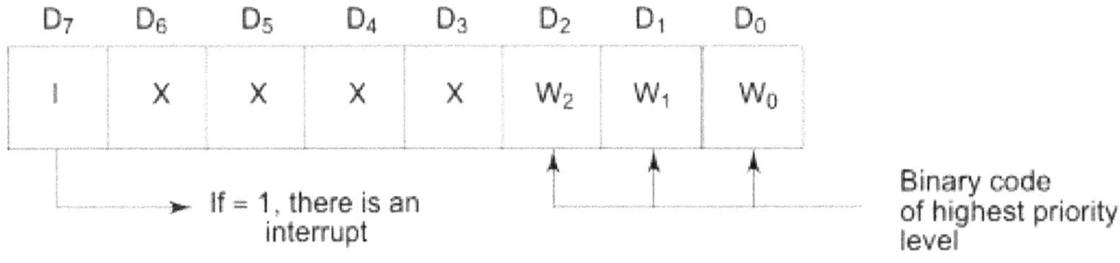

Fig. 6.19 *Data Word of 8259*

Special Fully Nested Mode: This mode is used in more complicated system, where cascading is used and the priority has to be programmed in the master using ICW 4. This is somewhat similar to the normal nested mode.

In this mode, when an interrupt request from a certain slave is in service, this slave can further send request to the master, if the requesting device connected to the slave has higher priority than the one being currently served. In this mode, the master interrupts the CPU only when the interrupting device has a higher or the same priority than the one current being served. In normal mode, other requests than the one being served are masked out.

When entering the interrupt service routine the software has to check whether this is the only request from the slave. This is done by sending a non-specific EOI can be sent to the master, otherwise no EOI should be sent. This mode is important, since in the absence of this mode, the slave would interrupt the master only once and hence the priorities of the slave inputs would have been disturbed.

Buffered Mode: When the 83259A is used in the systems where bus driving buffers are used on data buses. The problem of enabling the buffers exists. The 8259A sends buffer enable signal on SP/ EN pin, whenever data is placed on the bus.

Cascade Mode: The 8259A can be connected in a system containing one master and eight slaves (maximum) to handle up to 64 priority levels. The master controls the slaves using CAS 0-CAS 2 which act as chip select inputs (encoded) for slaves.

In this mode, the slave INT outputs are connected with master IR inputs. When a slave request line is activated and acknowledged, the master will enable the slave to release the vector address during second pulse of INTA sequence.

The cascade lines are normally low and contain slave address codes from the trailing edge of the first INTA pulse to the trailing edge of the second INTA pulse. Each 8259A in the system must be separately initialized and programmed to work in different modes. The EOI command must be issued twice, one for master and the other for the slave. A separate address decoder is used to activate the chip select line of each 8259A. Following Fig shows the details of the circuit connections of 8259A in cascade scheme.

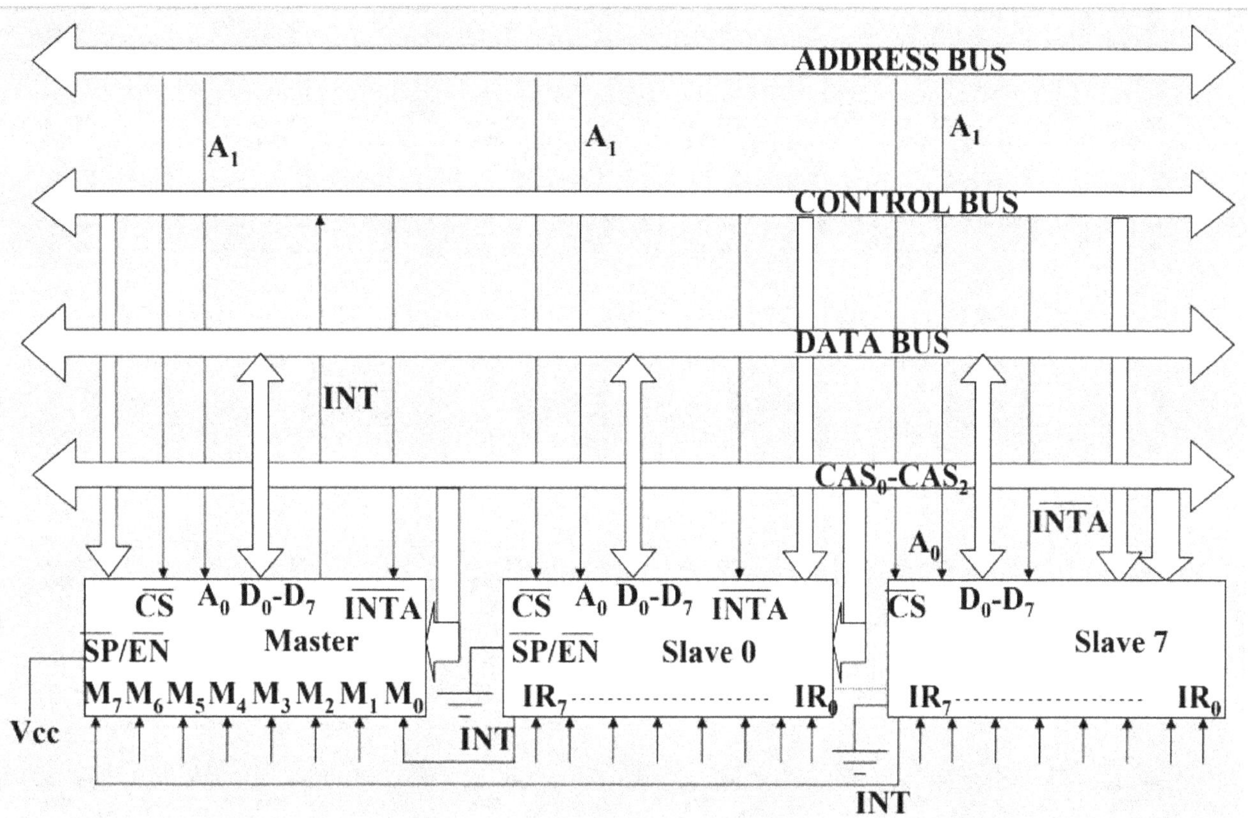

Fig : 8259A in Cascade Mode

CHAPTER FOUR

INTERFACING WITH 8086

- ### _Interfacing Memory_

- The memory interfacing circuit is used to access memory quit frequently to read instruction codes and data stored in the memory. The read / write operations are monitored by control signals.We have four common types of memory:
- Read only memory (ROM)
- Read Only Memory (RAM)
- Static Random access memory (SARAM)
- Dynamic Random access memory (DRAM)
-

Memory structure and its requirements

- The read / write memories consist of an array of registers in which each register has unique address. The size of memory is N * M as shown in figure.

-

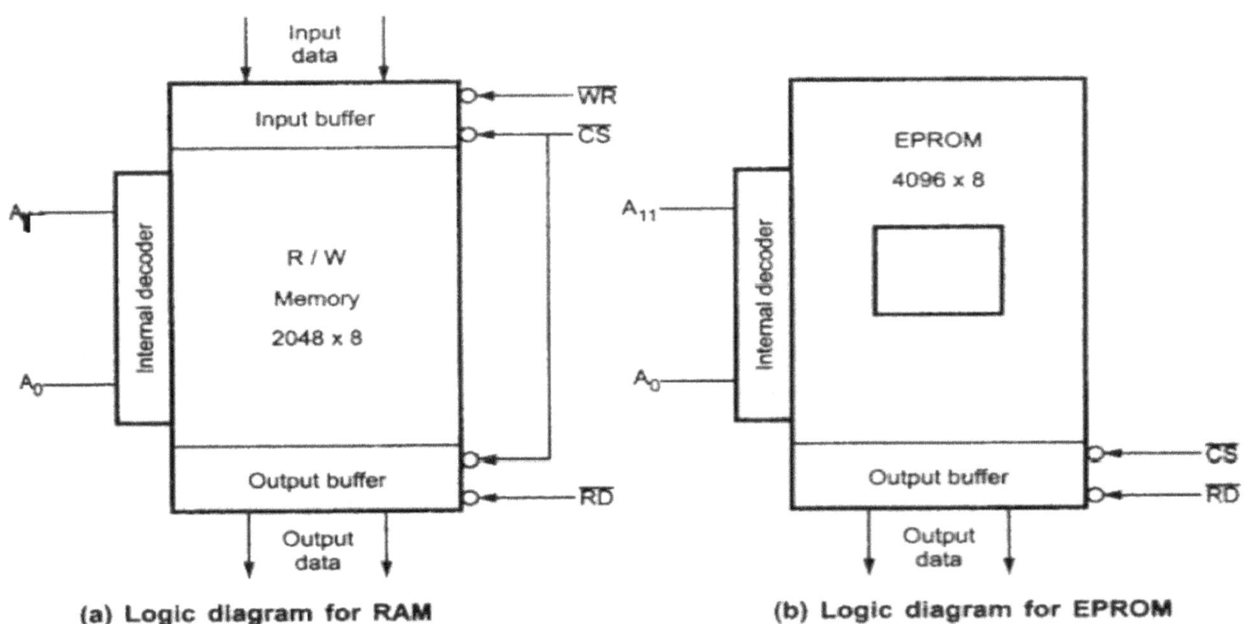

(a) Logic diagram for RAM   (b) Logic diagram for EPROM

- Where N is number of register and M is the word length, in number of bits.
- As shown in figure(a) memory chip has 12 address lines Ao–A11, one chip select (CS), and two control lines, Read (RD) to enable output buffer and Write (WR) to enable the input buffer. The internal decoder is used to decoder the address lines.
- Figure(b) shows the logic diagram of a typical EPROM (Erasable Programmable Read-Only Memory) with 4096 (4K) register. It has 12 address lines Ao – A11, one chip select (CS), one read control signal. Since EPROM does not require the (WR) signal.
- The Following Table Summarizes the Memory Capacity and Address Lines required for Memory Interfacing.
-

Memory Capacity	Address Lines Required
1K = 1024 memory locations	10
2K = 2048 memory locations	11
4K = 4096 memory locations	12
8K = 8192 memory locations	13
16K = 16384 memory locations	14
32K = 32768 memory locations	15
64K = 65536 memory locations	16

-

- Example :
- If memory is having 12 address lines and 16 data lines, then Number of registers /memory locations = $2 \wedge N = 2 \wedge 12$
- = 4096
- Word length = M bits
- = 16 bits
-

Basic Concepts in memory interfacing

- For interfacing memory devices to microprocessor 8086 following important points are to be kept in mind. Microprocessor 8086 can access 1 Mbytes memory since address bus is 20-bit. But it is not always necessary to use full 1 Mbytes address space. The total memory space depends upon the application.
- Generally EPROM (or EPROMs) is used as a program memory and RAM (or RAMs) as a data memory. When both, EPROM and RAM are used, the total address space 1 Mbytes is shared by them.
- The individual capacities of program memory and data memory depends on the application. It is not always necessary to select 1 EPROM and 1 RAM. We can have multiple EPROMs and multiple RAMs as per the requirement of application. We can place EPROM/RAM anywhere in full 1 Mbytes address space. But program

memory (EPROM) should be located at last memory page so that the starting address FFFF0H will lie within the program memory range.

- To provide facility to set addresses in the interrupt vector table we must provide RAM at page 0 of memory. So that the interrupt vector table lie with the read/write memory range. It is not always necessary to locate EPROM and RAM in consecutive memory addresses. However, it is advised to do that. While interfacing memory to 8086 we have to provide odd and even banks of memory. Even banks is selected when Ao = 0 and odd bank is selected when BHE = 0.
- The Memory Interfacing requires to :
- Select the chip
- Identify the register
- Enable the appropriate buffer
-

Program 5.1

Interface two 4K × 8 EPROMS and two 4K × 8 RAM chips with 8086. Select suitable maps.

Solution   We know that, after reset, the IP and CS are initialised to form address FFFF0H. Hence, this address must lie in the EPROM. The address of RAM may be selected any where in the 1MB address space of 8086, but we will select the RAM address such that the address map of the system is continuous, as shown in Table 5.1.

Table 5.1   *Memory Map for Problem 5.1*

Address	A_{19}	A_{18}	A_{17}	A_{16}	A_{15}	A_{14}	A_{13}	A_{12}	A_{11}	A_{10}	A_{09}	A_{08}	A_{07}	A_{06}	A_{05}	A_{04}	A_{03}	A_{02}	A_{01}	A_{00}
FFFFFH	1	1	1	1	1	1	1	1	1	1	1	1	1	1	1	1	1	1	1	1
				EPROM								8K × 8								
FE000H	1	1	1	1	1	1	1	0	0	0	0	0	0	0	0	0	0	0	0	0
FDFFFH	1	1	1	1	1	1	0	1	1	1	1	1	1	1	1	1	1	1	1	1
				RAM								8K × 8								
FC000H	1	1	1	1	1	1	0	0	0	0	0	0	0	0	0	0	0	0	0	0

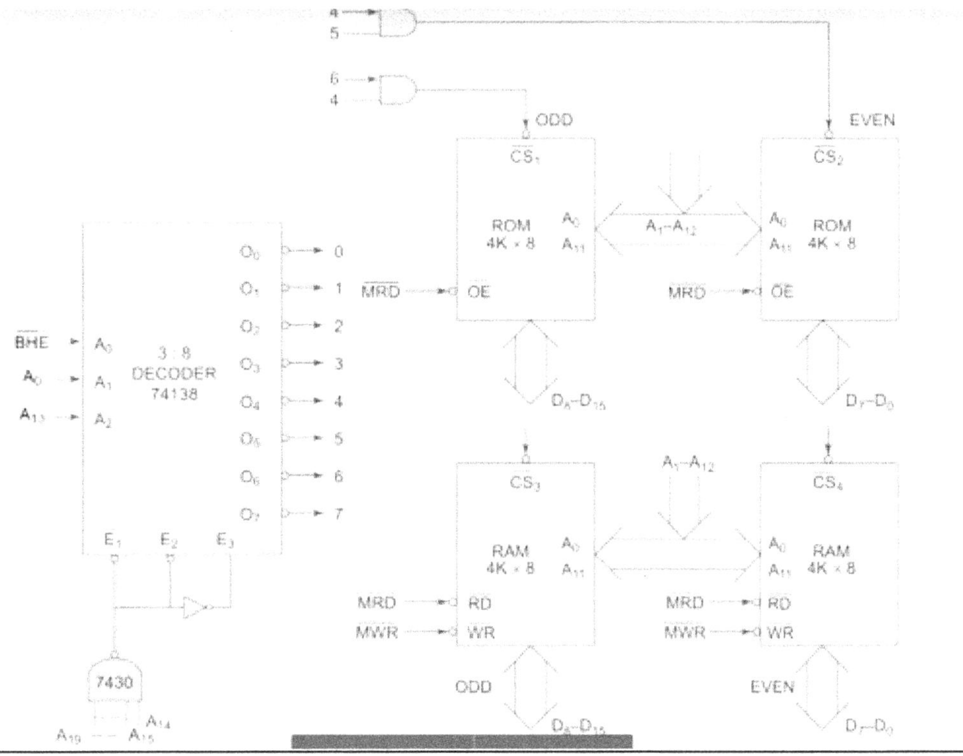

Fig. 5.1   *Interfacing Problem 5.1*

Total 8K bytes of EPROM need 13 address lines A_0–A_{12} (since $2^{13} = 8K$). Address lines A_{13}–A_{19} are used for decoding to generate the chip select. The $\overline{BHE}$ signal goes low when a transfer is at odd address or higher byte of data is to be accessed. Let us assume that the latched address, $\overline{BHE}$ and demultiplexed data lines are readily available for interfacing. Figure 5.1 shows the interfacing diagram for the memory system.

The memory system in this example contains in total four 4K × 8 memory chips.

The two 4K × 8 chips of RAM and ROM are arranged in parallel to obtain 16-bit data bus width. If A_0 is 0, i.e. the address is even and is in RAM, then the lower RAM chip is selected indicating 8-bit transfer at an even address. If A_0 is 1, i.e. the address is odd and is in RAM, the $\overline{BHE}$ goes low, the upper RAM chip is selected, further indicating that the 8-bit transfer is at an odd address. If the selected addresses are in ROM, the respective ROM chips are selected. If at a time A_0 and $\overline{BHE}$ both are 0, both the RAM or ROM chips are selected, i.e. the data transfer is of 16 bits. The selection of chips here takes place as shown in Table 5.2.

Table 5.2 *Memory Chip Selection for Problem 5.1*

Decoder I/P → *Address/* $\overline{BHE}$ →	A_2 A_{13}	A_1 A_0	A_0 $\overline{BHE}$	*Selection/* *Comment*
Word transfer on D_0 – D_{15}	0	0	0	Even and odd addresses in RAM
Byte transfer on D_7 – D_0	0	0	1	Only even address in RAM
Byte transfer on D_8 – D_{15}	0	1	0	Only odd address in RAM
Word transfer on D_0 – D_{15}	1	0	0	Even and odd addresses in ROM
Byte transfer on D_0 – D_7	1	0	1	Only even address in ROM
Byte transfer on D_8 – D_{15}	1	1	0	Only odd address in ROM

Design an interface between 8086 CPU and two chips of 16K × 8 EPROM and two chips of 32K × 8 RAM. Select the starting address of EPROM suitably. The RAM address must start at 00000H.

Solution   The last address in the map of 8086 is FFFFFH. After resetting, the processor starts from FFFF0H. Hence this address must lie in the address range of EPROM. Figure 5.2 shows the interfacing diagram, and Table 5.3 shows complete map of the system.

Table 5.3   *Address Map for Problem 5.2*

Addresses	A_{19}	A_{18}	A_{17}	A_{16}	A_{13}	A_{14}	A_{15}	A_{12}	A_{11}	A_{10}	A_{09}	A_{08}	A_{07}	A_{06}	A_{05}	A_{04}	A_{03}	A_{02}	A_{01}	A_{00}
FFFFFH	1	1	1	1	1	1	1	1	1	1	1	1	1	1	1	1	1	1	1	1
								32KB			EPROM									
F8000H	1	1	1	1	1	0	0	0	0	0	0	0	0	0	0	0	0	0	0	0
0FFFFH	0	0	0	0	1	1	1	1	1	1	1	1	1	1	1	1	1	1	1	1
							64KB RAM													
00000H	0	0	0	0	0	0	0	0	0	0	0	0	0	0	0	0	0	0	0	0

It is better not to use a decoder to implement the above map because it is not continuous, i.e. there is some unused address space between the last RAM address (0FFFFH) and the first EPROM address (F8000H). Hence the logic is implemented using logic gates, as shown in Fig. 5.2.

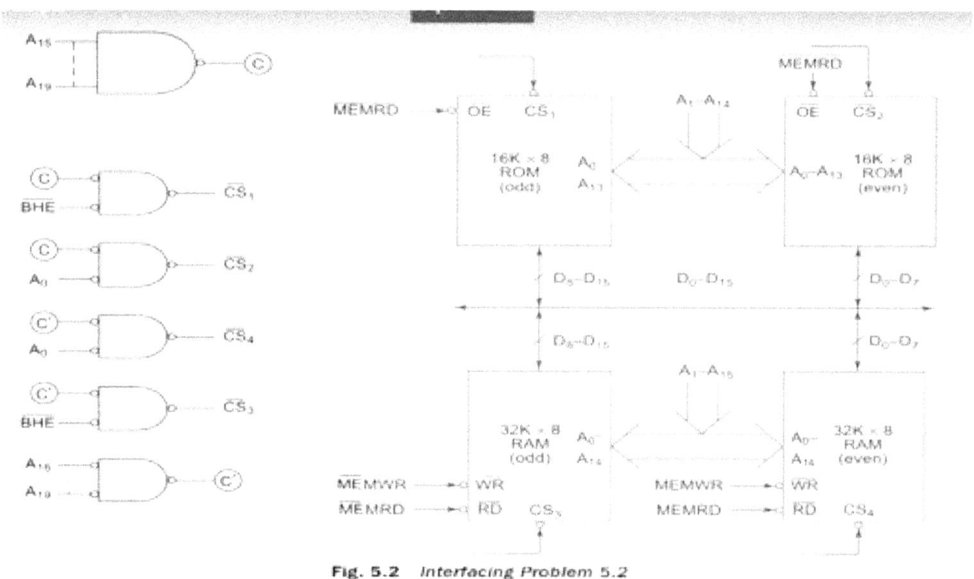

Fig. 5.2   *Interfacing Problem 5.2*

Let us select a variable C for memory address pulse, i.e. output of 6-input NAND gate. BHE is abbreviated as B. The chip selection logic can be designed as shown in Table 5.4.

Table 5.4

I/P		O/P	
A_0	$B(\overline{BHE})$	C_1	C_2
0	0	0	0
0	1	1	0
1	0	0	1
1	1	1	1

$$C_2 = A_0$$
$$C_1 = \overline{BHE}$$

To find out $\overline{CS_1}$ and $\overline{CS_2}$ we will have to combine C_1 and C_2 with C.

•

o

•

Table 5.5

I/P				O/P	
C_1	C_2	C		$\overline{CS_1}$	$\overline{CS_2}$
0	0	0		0	0
1	0	0		1	0
1	1	0		1	1
0	1	0		0	1

Table 5.5 shows that

$$\overline{CS_1} = C + C_1 = C + \overline{BHE} \quad \text{and} \quad \overline{CS_2} = C + C_2 = C + A_0$$

Similarly we can find out CS_3 and CS_4.

•

o

• <u>Interfacing I/O Ports</u>

- I/O ports or input/output ports are the devices through which the microprocessor communicates with other devices or external devices. Input activity, is the activity that enables the microprocessor to read data from external devices, for example keyboard, joysticks, mouser etc. The devices are known as input devices as they feed data into a microprocessor system.

- Output activity transfers data from the microprocessor top the external devices, for example CRT display, 7 segments displays, printer, etc, the devices that accept the data from a microprocessor system are called output devices.

- ### Steps in Interfacing an I/O Device

- The following steps are performed to interface a general I/O device with a CPU:
- 1. Connect the data bus of the microprocessor system with the data bus of the I/O port.
- 2. Derive a device address pulse by decoding the required address of the device and use it as the chip select of the device.
- 3. Use a suitable control signal, i.e. IORD and /or IOWR to carry out device operations, i.e. connect IORD to RD input of the device if it is an input devise, and otherwise connect IOWR to WR input of the device.
- **Input Port**
- The input device is connected to the microprocessor through buffer. The simplest form of an input port is a buffer as shown in the figure.
-

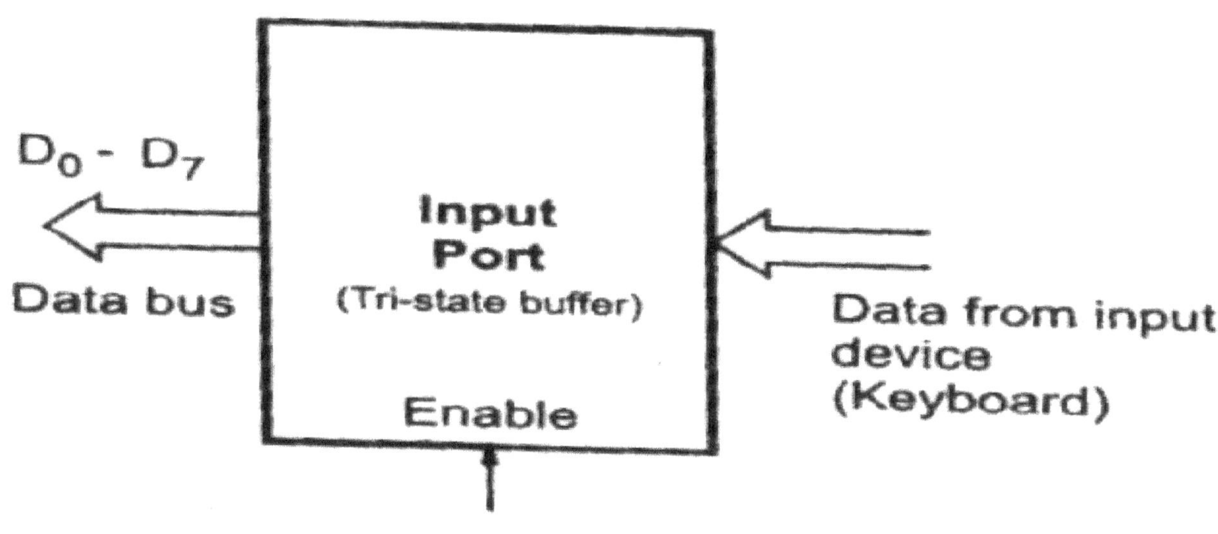

-

o

- When microprocessor wants to read data from the input device (keyboard), the control signals from the microprocessor activates the buffer by asserting enable input of the buffer. Once the buffer is enabled, data from the device is available on the data bus. Microprocessor reads this data by initiating read command.
- **Output Port**
- It is used to send the data to the output device such as display from the microprocessor. The simplest form of the output port is a latch.
-

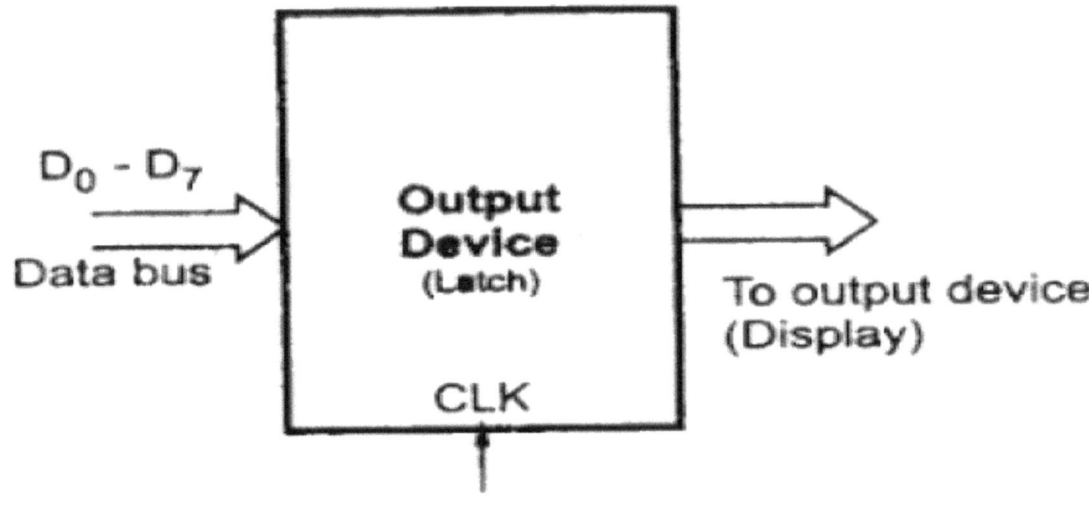

-
  o

- The output device is connected to the microprocessor through latch as shown in the figure. When microprocessor wants to send data to the output device it puts the data on the data bus and activates the clock signal of the latch, latching the data from the data bus at the output of latch. It is then available at the output of latch for the output device.

-

I/O Interfacing Techniques

- Input/output devices can be interfaced with microprocessor systems in two ways :
- 1. I/O mapped I/O
- 2. Memory mapped I/O
-

Difference between Memory Mapped I/O & I/O mapped I/O

Memory Mapped I/O	I/O Mapped I/O
Memory & I/O share the entire address range of processor	Processor provides separate address range for memory & I/O
Processor provides more address lines for accessing memory	Less address lines for accessing I/O
More Decoding is required	Less decoding is required
Memory control signals used to control Read & Write I/O operations	I/O control signals are used to control Read & Write I/O operations

- **Problem:**
- Interface an input port 74LS245 to read the status of the switches SW1 to SW8. the switches when shorted, input a '1' else input a '0' to the microprocessor system. Store the status in register BL. The address of the port is **0740H**

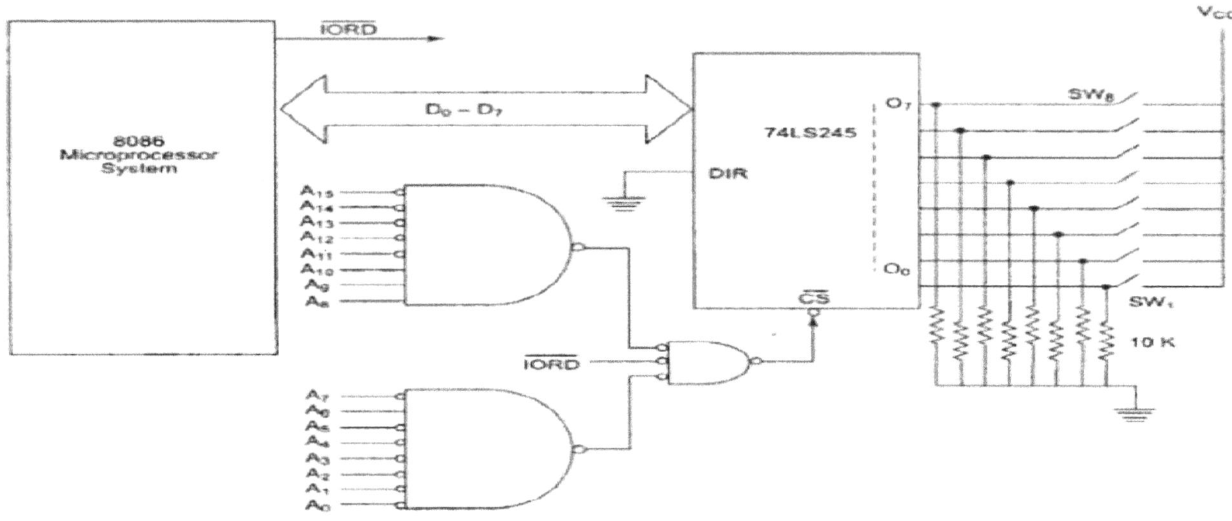

Fig. *Interfacing Input Port 74LS245*

- **Solution:**
- The hardware interface circuit is shown in figure. The address, control and data lines are assumed to be readily available at the microprocessor system The ALP is given as follows:
-
- MOV BL, 00H ; clear BL for status
- MOV DX, 0740H ; 16-bit Port address in DX
- IN AL,DX ; Read Port 0740H for switch positions.
- MOV BL, AL ; Store status of switches from AL into BL
- HLT ; Stop
-
- Here LSB bit of BL corresponds to the status of SW1 and likewise the MSB of BL corresponds to the status of SW8.
- <u>Problem :</u>
- Design an interface of input port 74LS245 to read the status of switches SW1 to SW8 and output port 74LS373 with 8086. Display the number of key that is pressed with the help of output port on 7 segment display. Write an ALP for this task. The input port address is 08H and output port address is 0AH.
- Solution : Status of the switches is first read into the AL. Displaying the shorted switch number in the 7 segment display. Instead of using 16 address lines, one may use only A3– A0.
-

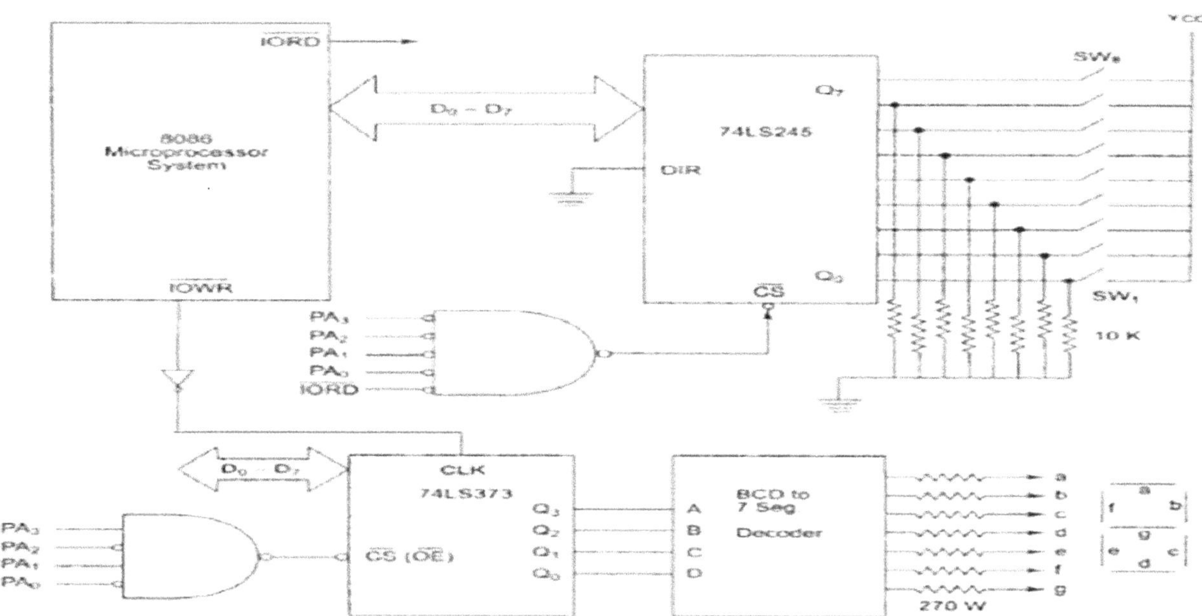

Fig. *Interfacing Switches and Displays for Problem*

-
  -

- **I/O Interfacing of 8086 Using 8255A**
- **8255A Programmable Peripheral Interface**
-

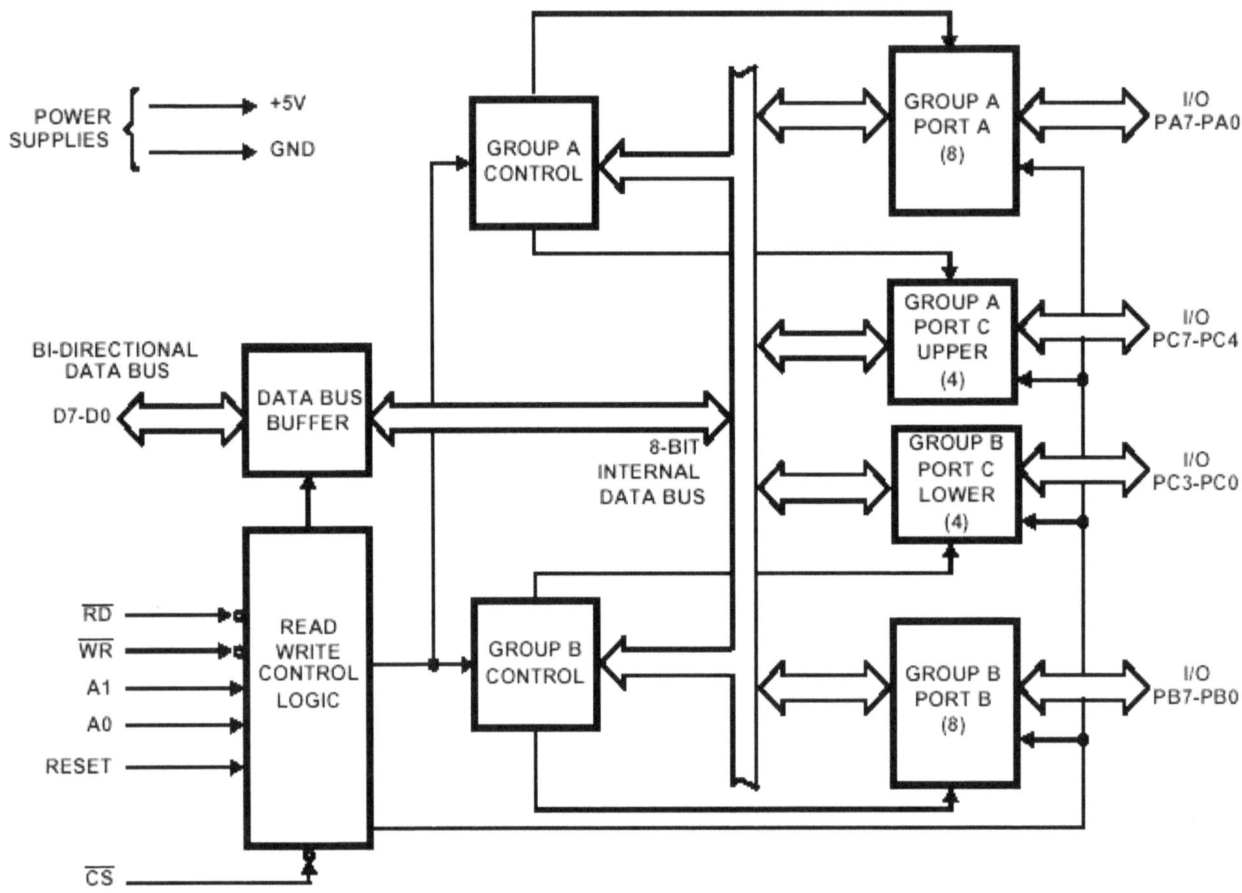

- The **Intel 8255** (or **i8255**) Programmable PeripheralInterface (PPI) chip was developed and manufactured by Intel in the first half of the 1970s for the Intel 8080 microprocessor. The 8255 provides 24 parallel input/output lines with a variety of programmable operating modes.
- The 8255 has 24 I/O pins that can be grouped primarily into two 8 bit parallel ports: A and B, with the remaining 8 bits as Port C.
- Port A and port B can be used as 8-bit input/output ports. Port C can be used as an 8-bit input/output port or as two 4-bit input/output ports or to produce handshake signals for ports A and B.
- The three ports are further grouped as follows:
- Group A consisting of port A and upper part of port C. [The port A lines are identified by symbols PA0-PA7 while the port C lines are identified as PC4-PC7.]
- Group B consisting of port B and lower part of port C. [Port B, containing lines PB0- PB7 and a 4-bit port C with lower bits PC0-PC3].
- The 8 bits of port C can be used as individual bits or be grouped into two 4 bit ports represented as: CUpper (CU) and CLower (CL).
- The functions of these ports are defined by writing a control word in the control register. The port C upper and port C lower can be used in combination as an 8-bit port C.
- All of these ports can function independently either as input or as output ports. This can be achieved by programming the bits of an internal register of 8255 called as control word register (CWR).

- **Data Bus Buffer**
- This three-state bi-directional 8-bit buffer is used to interface the 8255A to the system data bus. Data is transmitted or received by the buffer upon execution of input or output instructions by the CPU.
- Control words and status information are also transferred through the data bus buffer.
- Eight data lines (D0–D7) are available (with an 8-bit data buffer) to read/write data into the ports or control register under the status of the ${\displaystyle {\neg }}RD$ (pin 5) and ${\displaystyle {\neg }}WR$ (pin 36), which are active-low signals for read and write operations respectively.
- **Read/Write and Control Logic**- The function of this block is to manage all of the internal and external transfers of both Data and Control or Status words.
- **(A0 and A1) Port Select 0 and Port Select 1** : These input signals, in conjunction with the RD and WR inputs, control the selection of one of the three ports or the control word register.
- Address lines A_1 and A_0 allow to access a data register for each port or a control register, as listed below:
-

A_1	A_0	Port selected
0	0	port A
0	1	port B
1	0	port C
1	1	control register

-

  ○

- **(CS) Chip Select** : A "low" on this input pin enables the communication between the 82C55A and the CPU.
- The control signal chip select ${\displaystyle {\neg }}CS$ (pin 6) is used to enable the 8255 chip. It is an active-low signal, i.e., when ${\displaystyle {\neg }}CS = 0$, the 8255 is enabled.
- **(RD) Read :** A "low" on this input pin enables 82C55A to send the data or status information to the CPU on the data bus. In essence, it allows the CPU to "read from" the 82C55A.
- **(WR) Write :** A "low" on this input pin enables the CPU to write data or control words into the 82C55A.
- **RESET:**Logic high on this line clears the control word register of 8255. The **RESET** input (pin 35) is connected to the RESET line of system like 8085, 8086, etc., so that when the system is reset, all the ports are initialized as

input lines.
- The control register (or the control logic, or the command word register) is an 8-bit register used to select the modes of operation and input/output designation of the ports
- **<u>Group A and Group B controls</u>**:
- Group A and B get the Control Signal from CPU and send the command to the individual control blocks.
- Group A send the control signal to port A and Port C (Upper) PC7-PC4.
- Group B send the control signal to port B and Port C (Lower) PC3-PC0.
- <u>PORT A:</u>
- This is an 8-bit buffered I/O latch.
- It can be programmed by mode 0 , mode 1, mode 2 .
- <u>PORT B:</u>
- This is an 8-bit buffer I/O latch.
- It can be programmed by mode 0 and mode 1.
- <u>PORT C:</u>
- This is an 8-bit Unlatched buffer Input and an Output latch.
- It is divided into two parts.
- It can be programmed by bit set/reset operation.
-

Pin Description of 8255

-

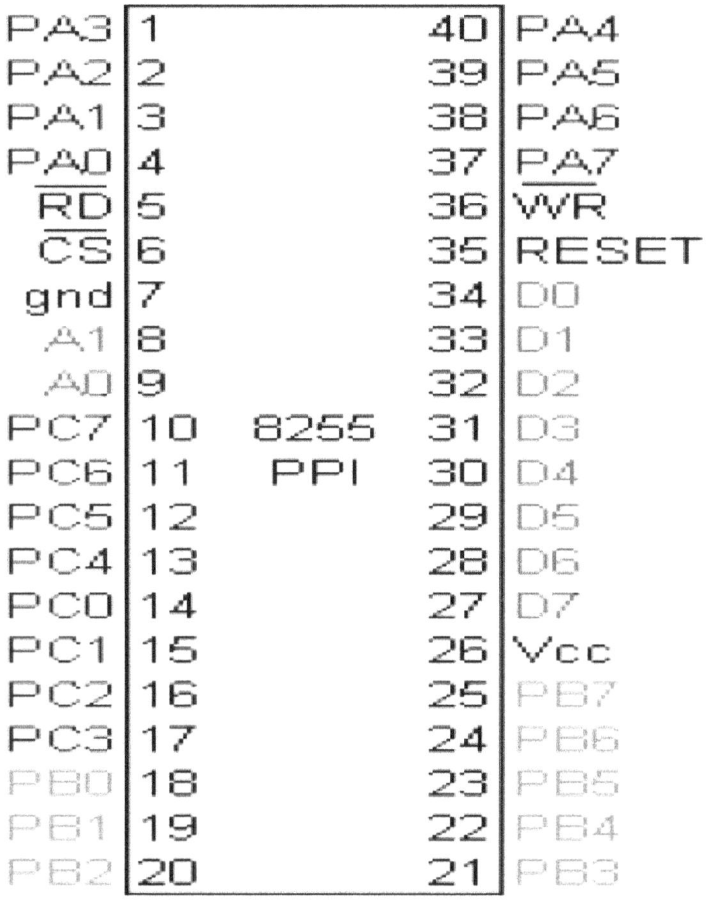

Fig. 6.1 Pin Configuration of 8255

• **Working Modes of 8255 Mode Selection**

- There are two basic operational modes of 8255:
- Bit Set/Reset mode (BSR mode).
- Input/output mode (I/O mode).
-
- Bit Set/Reset (BSR) mode
- The Bit Set/Reset (BSR) mode is available on port C only.
- Each line of port C (PC_0 - PC_7) can be set or reset by writing a suitable value to the control word register.
- BSR mode and I/O mode are independent and selection of BSR mode does not affect the operation of other ports in I/O mode
- The control word format of BSR mode is as shown in the figure below
-

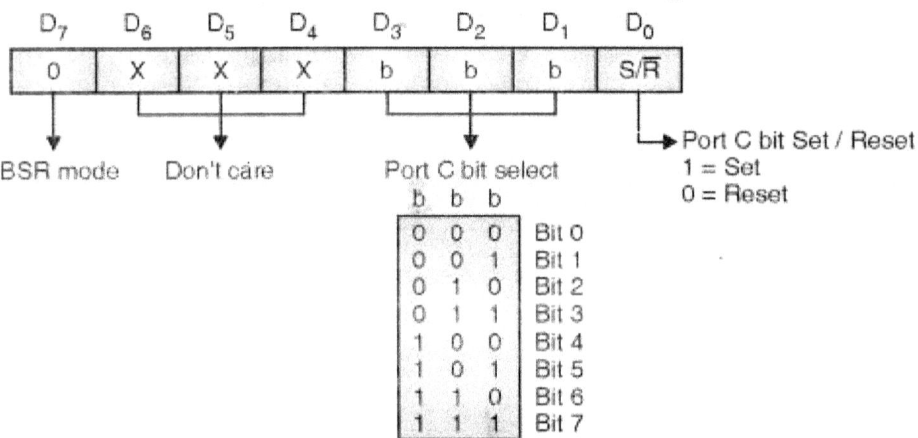

BSR control word format

- D_7 bit is always 0 for BSR mode.
- Bits D_6, D_5 and D_4 are don't care bits.
- Bits D_3, D_2 and D_1 are used to select the pin of Port C.
- Bit D_0 is used to set/reset the selected pin of Port C.
- Selection of port C pin is determined as follows:

D3	D2	D1	Bit/pin of port C selected
0	0	0	PC_0
0	0	1	PC_1
0	1	0	PC_2
0	1	1	PC_3
1	0	0	PC_4
1	0	1	PC_5
1	1	0	PC_6
1	1	1	PC_7

- As an example, if it is needed that PC_5 be set, then in the control word,
- Since it is BSR mode, D_7 = '**0**'.
- Since D_4, D_5, D_6 are not used, assume them to be '**0**'.
- PC_5 has to be selected, hence, D_3 = '**1**', D_2 = '**0**', D_1 = '**1**'.
- PC_5 has to be set, hence, **D0** = '**1**'.
- Thus, as per the above values, 0B (Hex) will be loaded into the Control Word Register (CWR).

D7	D6	D5	D4	D3	D2	D1	D0

- Input/Output mode
- This mode is selected when D_7 bit of the Control Word Register is 1. There are three I/O modes
- Mode 0 - Simple I/O
- Mode 1 - Strobed I/O
- Mode 2 - Strobed Bi-directional I/O
-

Control word

| D7 | D6 | D5 | D4 | D3 | D2 | D1 | D0 |

Group B

Port C (Lower)
1 = Input
0 = Output

Port B
1 = Input
0 = Output

Mode Selection
0 = Mode 0
1 = Mode 1

Group B

Port C (Lower)
1 = Input
0 = Output

Port A
1 = Input
0 = Output

Mode Selection
00 Mode 0
01 = Mode 1
1X = Mode 2

Mode Set Flag
1 = Active

-
-

- D_0, D_1, D_3, D_4 are assigned for port C lower, port B, port C upper and port A respectively. When these bits are **1**, the corresponding port acts as an input port. For e.g., if $D_0 = D_4 = 1$, then lower port C and port A act as input ports. If these bits are **0**, then the corresponding port acts as an output port. For e.g., if $D_1 = D_3 = 0$, then port B and upper port C act as output ports.

- D_2 is used for mode selection of Group B (port B and lower port C). When $D_2 = 0$, mode 0 is selected and when $D_2 = 1$, mode 1 is selected.
- D_5 & D_6 are used for mode selection of Group A (port A and upper port C). The selection is done as follows:
-

D_6	D_5	Mode
0	0	0
0	1	1
1	X	2

❖ As it is I/O mode, $D_7 = 1$.

-

Mode 0 - simple I/O

- This mode is also called as basic input/output Mode. This mode provides simple input and output capabilities using each of the three ports. Data can be simply read from and written to the input and output ports respectively, after appropriate initialization.
- In this mode, the ports can be used for simple I/O operations without handshaking signals. Port A, port B provide simple I/O operation. The two halves of port C can be either used together as an additional 8-bit port, or they can be used as individual 4-bit ports. Since the two halves of port C are independent, they may be used such that one-half is initialized as an input port while the other half is initialized as an output port.
- The salient features of this mode are as listed below:
- 1. Two 8-bit ports (port A and port B) and two 4-bit ports (port C upper and lower) are available. The two 4-bit ports can be combined used as a third 8-bit port.
- 2. Any port can be used as an input or output port.
- 3. Output ports are latched. Input ports are not latched.
- 4. A maximum of four ports are available so that overall 16 I/O configurations are possible.
- 'Latched' means the bits are put into a storage register (array of flip-flops) which holds its output constant even if the inputs change after being latched.
- The 8255's outputs are latched to hold the last data written to them. This is required because the data only stays on the bus for one cycle, so without latching the outputs would become invalid as soon as the write cycle finished.
- The inputs are not latched because the CPU only has to read their current values, and then store the data in a CPU register or memory if it needs to be referenced at a later time. If an input changes while the port is being read then the result may be indeterminate.
- *Mode 0 – Input mode*

- In the input mode, the 8255 gets data from the external peripheral ports and the CPU reads the received data via its data bus.
- The CPU first selects the 8255 chip by making $\overline{CS}$ low. Then it selects the desired port using A_0 and A_1 lines.
- The CPU then issues an $\overline{RD}$ signal to read the data from the external peripheral device via the system data bus.
- *<u>Mode 0 - Output mode</u>*
- In the output mode, the CPU sends data to 8255 via system data bus and then the external peripheral ports receive this data via 8255 port.
- CPU first selects the 8255 chip by making $\overline{CS}$ low. It then selects the desired port using A_0 and A_1 lines.
- CPU then issues a $\overline{WR}$ signal to write data to the selected port via the system data bus. This data is then received by the external peripheral device connected to the selected port.
-

- **<u>Mode1 (Strobed Input / Output):</u>**
- The Port A and Port B Can be designed to operate this mode of operation
- The transferring of of IO data to or from a specific port , is made possible with help of strobes or handshake signals
- In this mode the ports are divided in to two groups Group A and Group B
- Each group contain one 8 bit port and one 4 bit port
- In Mode 1 handshake signals are exchanged between the processor and peripherals prior to data transfer
- Port C pins are used for Handshake signals
- PCO, PC1, PC2 are used for control of port B When it can be used as either Input or Output port
- In case of Port A when its operated as input mode Port PC3, PC4, PC5 are used as handshake signals
- In case of Port A when its operated as output mode Port PC3, PC6 are used as handshake signals
-

- **Input control signal definitions (mode 1):**
- **STB** (Strobe input) – If this lines falls to logic low level, the data available at 8-bit input port is loaded into input latches.
- **IBF** (Input buffer full) – If this signal rises to logic 1, it indicates that data has been loaded into latches, i.e. it works as an acknowledgement. IBF is set by a low on STB and is reset by the rising edge of RD input.
- **INTR** (Interrupt request) – This active high output signal can be used to interrupt the CPU whenever an input device requests the service. INTR is set by a high STB pin and a high at IBF pin. INTE is an internal flag that can be controlled by the bit set/reset mode of either PC4 (INTEA) or PC2 (INTEB) as shown in fig.
- INTR is reset by a falling edge of RD input. Thus an external input device can be request the service of the processor by putting the data on the bus and sending the strobe signal.
-

Input control signal definitions in Mode 1

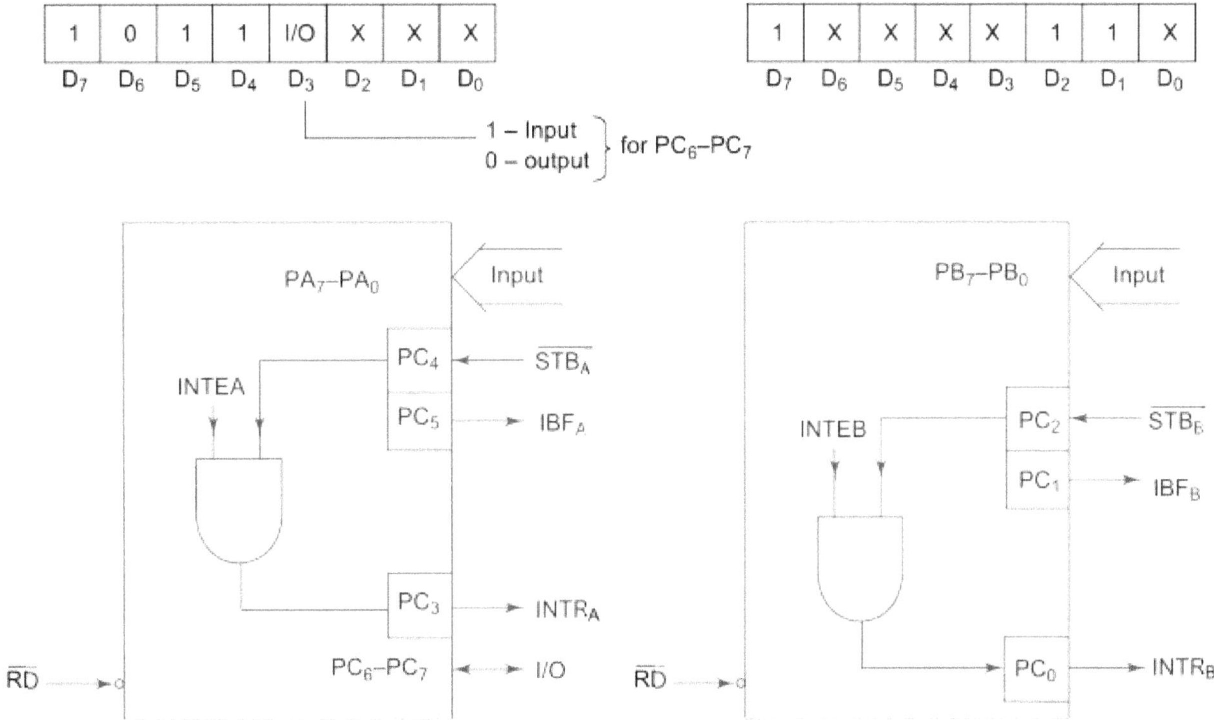

Fig. 5.27 *(a) Mode1 Control Word Group A I/P (b) Mode 1 Control Word Group B I/P*

- The input is the strobe input to 8255. Whenever an input is given to 8255, it will output an IBF indicating the output buffer full. It is the indication regarding no more inputs until the first one is processed. After an input is loaded the CPU is informed regarding the incoming instruction by INTR signal. INTE is an internal flag.
- STB_A shows input to Port A. STB_B shows input to port B.
- **Output control signal definitions (mode 1):**
- **OBF** (Output buffer full) – This status signal, whenever falls to low, indicates that CPU has written data to the specified output port. The OBF flip- flop will beset by a rising edge of WR signal and reset by a low going edge at the ACK input.
- **ACK** (Acknowledge input) – ACK signal acts as an acknowledgement to be given by an output device. ACK signal, whenever low, informs the CPU that the data transferred by the CPU to the output device through the port is received by the output device.
- **INTR** (Interrupt request) – Thus an output signal that can be used to interrupt the CPU when an output device acknowledges the data received from the CPU.INTR is set when ACK, OBF and INTE are 1. It is reset by a falling edge on WR input. The INTEA and INTEB flags are controlled by the bit set-reset mode ofPC6 and PC2 respectively.

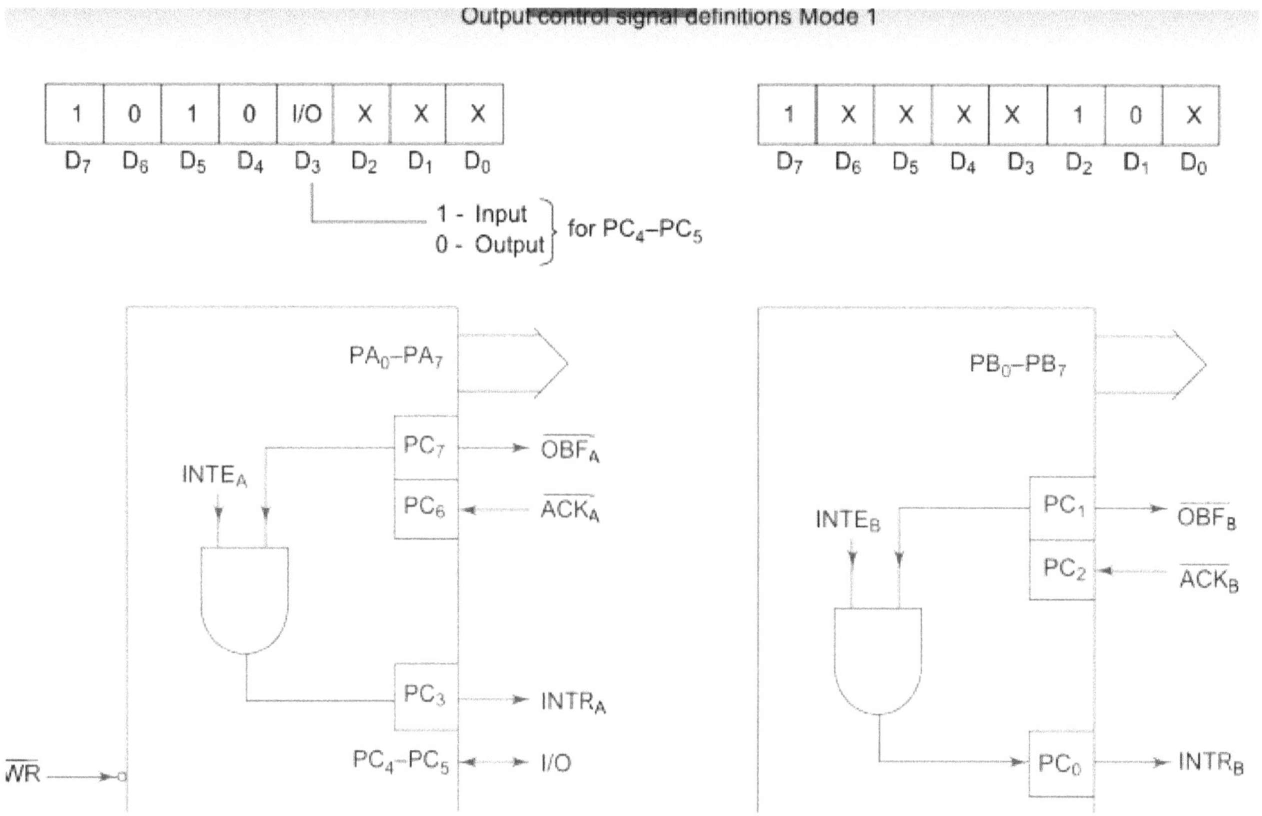

Output control signal definitions Mode 1

Fig. 5.29 *(a) Mode 1 Control Word Group A o/p (b) Mode 1 Control Word Group B o/p*

- **Mode 2 Basic Functional Definitions:**
- (i) Used in Group A only
- (ii) One 8-bit, bi-directional bus Port (Port A) and a 5-bit control Por t (Por t C)
- (iii) Both inputs and outputs are latched
- (iv) The 5-bit control port (Port C) is used for control and status for the 8-bit, bi-directional bus port
- (Port A)
- **Control signal definitions in mode 2:**
- **INTR** – (Interrupt request) as in mode 1, this control signal is active high and is used to interrupt the microprocessor to ask for transfer of the next data byte to/from it. This signal is used for input (read) as well as output (write) operations.
- **Control Signals for Output operations:**
- **OBF (Output buffer full)** – This signal, when falls to low level, indicates that the CPU has written data to port A.
- **ACK (Acknowledge):** This control input, when falls to logic low level, Acknowledges that the previous data byte is received by the destination and next byte may be sent by the processor. This signal enables the internal tristate buffers to send the next data byte on port A.
- **INTE1** (A flag associated with OBF): this can be controlled by bit set/resetmode with PC6.
- **Control signals for input operations:**
- **STB (Strobe input):** a low on this line is used to strobe in the data into the input Latches of 8255.
- **IBF (Input buffer full):** when the data is loaded into input buffer, this signal rises to logic „1". This can be used as an acknowledge that the data has been received by the receiver.

- The waveforms in fig show the operation in Mode 2 for output as well as input port.
- Note: WR must occur before ACK and STB must be activated before RD.
  - **Problems**
- **Example 1**
- I/O Interfacing (LED's Interfaced with 8086) Example 1:- Interface an 8255 chip with 8086 to work as an I/O port. Initialize port A as output port, Port B as I/P port and Port C as O/P port. Port A address should be 0740H. Write an ALP to sense switch positions SW0–SW7 connected at port B. The sensed pattern is to be displayed on port A, to which 8 LED's are connected, while port C lower displays number of on switches out of the total eight switches ?

-

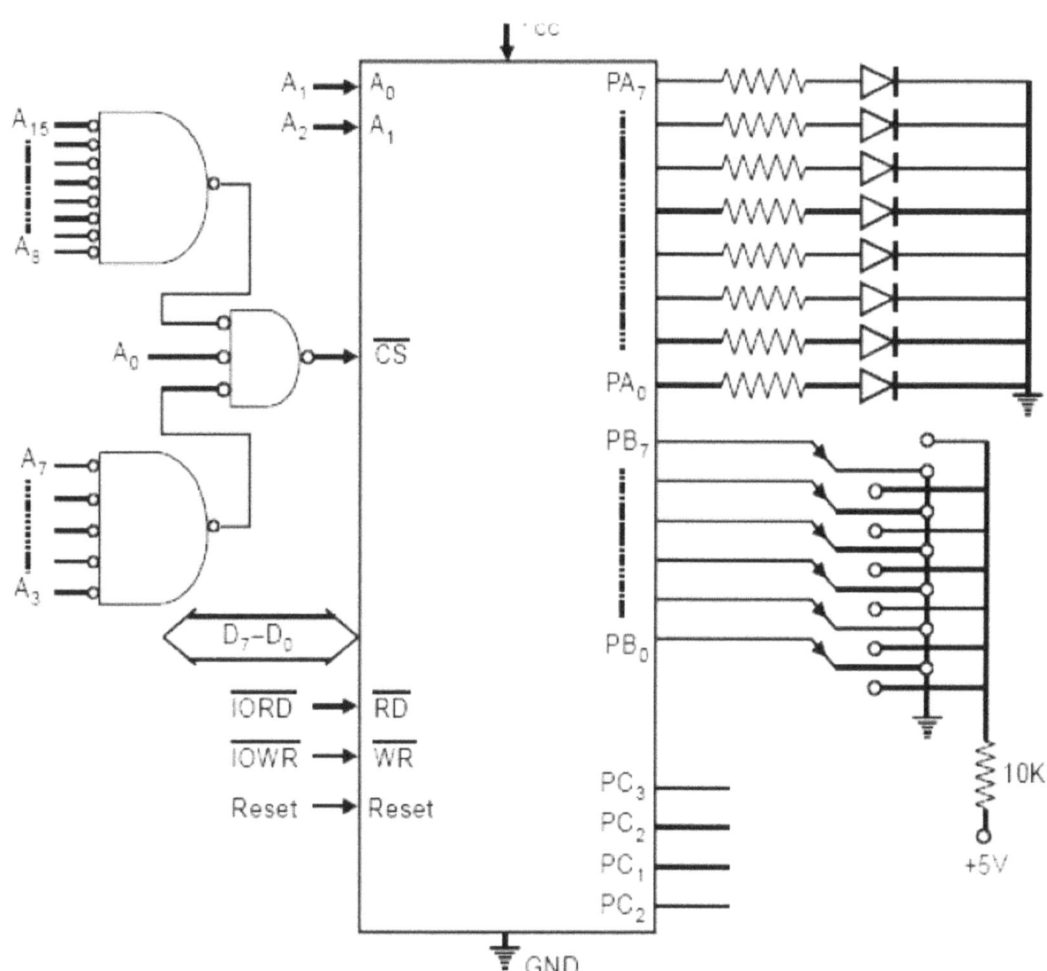

-

  ○

- **Example 2**
- **Interface a 4* 4 keyboard with 8086 using 8255, and write an ALP for detecting key closure and return the key code in AL. The debouncing period for a key in 20 ms?**

-

The interface circuit for the problem is as shown below :

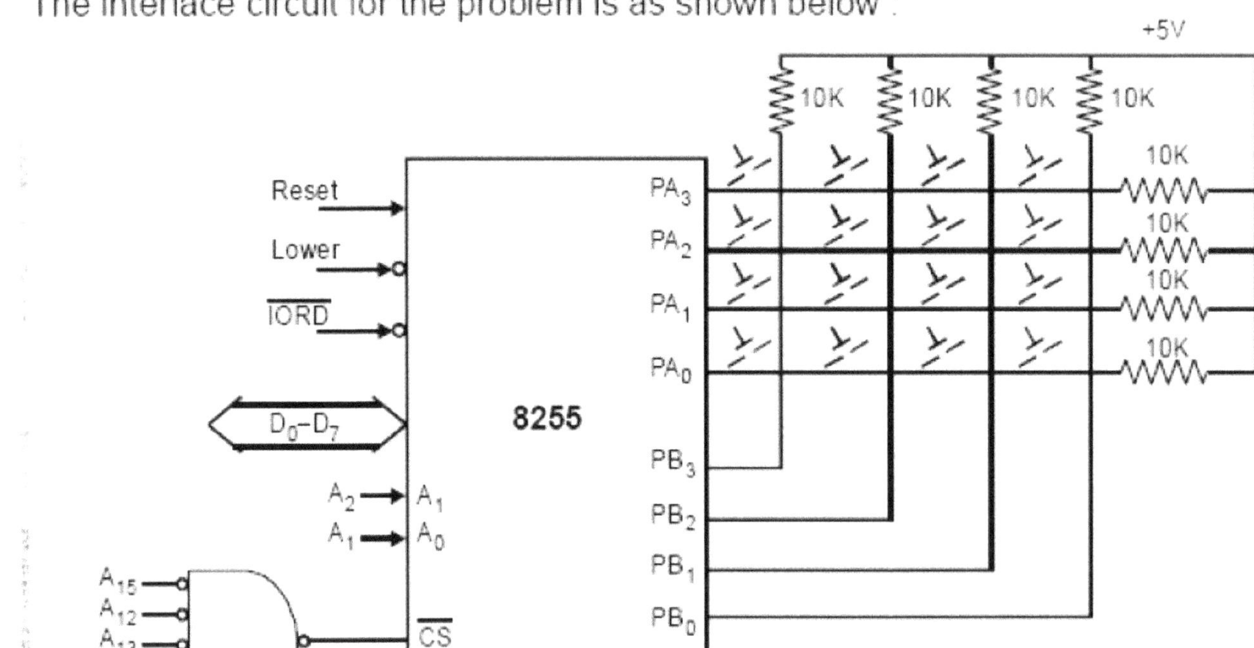

- Here we use port A as output port for selecting a row of keys while port B is used as an input port for sensing a closed key.
- •Hence the keyboard lines are selected one by one through Port A and the Port B lines are polled continuously till a key closure is sensed.
- •The higher order lines of Port A and Port B are left unused. The flowchart of the ALP is as shown below:
-

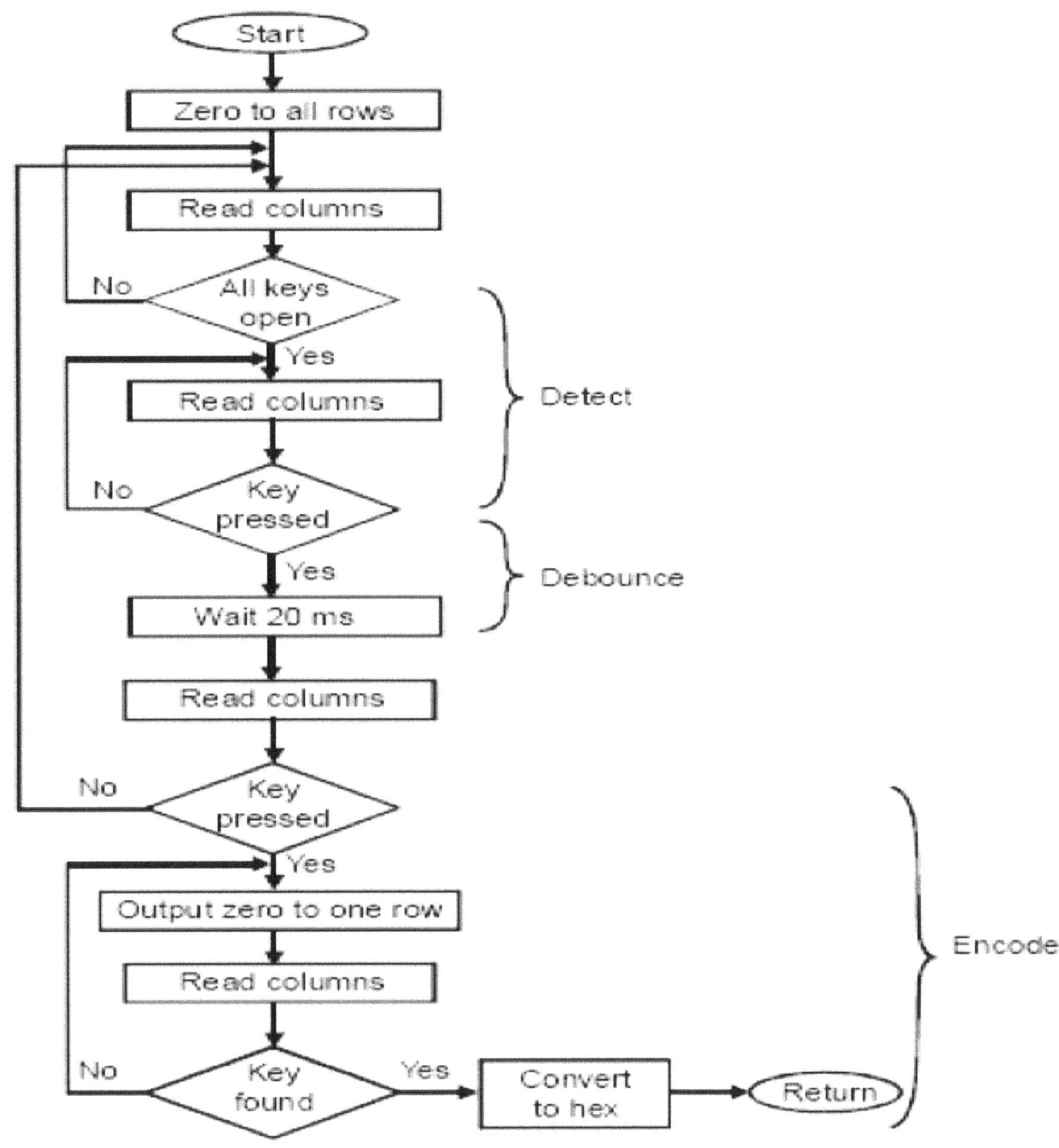

- We suppose that we use simple mechanical switches. For keyboard, then to get the meaningful data from a keyboard requires three steps:
- (1) Detect a key press
- (2) Debounce the key press
- (3) Encode the key press
- The three tasks can be done with hardware, software or a combination of the two.
- The rows of the matrix are connected to four output port lines. The column line of the matrix are connected to four input port lines
- **<u>Example 3</u>**

- **Interfacing 7-Seg Display with 8086**
- Interface an 8255 with 8086 at 80H as an I/O address of Port A.Interface five7segment displays with the 8255.Write an ALP to display1,2,3,4 and5over the 5 displays continuously as per their positions starting with1at the least significant position?

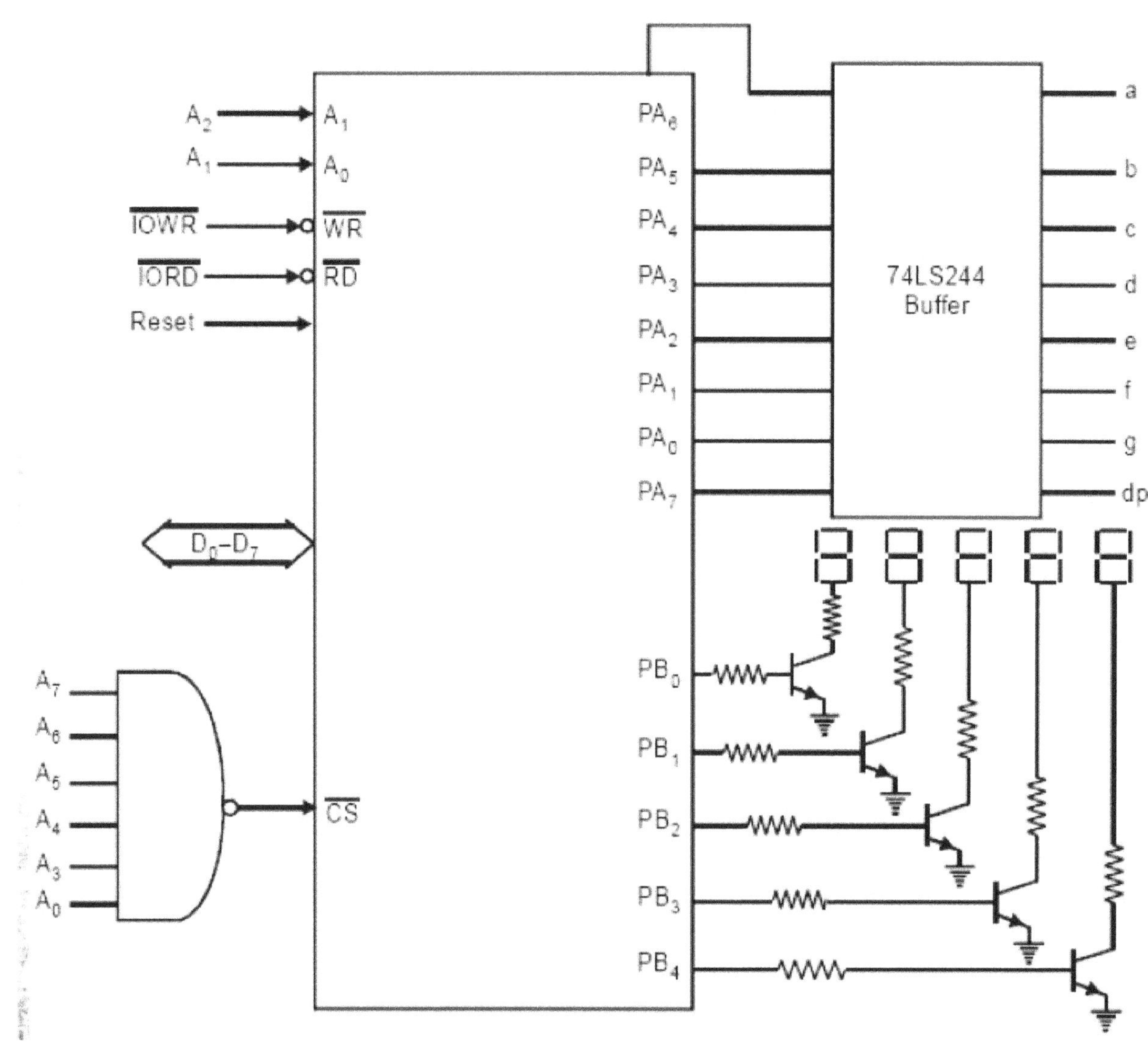

<u>*8279 – Programmable Keyboard/Display Interface*</u>

- 8255 can be used in interfacing keyboard and displays. The disadvantage of this method is that the processor has to refresh the display and check the status of the keyboard periodically using Polling technique. Thus CPU time is wasted; reducing the system operating speed.

- Intel's 8279 is a general purpose Keyboard Display controller that simultaneously drives the display of a system and interfaces a Keyboard with the CPU.
- The Keyboard Display interface scans the Keyboard to identify if any key has been pressed and sends the code of the pressed key to the CPU. It also transmits the data received from the CPU to the display device.
- Both of these functions are performed by the controller in repetitive fashion without involving the CPU. The Keyboard is interfaced either in the **interrupt or the polled mode.**In the interrupt mode, the processor is requested service only if any key is pressed, otherwise the CPU can proceed with its main task.
- In the polled mode, the CPU periodically reads an internal flag of 8279 to check for a key pressure.
- **Two sections of 8279**
- The **Keyboard section** can interface an array of a maximum of 64 keys with the CPU. The Keyboard entries (key codes) are debounced and stored in an 8-byte FIFO RAM that is further accessed by the CPU to read the key codes. If more than eight characters are entered in the FIFO (i.e. more that eight keys are pressed), before any FIFO read operation, the overrun status is set. If a FIFO contains a valid key entry, the CPU is interrupted (in interrupt mode) or the CPU checks the status (in polling) to read the entry.
- Once the CPU reads a key entry, the FIFO is updated, i.e. the key entry is pushed out of the FIFO to generate space for new entries. The 8279 normally provides a maximum of sixteen 7-seg **display interface** with CPU It contains a 16-byte display RAM that can be used either as an integrated block of 16x8-bits or two 16x4-bit block of RAM. The data entry to RAM block is controlled by CPU using the command words of the 8279.
-

-

- ## Architecture and Signal Descriptions of 8279
-

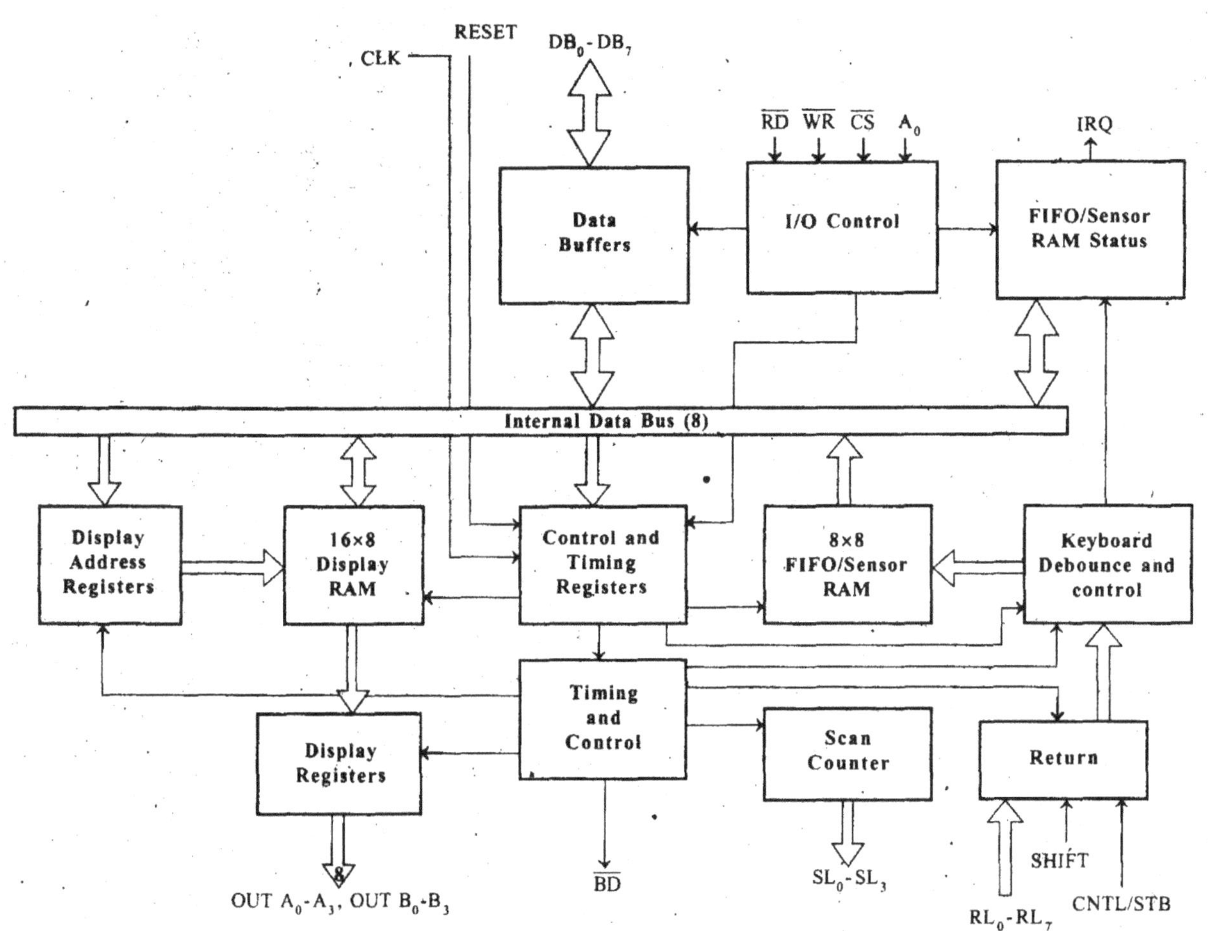

- ## I/O Control and Data Buffer
- The I/O control section controls the flow of data to/from the 8279. The data buffer interfaces the external bus of the system with internal bus of 8279.
- ## Control and Timing Register and Timing Control
- These registers store the keyboard and display modes and other operating conditions programmed by CPU. The registers are written with Ao=1 and WR =0. The timing and control unit controls the basic timings for the operation of the circuit.
- ## Scan Counter
- The Scan Counter has two modes to scan the key matrix and refresh the display. In the <u>Encoded mode</u>, the counter provides a binary count that is to be externally decoded to provide the scan lines for keyboard and display.In the <u>decoded scan mode</u>, the counter internally decodes the least significant 2 bits and provides a decoded 1 out of 4 scan on SL0-SL3 (four internally decoded scan lines may drive up to 4 Displays). The Keyboard and Display both are in the same mode at a time.
- ## Return Buffers and Keyboard Debounce and Control

- This section scans for a Key closure row-wise. If it is detected, the Keyboard debounce unit debounces the key entry (i.e. wait for 10 ms). After the debounce period, if the key continues to be detected. The code of the Key is directly transferred to the sensor RAM along with SHIFT and CONTROL key status.
- **FIFO/Sensor RAM and Status Logic**
- In Keyboard or strobed input mode, this block acts as 8-byte first-in-first-out (FIFO) RAM. Each key code of the pressed key is entered in the order of the entry, and in the meantime, read by the CPU, till the RAM becomes empty. The status logic generates an interrupt request after each FIFO read operation till the FIFO is empty.
- In scanned sensor matrix mode, this unit acts as sensor RAM. Each row of the sensor RAM is loaded with the status of the corresponding row of sensors in the matrix. If a sensor changes its state, the IRQ line goes high to interrupt the CPU.
- **Display Address Registers and Display RAM.**
- The Display address registers hold the addresses of the word currently being written or read by the CPU to or from the display RAM. The contents of the registers are automatically updated by 8279 to accept the next data entry by CPU. The 16-byte display RAM contains the 16-byte of data to be displayed on the sixteen 7-seg displays in the encoded scan mode.
- **Pin diagram of 8279**
-

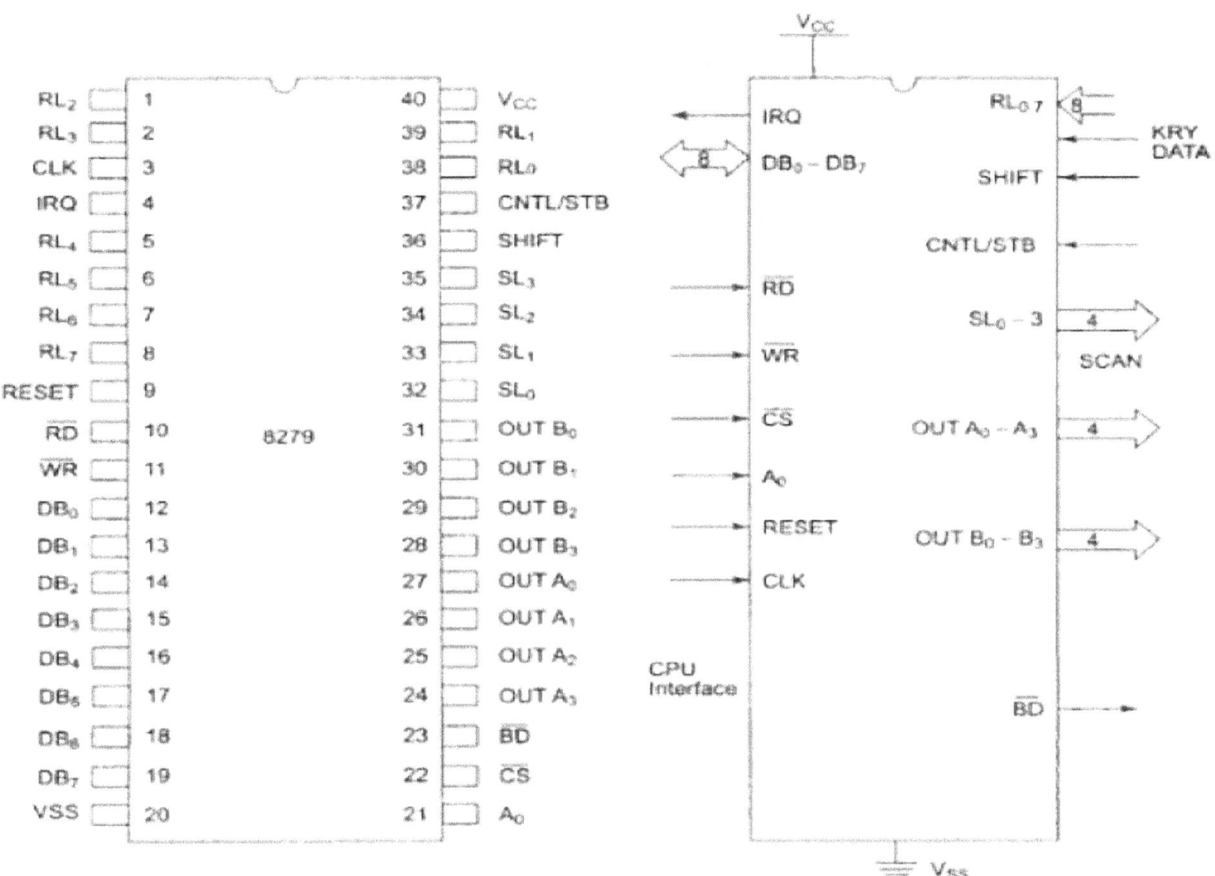

- **Ao :**A high on the Ao line indicates the transfer of a command or status information. A low on this line indicates the transfer of data. This is used to select one of the internal registers of 8279.

- **IRQ:**
- This interrupt output line goes high when there is data in the FIFO sensor RAM. The interrupt line goes low with each FIFO RAM read operation. However, if the FIFO RAM further contains any Key-code entry to be read by the CPU, this pin again goes high to generate an interrupt to the CPU.
- **SL0-SL3 – Scan Lines:**
- These lines are used to scan the keyboard matrix and display digits. These lines can be programmed as encoded or decoded, using the mode control register.
- **RL0-RL7 – Return Lines:**
- These are the input lines which are connected to one terminal of keys, while the other terminal of the keys is connected to the decoded scan lines. These are normally high, but pulled low when a key is pressed.
-
- **SHIFT:**
- The status of the Shift input line is stored along with each key code in FIFO in the scanned keyboard mode. Till it is pulled low with a key closure it is pulled up internally to keep it high.
- **CNTL/STB-CONTROL/STROBED I/P Mode:**
- In the Keyboard mode, this line is used as a control input and stored in FIFO on a key closure. The line is a strobe line that enters the data into FIFO RAM, in the strobed input mode. It has an internal pull up. The line is pulled down with a Key closure.
- **BD – Blank Display:**
- This output pin is used to blank the display during digit switching or by a blanking command.
- **OUTA0 – OUTA3 and OUTB0 – OUTB3:**
- These are the output ports for two 16x4 (or one 16 x 8) internal display refresh registers. The data from these lines is synchronized with the scan lines to scan the display and keyboard. The two 4-bit ports may also be used as one 8-bit port.
- <u>**The Modes of operation of 8279**</u>
- i. Input (Keyboard) modes
- ii. Output (Display) modes
- **Input/Keyboard Modes**
- **1. Scanned Key board mode:**
- **1.Scanned Keyboard Mode with 2 Key Lockout**
- 2 key lockout- if two keys are pressed with in a debounce cycle (simultaneously), no key is recognized till one of them remain closed and the other is released. The last key remains pressed is considered as single key press.In this mode of operation, when a key is pressed, a debounce logic comes into operation. The Key code of the identified key is entered into the FIFO with SHIFT and CNTL status, provided the FIFO is not full.
- **2. Scanned Keyboard with N-key Rollover**
- In this mode, each key depression is treated independently. When a key is pressed, the debounce circuit waits for 2 keyboard scans and then checks whether the key is still depressed. If it is still depressed, the code is entered in FIFO RAM. Any **number of keys can be pressed simultaneously and recognized in the order**, the Keyboard scan record them.
- **3. Scanned Keyboard Special Error Mode**
- This mode is valid only under the N-Key rollover mode. This mode is programmed using end interrupt/error mode set command. If during a single debounce period (two Keyboard scan) two keys are found pressed, this is considered a simultaneous depression and an error flag is set. This flag, if set, prevents further writing in FIFO but allows generation of further interrupts to the CPU for FIFO read.
- **4. Sensor Matrix Mode**
- In the Sensor Matrix mode, the debounce logic is inhibited the 8-byte memory matrix. The status of the sensor switch matrix is fed directly to sensor RAM matrix Thus the sensor RAM bits contains the row-wise and column-wise status of the sensors in the sensor matrix.

- **<u>Display modes:</u>**
- There are various options of data display The first one is known as left entry mode or type writer mode. Since in a type writer the first character typed appears at the left-most position, while the subsequent characters appears successively to the right of the first one. The other display format is known as right entry mode, or calculator mode, since the calculator the first character entered appears at the right-most position and this character is shifted one position left when the next character is entered.
-
  Scanned Keyboard Special Error Mode :
<ul><li>This mode is valid only under the N-Key
- rollover mode.

-
- **1. Left Entry Mode**
- In the Left entry mode, the data is entered from the left side of the display unit. Address0 of the display RAM contains the leftmost display character and address 15 of the RAM contains the rightmost display character.
- **2. Right Entry Mode**
- In the right entry mode, the first entry to be displayed is entered on the rightmost display.The next entry is also placed in the right most display but after the previous display is shifted left by one display position.
- **<u>Command Words of 8279</u>**
- All the Command words or status words are written or read with Ao = 1 and CS = 0 to or from 8279.
- **a. Keyboard Display mode set**
- The format of the command word to select different modes of operation of 8279 is given below with its bit definitions.
-

D_7	D_6	D_5	D_4	D_3	D_2	D_1	D_0	A_0
0	0	0	D	D	K	K	K	1

D	D	Display modes
0	0	Eight 8-bit character Left entry
0	1	Sixteen 8-bit character Left entry (Default after reset)
1	0	Eight 8-bit character Right entry
1	1	Sixteen 8-bit character Right entry

K	K	K	Keyboard modes
0	0	0	Encoded scan, 2 key lockout (Default after reset)
0	0	1	Decoded scan, 2 key lockout
0	1	0	Encoded scan N-Key roll over
0	1	1	Decoded scan N-Key roll over
1	0	0	Encoded scan sensor matrix
1	0	1	Decoded scan sensor matrix
1	1	0	Strobed Input Encoded scan
1	1	1	Strobed Input Decoded scan

b. Programmable Clock

The clock for operation of 8279 is obtained by dividing the external clock input signal by a programmable constant called prescaler.

D_7	D_6	D_5	D_4	D_3	D_2	D_1	D_0	A_0
0	0	1	P	P	P	P	P	1

PPPPP is a 5-bit binary constant. The input frequency is divided by a decimal constant ranging from 2 to 31, decided by the bits of an internal prescalar, PPPPP.

c. Read FIFO/Sensor RAM

The format of this command is given as shown below

D_7	D_6	D_5	D_4	D_3	D_2	D_1	D_0	A_0
0	1	0	AI	X	A	A	A	1

X - don't care

AI - Auto increment flag

AAA - Address pointer to 8 bit FIFO RAM

This word is written to set up 8279 for reading FIFO/Sensor RAM. In scanned keyboard mode, AI and AAA bits are of no use. The 8279 will automatically drive data bus for each subsequent read, in the same sequence, in which the data was entered.

d. Read Display RAM

This command enables a programmer to read the display RAM data

D_7	D_6	D_5	D_4	D_3	D_2	D_1	D_0	A_0
0	1	1	AI	A	A	A	A	1

The CPU writes this command word to 8279 to prepare it for display RAM read operation. AI is auto incremented flag and AAAA, the 4-bit address, points to the 16-byte display RAM that is to be read. If AI = 1, the address will be automatically, incremented after each read or write to the display RAM.

e. Write Display RAM

The format of this command is given as shown below

D_7	D_6	D_5	D_4	D_3	D_2	D_1	D_0	A_0
1	0	0	AI	A	A	A	A	1

AI - Auto increment flag

AAAA - 4-bit address for 16-bit display RAM to be written

other details of this command are similar to the 'Read Display RAM Command.

f. Display Write Inhibit/Blanking

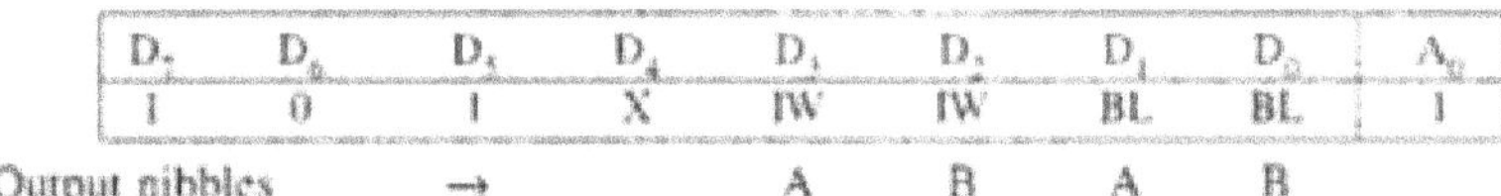

D_7	D_6	D_5	D_4	D_3	D_2	D_1	D_0	A_0
1	0	1	X	IW	IW	BL	BL	1

| Output nibbles | $\rightarrow$ | | | A | B | A | B | |

The IW (Inhibit write flag) bits are used to mask the individual nibble Here Do and D2 corresponds to OUTB0 – OUTB3 while D1 and D3 corresponds to OUTA0-OUTA3 for blanking and masking respectively.

g. Clear Display RAM

D_7	D_6	D_5	D_4	D_3	D_2	D_1	D_0	A_0
1	1	0	CD_2	CD_1	CD_0	CF	CA	1

The CD2, CD1, CD0 is a selectable blanking code to clear all the rows of the display RAM as given below. The characters A and B represent the output nibbles.

CD	CD1	CDo	
1	0	x	All Zeros (x don't care) AB = 00
1	1	0	A3-Ao = 2(0010) and B3-Bo = 00(0000)
1	1	1	All ones (AB = FF), i.e. clear RAM

Here, CA represents clear All and CF represents Clear FIFO RAM

End Interrupt/Error Mode Set

D_7	D_6	D_5	D_4	D_3	D_2	D_1	D_0	A_0
1	1	1	E	x	x	x	x	1

x—do not care

For the sensor matrix mode, this command lowers the IRQ line and enables further writing into the RAM. Otherwise, if a charge in sensor value is detected, IRQ goes high that inhibits

- writing in the sensor RAM.

  o

-
- **Interfacing and Programming 8279**
- **Problem:**
- Interface keyboard and display controller 8279 with 8086 at address 0080H. Write an ALP to set up 8279 in scanned keyboard mode with encoded scan, N-Key rollover mode. Use a 16 character display in right entry display format. Then clear the display RAM with zeros. Read the FIFO for key closure. If any key is closed, store its code to register CL. Then write the byte 55 to all the displays, and return to DOS. The clock input to 8279 is 2MHz, operate it at 100 KHz.
- **Solution:**
- The 8279 is interfaced with lower byte of the data bus, i.e. D0-D7. Hence the A0 input of 8279 is connected with address lineA1.
- The data register of 8279 is to be addressed as 0080H, i.e.A0=0.
- For addressing the command or status word A0 input of 8279 should be 1.
- The next step is to write all the required command words for this problem.
- **Figure shows the interfacing schematic**
-

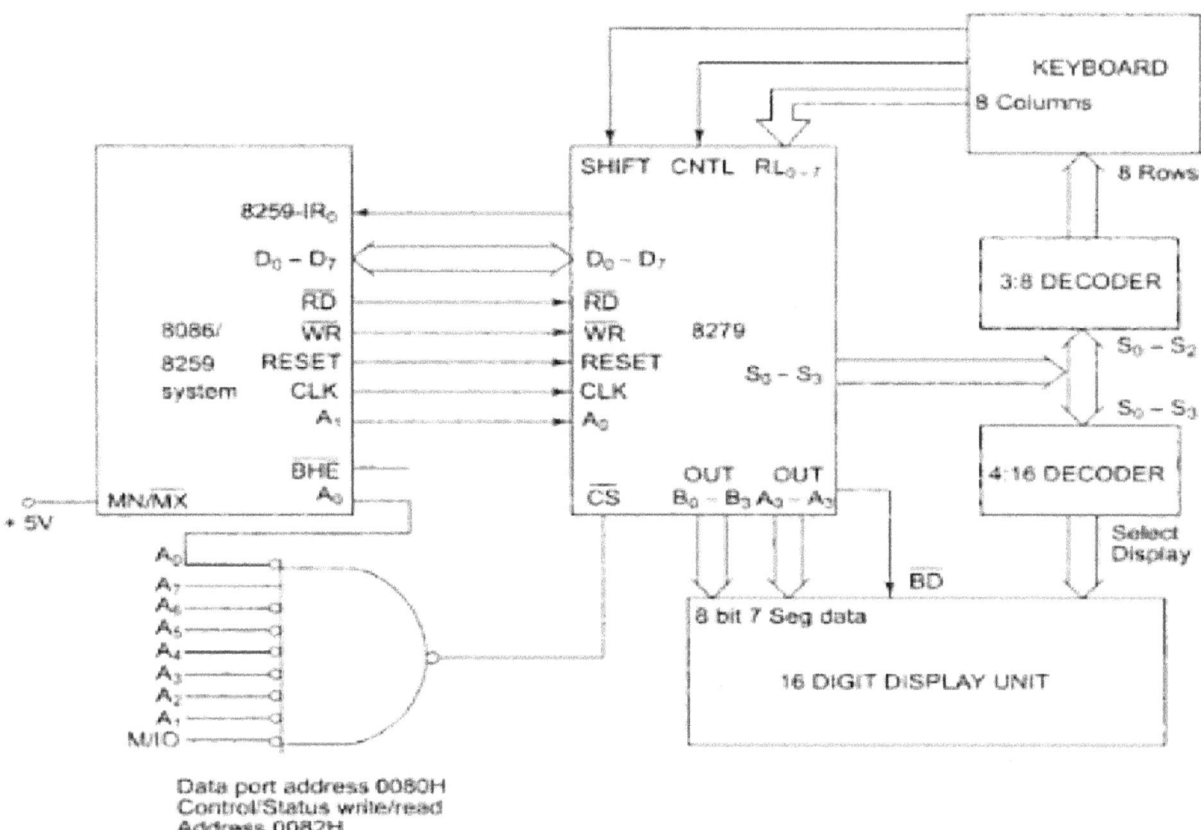
KEYBOARD
8 Columns
8 Rows
SHIFT CNTL RL$_{0-7}$
8259-IR$_0$
D$_0$ – D$_7$
D$_0$ – D$_7$
$\overline{RD}$
$\overline{WR}$
RESET
CLK
A$_1$
8086/
8259
system
$\overline{RD}$
$\overline{WR}$
RESET
CLK
A$_0$
8279
S$_0$ – S$_3$
3:8 DECODER
S$_0$ – S$_2$
S$_0$ – S$_3$
4:16 DECODER
Select
Display
$\overline{BHE}$
A$_0$
MN/$\overline{MX}$
+ 5V
$\overline{CS}$
OUT
B$_0$ – B$_3$
OUT
A$_3$ – A$_3$
$\overline{BD}$
8 bit 7 Seg data
16 DIGIT DISPLAY UNIT
A$_0$
A$_7$
A$_6$
A$_5$
A$_4$
A$_3$
A$_2$
A$_1$
M/IO
Data port address 0080H
Control/Status write/read
Address 0082H

-

  ○

-
-

Keyboard/Display Mode Set CW:

This command byte sets the 8279 in 16-character right entry and encoded scan N-Key rollover mode.

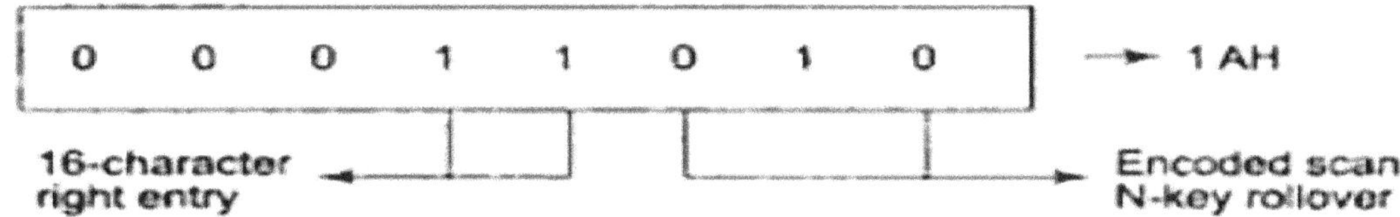

Program clock selection:

The clock input to 8279 is 2MHz, but the operating frequency is to be 100KHz, i.e. the clock input is to be divided by 20 (10100). Thus the prescalar value is 10100 and the command byte is set as given.

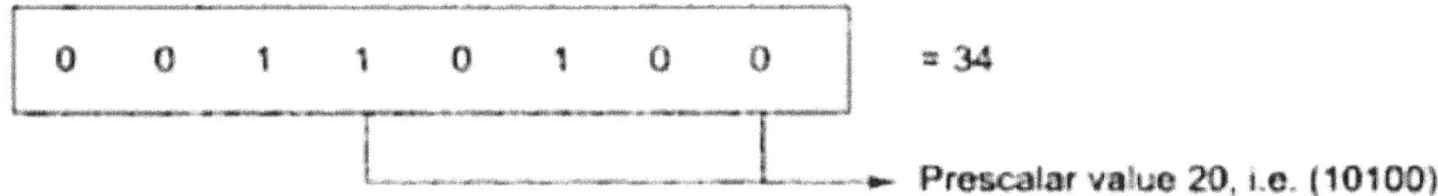

Clear Display RAM:

This command clears the display RAM with the programmable blanking code.

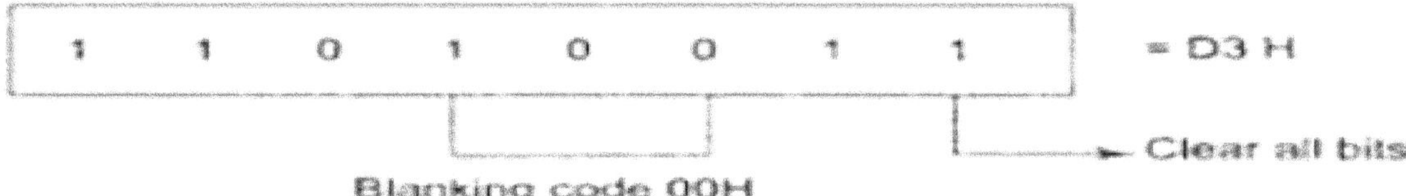

Read FIFO:

This command byte enables the programmer to read a key code from the FIFO RAM

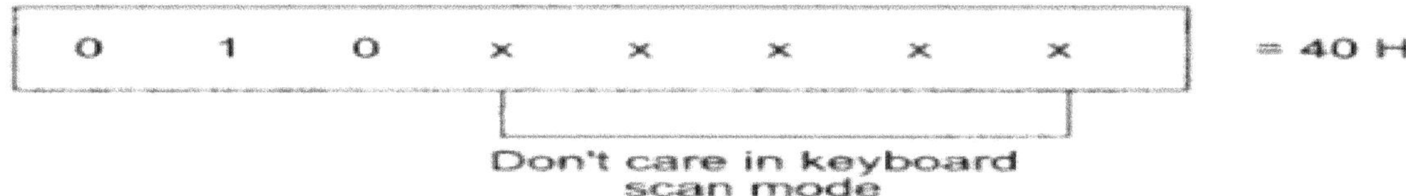

Write Display RAM:

This command enables the programmer to write the addressed display locations of the RAM as presented below.

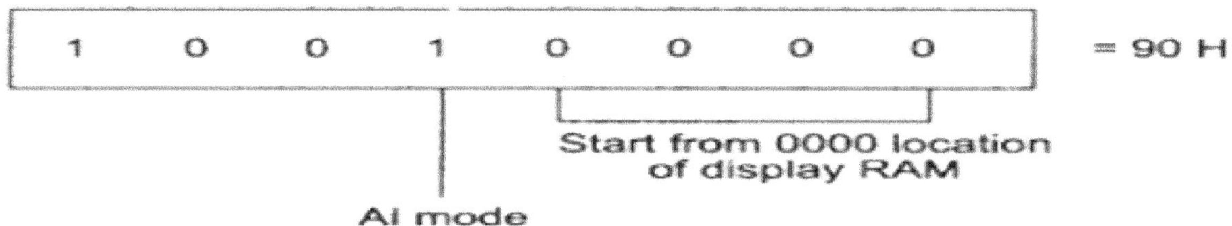

-
  -
-

Program gives the ALP required to initialize the 8279 as required:

```
        Assume CS        : Code
        Code  Segment
Start : MOV AL, 1AH      :    Set 8279 in Encoded scan,
        OUT 82H, AL      :    N Key rollover, 16 display, Right entry mode.
        MOV AL, 34H      :    Set clock prescalar to
        OUT 82H, AL      :    100KHz
        MOV AL, 0D3H     :    Clear display ram
        OUT 82H, AL      :    command
        MOV AL, 40H      :    Read FIFO command
        OUT 82H, AL      :    for checking display RAM
Wait :  IN AL, 82H       :    Wait for clearing of
        AND AL, 80H      :    Display RAM by reading
        CMP AH, 80H      :    FIFO Du bit of the status word i.e.
        JNZ Wait         :    If Du bit is not set wait, else proceed.
        MOV AH, 40H      :    Read FIFO command
        OUT 82H, AL      :    for check key closure
        IN AL, 82H       :    Read FIFO status
        AND AH, 07H      :    Mask all bits except the
        CMP AH, 00       :    number of characters bits
        JNZ Key code     :    if any key is pressed, take

Warm:   MOV AL, 90H      :       required action. otherwise
        OUT 82H, AL      :       Proceed to write display
        MOV AL, 55H      :       RAM by using write display
        MOV CL, 10H      :       command. Write the byte
Next:   OUT 80H, AL      :       55H to all display RAM
        DEC CL           :       Locations
        JNZ Next         :
        JMP Stop         :
Key code: Call Read code :       Call routine to read the key
        JMP Warm    :    Code of the pressed key is
        assumed available
Stop    MOV AH, 4CH      :       stop
        INT 21H


        CODE      ENDS
                  END  START
```

CHAPTER FIVE

MICROCONTROLLERS

Q.How does microprocessor differ from Microcontroller?

Q.List out the applications of microprocessor and microcontrollers?

Introduction to microcontrollers- Comparison with microprocessors

Microcontrollers are small computing systems on a single chip.

A microcontroller will also be referred to as an MCU.

Central Processing Unit (CPU)

Program memory

Random Access Memory (RAM)

EEPROM - Electrically Erasable Programmable Read Only Memory

USARTs, Timer/Counters, ADC, DAC, I/O Ports, CANs, SPIs, etc.

Applications

Cell phone, Pager, Watch, Calculator, video games. Alarm clock. Air conditioner,

TV remote, Microwave oven, Washing machines, Robotic system

Comparison

Microprocessor

CPU is stand alone, RAM, ROM, IO, Timer are separate.

Designer can decide on the amount of RAM, ROM and IO ports.

Expansive

Versatility

General purpose

Examples: 8085,8086

Microcontroller

CPU, RAM, ROM, IO and timer are all on a single chip.

Fix amount of on chip ROM, RAM, IO ports.

Highly bit addressable

For applications in which cost, power and space are critical.

Single purpose

Examples

Motorola's 6811

Intel's 8051

Zilog's Z8

PIC 16X.

Q.What are the minimum structural units and devices needed in a microcontroller?

Ans:(: Describe various blocks in the block diagram given below)

Microprocessor	Microcontroller
Block diagram of microprocessor	Block diagram of microcontroller
Microprocessor contains ALU, General purpose registers, stack pointer, program counter, clock timing circuit, interrupt circuit	Microcontroller contains the circuitry of microprocessor, and in addition it has built in ROM, RAM, I/O Devices, Timers/Counters etc.
It has many instructions to move data between memory and CPU	It has few instructions to move data between memory and CPU
Few bit handling instruction	It has many bit handling instructions
Less number of pins are multifunctional	More number of pins are multifunctional
Single memory map for data and code (program)	Separate memory map for data and code (program)
Access time for memory and IO are more	Less access time for built in memory and IO.
Microprocessor based system requires additional hardware	It requires less additional hardwares
More flexible in the design point of view	Less flexible since the additional circuits which is residing inside the microcontroller is fixed for a particular microcontroller
Large number of instructions with flexible addressing modes	Limited number of instructions with few addressing modes

Types of microcontrollers

Q.Explain types of microcontrollers?

Q.Distinguish CISC and RISC Architecture microcontrollers?

Q.How the Harvard architecture microcontroller differ from Princeton memory architecture microcontrollers.?

Q.What are embedded microcontrollers and embedded processors, and explain when each of them is used? When do we use external memory with in an MCU?

Q.What are different ways of classifying the types of the microcontrollers?

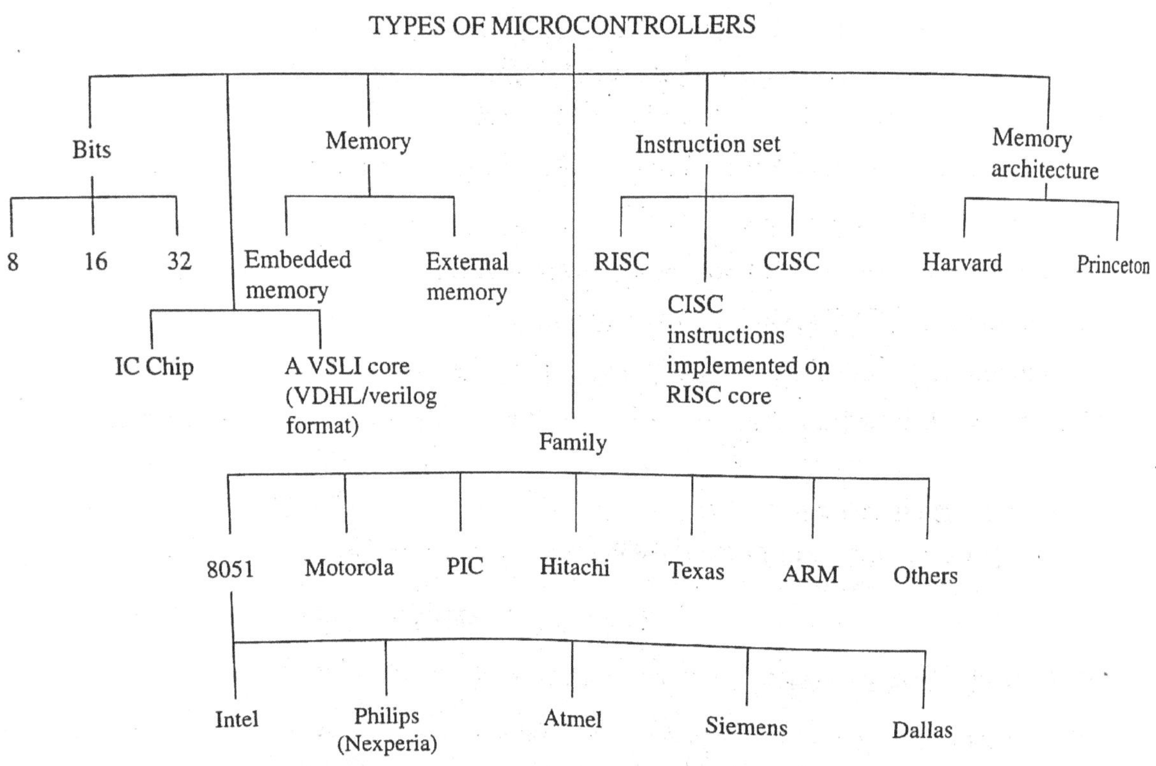

Figure 1.5 Various Types of Microcontrollers

1.2.1 The 8, 16 and 32-Bit Microcontrollers

8-bit microcontroller: When internal bus in an MCU is 8-bit bus and the ALU performs the arithmetic and logic operations on a byte at an instruction, the MCU is 8-bit microcontroller. Examples of 8-bit MCUs are Intel 8031/8051, PIC1x and Motorola MC68HC11 families.

16-bit microcontroller: When internal bus in an MCU is 16-bit bus and the ALU performs arithmetic and logic operations on the operand words of 16 bits at the instructions, the MCU is 16-bit microcontroller. Important 16-bit MCUs are Extended 8051XA, PIC2x, Intel 8096 and Motorola MC68HC12 families. 16-bit MCU provides greater precision and performance as compared to the 8-bit MCU.

32-bit microcontroller: When internal bus for the data transfer operations in an MCU is 32-bit bus and the ALU performs arithmetic and logic operations on operand words of 32 bits at the instructions, the MCU is 32-bit microcontroller. Important 32-bit MCUs are Intel/Atmel 251 family, PIC3x, Motorola M683xx and ARM 7 or 9 or 11 processor-based microcontroller families. These provide greater precision and performance compared to the 16-bit MCUs. They find applications in embedded

computing systems for applications—mobile phones, MP3 audio systems, MPEG processing, image-processing-based products and aerospace systems, are the examples.

1.2.2 Embedded and External Memory Microcontrollers

Embedded microcontroller: When an embedded system has an MCU that has all the hardware and software units in a single unit, the MCU is called embedded microcontroller. Very few or no other external unit or system is present for processing during the control or use of the external devices. For example, a telephone handset circuit uses an embedded microcontroller.

External memory microcontroller: When an embedded system has an MCU that has all the hardware and software units present not as a single unit and has all or part of the memory unit externally interfaced using an interfacing circuit which is called the glue circuit, the MCU is called an external memory microcontroller. For example, 8031 has the program memory which is interfaced externally to it. The 8051 has both internal as well as external program memory.

1.2.3 CISC and RISC Architecture Microcontrollers

Complicated Instruction Set Computer (CISC) architecture microcontroller: When an MCU has an instruction set that supports many addressing modes for the arithmetic and logical instructions and when there are the memory accesses during the ALU operations and the data transfer instructions, the MCU is said to be possessing CISC-architecture.

CISC provides flexibility in choosing various ways of performing the data transfer, arithmetic and other operations. For example, it is feasible to add contents of two registers or add the register and memory or add the bits at two memory addresses in a CISC. Instructions are of variable number of bytes in the CISC. These can take varying amounts of time interval for execution. An example is Intel 8096.

Reduced Instruction Set Computer (RISC) microcontroller: When an MCU has an instruction set that supports a few addressing modes for the arithmetic and logical instructions and just a few (load, store, push and pop) instructions for the data transfer, the MCU is said to be of RISC architecture. RISC provides no flexibility in choosing the many different ways of performing the arithmetic and logic operations. These operations are performed after the load of operands in the registers, and the results of these operations are placed in registers. The register contents are later on stored in the memory. RISC implements each instruction in a single cycle using a distinct hardwired control. It uses a lesser amount of circuitry. It has less power dissipation. There is reduced instruction set. Instructions are of fixed number of bytes and take a fixed amount of time for execution. It has many registers. Therefore, operations can be performed using them. The need for external fetches from the memories are greatly reduced. (An external fetch is to be done by the CPU for an operand more frequently in the CISC). The RISC provides a higher performance in computing than the CISC. This is because little need of the external fetches, which takes a significant amount of processor time. High performance is also because of hardwired implementation of instructions. An example of RISC architecture is the ARM processor family-based MCU.

These days most microprocessor and microcontroller designs are based on RISC core, because the CISC features can always be provided for programming with an appropriate on-chip compiler or internal circuit which translates the codes for the RISC core.

1.2.4 Harvard and Princeton Memory Architecture Microcontrollers

Harvard memory architecture microcontroller: When an MCU has a distinct memory address space for the program and data memory, the MCU has Harvard memory architecture in the processor. The MCU has separate instructions, and hence separate control signal(s), for the data transfers from these two memories. For example, 8051 has an address space between 0x0000 and 0xFFFF for the program memory bank and separate memory between 0x0000 and 0xFFFF for the data memory bank. (Bank saves the money, a memory bank saves the bytes during operations.)

Princeton memory architecture microcontroller: When an MCU has a common memory address space usable for the program memory and data memory, the MCU has Princeton memory architecture in the processor. For example, 68HC11 has an address space between 0x0000 and 0xFFFF for the program memory codes and the same space between 0x0000 and 0xFFFF for the data bytes. It has no separate instructions, and hence no separate control signal(s) for data transfers from and to these two sets of memories. (Program and data can be stored on the same memory chip or unit within same address block.)

Criteria for selecting a microcontroller
Q.What are the different criteria's for the selection of microcontrollers?
(Refer Assignment or Pg.No.16-Microcontrollers,Raj Kamal)
Different criterias to be taken into consideration are:-
Checklist of the needed features and factors tken into consideration
Selection of processor and processor family
Selection of on-chip resources –base
Selection of Software building Blocks

Selection of development Tool –Base
Example Applications of Microcontrollers.
Q.Describe various aplications of Microcontrollers ?
Applications are:-
Automatic Process Control
Instrumentation Applications.
Biomedical instruments like an ECG LCD display cum Recorder
Communication systems like cellular phones,Cable TV ,Fax etc..
Robotic Systems
Target Tracker
Automatic Signal Tracker
Instruments like industrial process controller and electronic smart weight display system
Etc..
Characteristics and Resources of a microcontroller. Organization and design of these resources in a typical microcontroller - 8051.
Q.Write short notes on microcontroller on-chip resources.
Microcontroller on-chip resources are:-

1. Basic processing unit, internal buses and interrupt handler (Section 2.3.1).
2. On-chip program memory, Internal EEPROM and Flash (Section 2.3.2).
3. On-chip RAM (Section 2.3.2).
4. Interfacing capability to external program memory (Section 2.3.2).
5. Interfacing capability to external data memory (Section 2.3.2).
6. Ports (Section 2.3.3).
7. On-chip registers (Section 2.3.4).
8. Special function registers (Section 2.3.5).
9. UART (Section 2.3.6).
10. Serial synchronous (Section 2.3.7).
11. Timers/counters (Section 2.3.8).
12. Pulse width modulator (PWM) (Section 2.3.9).
13. On-chip ADC (Section 2.3.10).
14. Watchdog timer (Section 2.3.11).
15. Bitwise manipulation capability (Section 2.3.12).
16. Power-down mode (Section 2.3.13).
17. Real-time clock (Section 2.3.14).

<u>The Microcontroller -8051</u>

Q.Explain the internal architecture of 8051 with a neat diagram?

Q.Describe the features of 8051 microcontroller?

History of 8051 microcontroller

In the year 1980 Intel corporation introduced an 8 bit microcontroller called 8051.

It has 4K bytes of ROM,128 Bytes of RAM , a serial port, two 6-bit Timers and 32 I/O pins.

CPU can work with 8 bit of data at a time.

Data larger than 8 bit can be broken into 8 bit pieces to be processed by the CPU

Important Features of 8051

4K bytes ROM

128 bytes RAM

Four 8-bit I/O ports

Two 8/16 bit timers

Serial port

64K external code memory space

64K data memory space

Multiple internal and external interrupt sources

8051 ARCHIECTURE

Q.Write the use of following blocks of 8051:-

a) Program Status Word

b) Data pointer(DPTR)

c)Serial data buffer?

The block diagram and description of each block is given below:-

Accumulator: Acts as operand register for some instructions

B register : Special function register. Used to store one of the operand for multiply or divide

Program Status Word: Special purpose register This set of flags contain status information

Stack Pointer: Contains 8bit stack address.8 bit wide register is incremented before the data is stored in stack. Decremented when data pushed from stack. Not top down structure.

Data pointer(DPTR): 16 bit register. Contains higher byte (DPH) and lower byte(DPL) of a 16 bit external data RAM address. Can be used as 16 bit and 8bit register.

Port 0 to 3 Latches and Drivers: these 4 latches and driver pairs are allotted to 4 on chip i/o ports. These latches have been allotted address in special function register bank. Using allotted address they communicate with these ports. They are identified as P0,P1, P2 and P3

Serial Data Buffer: contains 2independent registers- transmit and receive buffers. Loading byte into transmit buffer initiates serial data transfer.

Timer Registers: TL0 and TL1these 2 16 bit registers can be accessed as their lower and upper bytes.

Control registers: the special function registers IP,IE,TMOD, TCON,SCON & PCON contain control and status information for interrupts, timers/counters and serial ports.

Timing and Control Unit: this unit derives all necessary timing and control signals required for internal operation of circuit. It also derives control signals for deriving external bus.

Oscillator: generates timing clock signal

Instruction Register: decodes the opcode of instruction to be executed and gives information to timing and control unit to generate necessary signals for execution.

EPROM and Program Address Register: these block provide an on chip EPROM and a mechanism to internally address it.

RAM and RAM address Register: provides 128 bytes of RAM and mechanism to address it internally

ALU: operands in temporary register TMP1 and TMP2

SFR register Bank: set of special function registers, which can be addressed using respective address which lie in rang 80H to FFH

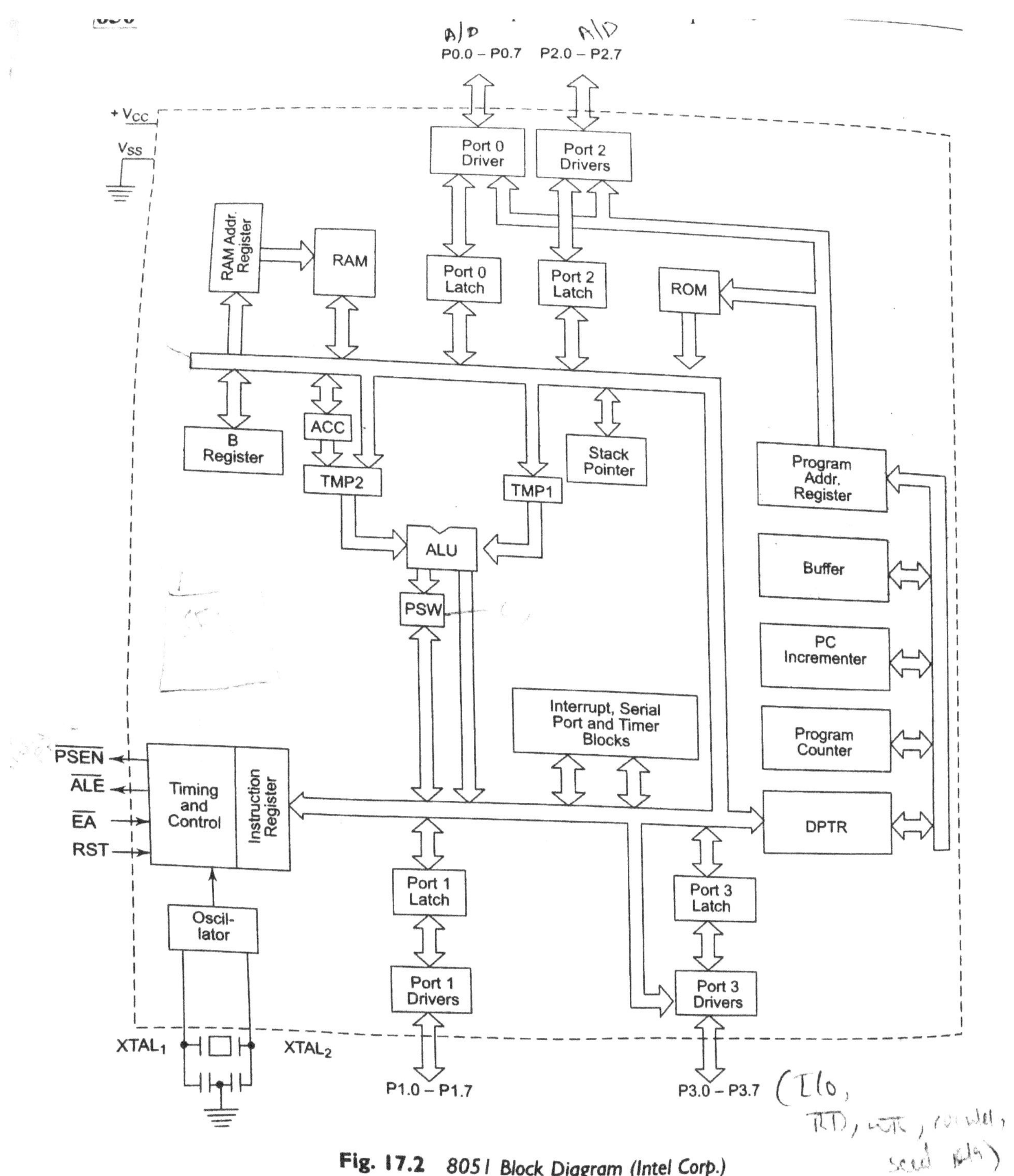

Fig. 17.2 *8051 Block Diagram (Intel Corp.)*

<u>**Internal RAM(128=7F bit) -Organisation of 8051**</u>

Q.Describe the internal RAM organization of 8051?

Q.Explain banked registers of 8051?

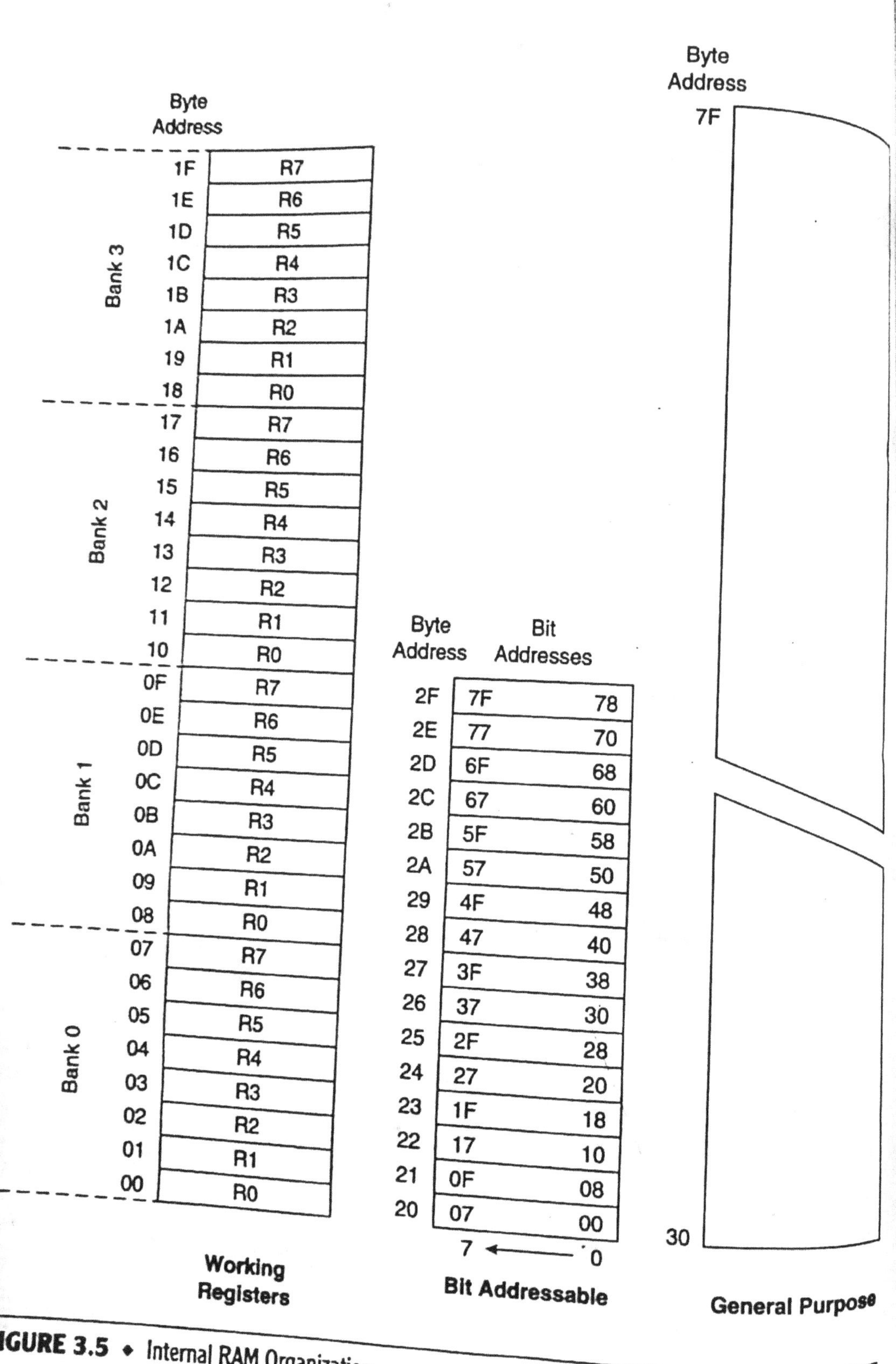

FIGURE 3.5 ◆ Internal RAM Organization

Internal RAM

The 128-byte internal RAM, which is shown generally in Figure 3.1 and in detail in Figure 3.5, is organized into three distinct areas:

1. Thirty-two bytes from address 00h to 1Fh that make up 32 working registers organized as four banks of eight registers each. The four register banks are numbered 0 to 3 and are made up of eight registers named R0 to R7. Each register can be addressed by name (when its bank is selected) or by its RAM address. Thus R0 of bank 3 is R0 (if bank 3 is currently selected) or address 18h (whether bank 3 is selected or not). Bits RS0 and RS1 in the PSW determine which bank of registers is currently in use at any time when the program is running. Register banks not selected can be used as general-purpose RAM. Bank 0 is selected on reset.

2. A *bit*-addressable area of 16 bytes occupies RAM *byte* addresses 20h to 2Fh, forming a total of 128 addressable bits. An addressable bit may be

specified by its *bit* address of 00h to 7Fh, or 8 bits may form any *byte* address from 20h to 2Fh. Thus, for example, bit address 4Fh is also bit 7 of byte address 29h. Addressable bits are useful when the program need only remember a binary event (switch on, light off, etc.). Internal RAM is in short supply as it is, so why use a byte when a bit will do?

3. A general-purpose RAM area above the bit area, from 30h to 7Fh, addressable as bytes.

Signal Descriptions of 8051

Q.Explain the signal descriptions of 8051?

Q.write the name of pins used for external memory access?(EA ,PSEN)?

Q.Describe the alternative functions of PORT 3?

The 8051 is a 40 pin device, but out of these 40 pins, 32 are used for I/O.

24 of these are dual purpose, i.e. they can operate as I/O or a control line or as part of address or data bus.

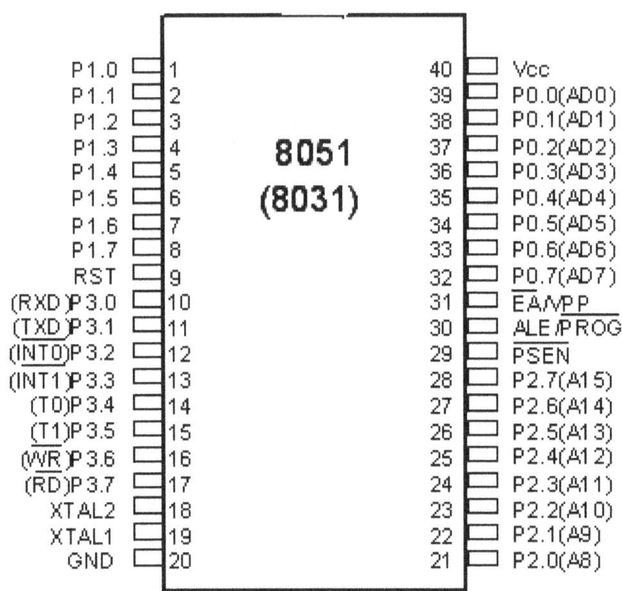

•

Vcc（pin 40）: Vcc provides supply voltage to the chip. The voltage source is +5V.

GND（pin 20）: ground

XTAL1 and XTAL2 : There is inbulit oscillator to derive clock frequency. XTAL1 is input to amplifier and XTAL2 is output

RESET : resets 8051,only when it goes high for 2 or more machine cycles

ALE/PROG : ALE indicates valid address are available in respective pins.ALE is valid for external memory access only. This pin acts as program pulse input during on chip EPROM programming.

EA/Vpp : External access enable pin. If low 8051 can execute a program in external memory. For execution in internal memory it is high

PSEN : Program store enable. Goes low during external memory accesses

PORT 0(P0.0 –P0.7) : 8 bit bidirectional bit **addressable I/O port**. acts as multiplexed address/data lines during external memory address. Port 0 receives code bytes during programming of internal EPROM

PORT 1(P1.1 – P1.7) : 8 bit bidirectional bit addressable port.

PORT 2(P2.1- P2.7) : 8 bit bidirectional bit **addressable I/O port**. During external memory accesses, it emits higher eight bit address which are valid. It also receives address during programming of EPROM

PORT 3(P3.1 – P3.7) : 8 bit bidirectional bit addressable I/O port. Also serve alternative functions as shown in the table below:-

PORT 3 PIN	ALTERNATIVE FUNCION
P 3.0	Acts as serial input data pin (RXD)
P 3.1	Acts as serial output data pin (TXD)
P 3.2	Acts as external interrupt pin 0 (INT0)
P 3.3	Acts as external interrupt pin 1(INT1)
P 3.4	Acts as external input to timer 0(T0)
P 3.5	Acts as external input to timer 1(T1)
P 3.6	Acts as write control signal for external data memory(WR)
P 3.7	Acts as read control signal for external data memory read RD)

<u>REGISTER SET OF 8051</u>

Q.Describe the register set of 8051?

Q.Explain the special function registers of 8051?

Has two 8 bit registers **A(ACC) and B** to store operands

Internal temporary registers are not user accessible

8051 has family of **special purpose registers** know as Special Function Registers (SFR)

There are **21 bit addressable 8 bit registers**

Starting 32 bytes of on chip RAM mast be used as general purpose registers. These 32 ,8 bit registers are divided into 4 groups of 8 registers each called **register banks**. At a time only one of these 4 groups are used and accessed using RS0 and RS1 bits of an internal register called psw(program status word)

21 Special function registers are :-

Table 17.3   *SFR Registers, their Addresses and Contents after Reset*

Register	Bit Addressable	Address (SFR)	Content After Reset
ACC	Y	0E0H	0000 0000
B	Y	0F0H	0000 0000
PSW	Y	0D0H	0000 0000
SP	N	81H	0000 0111
DPH	N	82H	0000 0000
DPL	N	83H	0000 0000
P0	Y	80H	1111 1111
P1	Y	90H	1111 1111
P2	Y	0A0H	1111 1111
P3	Y	0B0H	1111 1111
IP	Y	0B8H	XX0 0000
IE	Y	0A8H	0XX0 0000
TMOD	N	89H	0000 0000
TCON	Y	88H	0000 0000
TH0	N	8CH	0000 0000
TL0	N	8AH	0000 0000
TH1	N	8DH	0000 0000
TL1	N	8BH	0000 0000
SCON	Y	98H	0000 0000
SBUF	N	99H	Indeterminate
PCON	N	87H	HMOS 0XXX XXXX CHMOS 0XXX 0000

Y–Yes

N–Nom

X–Undefined

Registers **TH0,TL0 and TH1 ,TL1** indicates the upper and lower byte of the 16 bit timer register T0 and T1

P0,P1,P2,P3-Represents 4 port latches.Any communication with these ports established using SFR addresses of these registers

SP-Stack pointer register

IP-control Interrupt priority

IE-Enable and disable the interrupts

DPH and DPL(DPTR)- are higher and lower bytes of a 16 bit register DPTR,ie datapointer which is used for accessing external data memory

SBUFF register- acts as a serial data buffer for transmit and receive operations

Q.Explain the control word formats of a)PSW b)TMOD c)TCON d)SCON e)PCON?

Remaining registers(ie critical special function registers) are :-

PSW(Programme Status Word)
TMOD(timer/counter mode control register)
TCON(Timer/counter control register-)
SCON(Serial port control register)
PCON(Power control register)
Their register formats are explained as follows:-
PROGRAMME STATUS WORD(PSW)

The PSW register contains several status bits that reflect the current state of the CPU.

CY	AC	F0	RS1	RS0	OV	—	P

CY	PSW.7	Carry Flag
AC	PSW.6	Auxiliary Carry Flag
FO	PSW.5	Flag 0 available to the user for general purpose
RS1	PSW.4	Register Bank selector bit 1
RS0	PSW.3	Register Bank selector bit 0
OV	PSW.2	Overflow Flag
—	PSW.1	User definable flag
P	PSW.0	Parity flag. Set/cleared by hardware each instruction cycle to indicate an odd/even umber of '1' bits in the accumulator.

With RS1 and RS0 bits we can select the corresponding register bank.

RS1	RS0	Register Bank	Address
0	0	0	00H-07H
0	1	1	08H-0FH
1	0	2	10H-17H
1	1	3	18H-1FH

TMOD Register
TMOD is a 8-bit register
The lower 4 bits are for Timer 0
The upper 4 bits are for Timer 1
In each case, the lower 2 bits are used to set the timer mode
The upper 2 bits to specify the operation

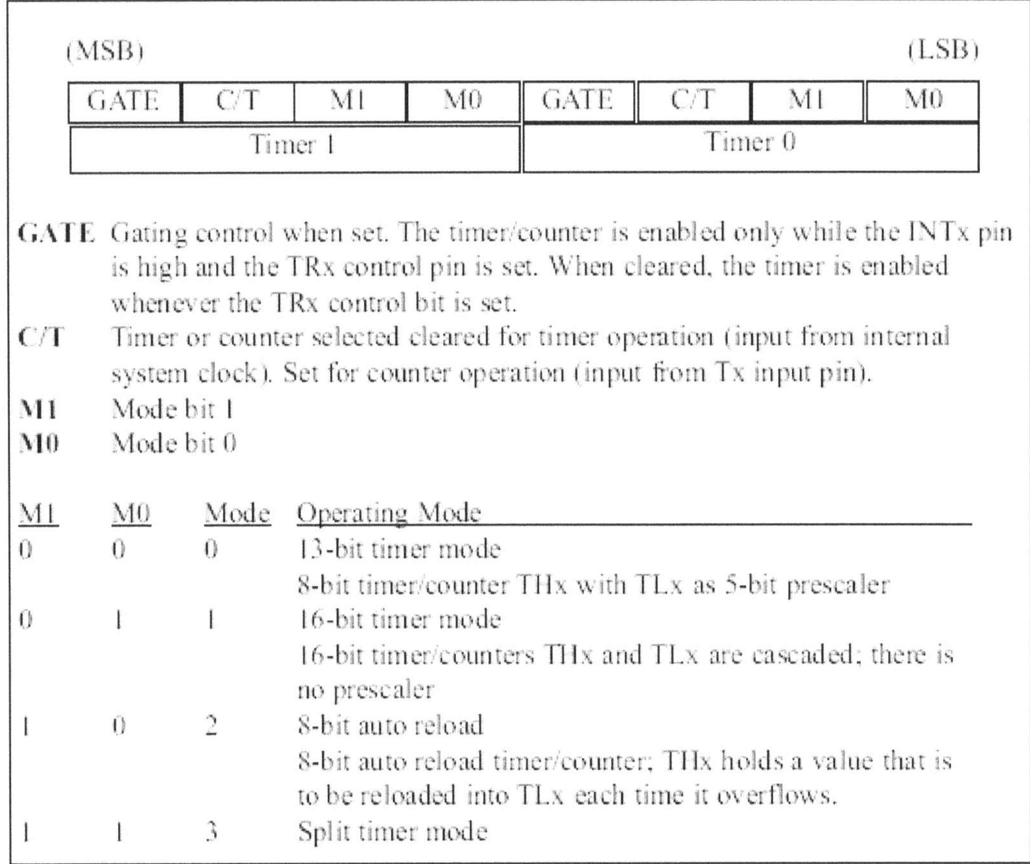

Figure 9-3. TMOD Register

TCON – Timer Control Register

D7	D6	D5	D4	D3	D2	D1	D0
TF1	TR1	TF0	TR0	IE1	IT1	IE0	IT0

Address: 88H (bit addressable)

TF1 – Timer 1 overflow flag

TR1 – Timer 1 run control bit

TF0 – Timer 0 overflow flag

TR0 – Timer 0 run control bit

IE1 – External interrupt 1 edge flag. Set to 1 when edge detected.

IT1 – Edge control bit for external interrupt 1. 1 = edge, 0 = level

IE0 – External interrupt 0 edge flag. Set to 1 when edge detectd

IT0 – Edge control bit for external interrupt 0. 1 = edge, 0 = level

Symbol	function
TF1	Timer 1 Overflow flag. Set when timer rolls from all 1's to 0. Cleared when processor vectors to execute interrupt service routine located at program address 001Bh.
TR1	Timer 1 run control bit. Set to 1 by program to enable timer to count; cleared to 0 by program to halt timer.
TF0	Timer 0 Overflow flag. Set when timer rolls from all 1's to 0. Cleared when processor vectors to execute interrupt service routine located at program address 000Bh.
TR0	Timer 0 run control bit. Set to 1 by program to enable timer to count; cleared to 0 by program to halt timer.
IE1	External interrupt 1 Edge flag. Set to 1 when a high-to-low edge signal is received on port 3.3 (INT1). Cleared when processor vectors to interrupt service routine at program address 0013h.
IT1	External interrupt 1 signal type control bit. Set to 1 by program to enable external interrupt 1 to be triggered by a falling edge signal. Set to 0 by program to enable a low-level signal on external interrupt 1 to generate an interrupt.
IE0	External interrupt 0 Edge flag. Set to 1 when a high-to-low edge signal is received on port 3.2 .Cleared when processor vectors to interrupt service routine at program address 0003h. Not related to timer operations.
IT0	External interrupt 0 signal type control bit. Set to 1 by program to enable external interrupt 1 to be triggered by a falling edge signal. Set to 0 by program to enable a low-level signal on external interrupt 0 to generate an interrupt.

SCON – Serial Control Register

D7	D6	D5	D4	D3	D2	D1	D0
SM0	SM1	SM2	REN	TB8	RB8	TI	RI

Address: 98H (bit-addressable)

SM0	SM1	Operation	Baud rate
0	0	Shift register	Osc/12
0	1	8-bit UART	Set by timer
1	0	9-bit UART	Osc/12 or Osc/64
1	1	9-bit UART	Set by timer

SM2 – Enables multiprocessor communication in modes 2 and 3.

REN – Receiver enable

TB8 – Transmit bit 8. This is the 9th bit transmitted in modes 2 and 3.

RB8 – Receive bit 8. This is the 9th bit received in modes 2 and 3.

TI – Transmit interrupt flag. Set at end of character transmission. Cleared in software.

RI – Receive interrupt flag. Set at end of character reception. Cleared in software.

PCON – Power Control Register

D7	D6	D5	D4	D3	D2	D1	D0
SMOD	x	x	x	GF1	GF0	PD	IDL

Address: 87H (not bit addressable)

SMOD – Serial mode bit used to determine the baud rate with Timer 1.

$$\text{Baud rate} = \frac{\text{Oscillator frequency in Hz}}{N[256 - (TH1)]}$$

If SMOD = 0 then N = 384. If SMOD = 1 then N = 192. TH1 is the high byte of timer 1 when it is in 8-bit autoreload mode.

GF1 and GF0 are General purpose flags not implemented on the standard device
PD is the power down bit. Not implemented on the standard device
IDL activate the idle mode to save power. Not implemented on the standard device

MEMORY and I/O ADDRESSING BY 8051

Q.Describe memory and I/O addressing of 8051?

Total memory of 8051 is divided into : **program memory and data memory**

Program memory stores the pgms to be executed

Data memory stores the data like intermediate results, variables and constants required for execution

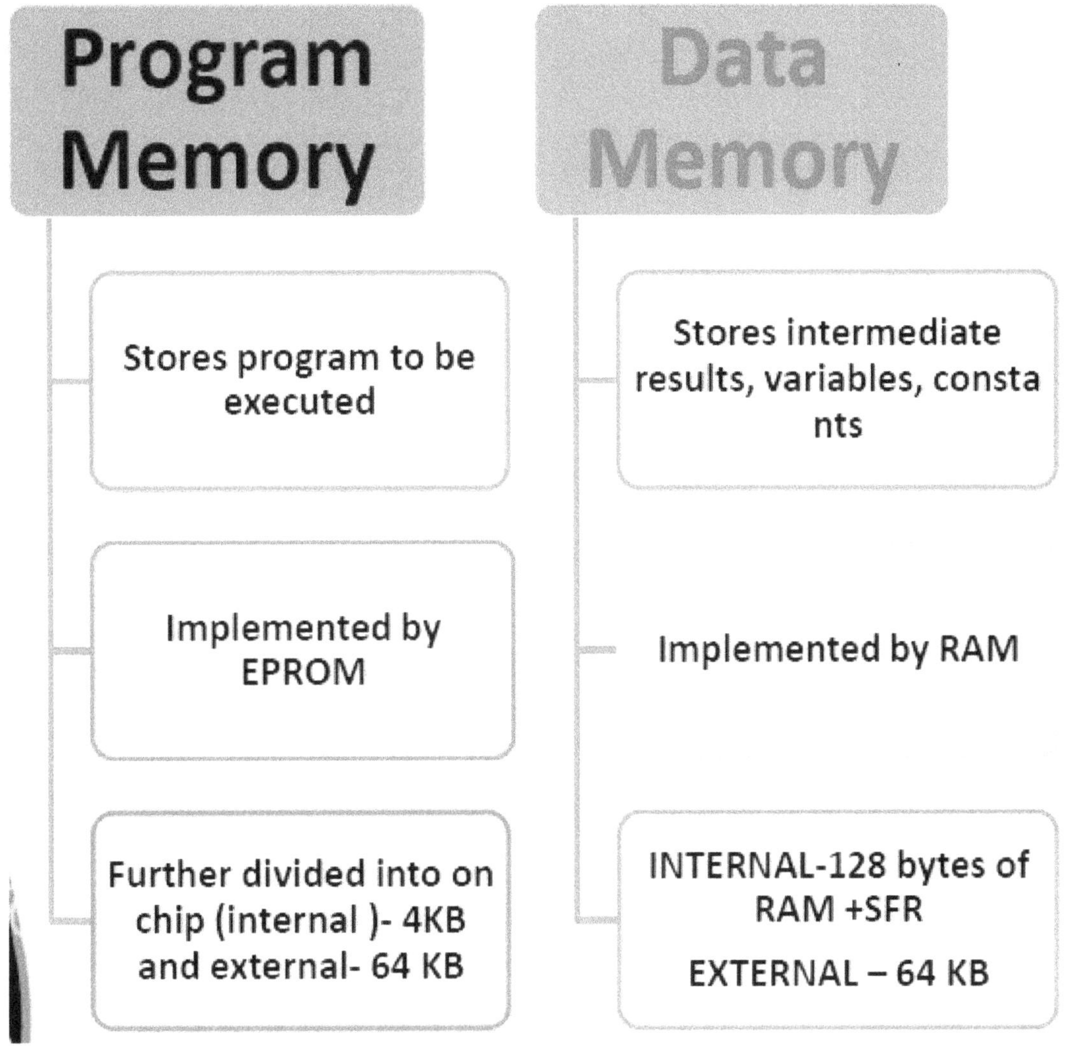

Program memory is implemented using EPROM

Data memory is implemented using RAM

Program memory and data memory may be categorized **as on-chip(internal)and external memory,** depending upon weather memory physically exists on chip or externaly interfaced.

8051 can address upto 4 Kb on chip(0000-0FFFH) and 64KB external program memory(0000-FFFFH) under the control of PSEN

There is **overlap b/w internal and external memory** which is distinguished by **PSEN signal.as shown in figure below.**

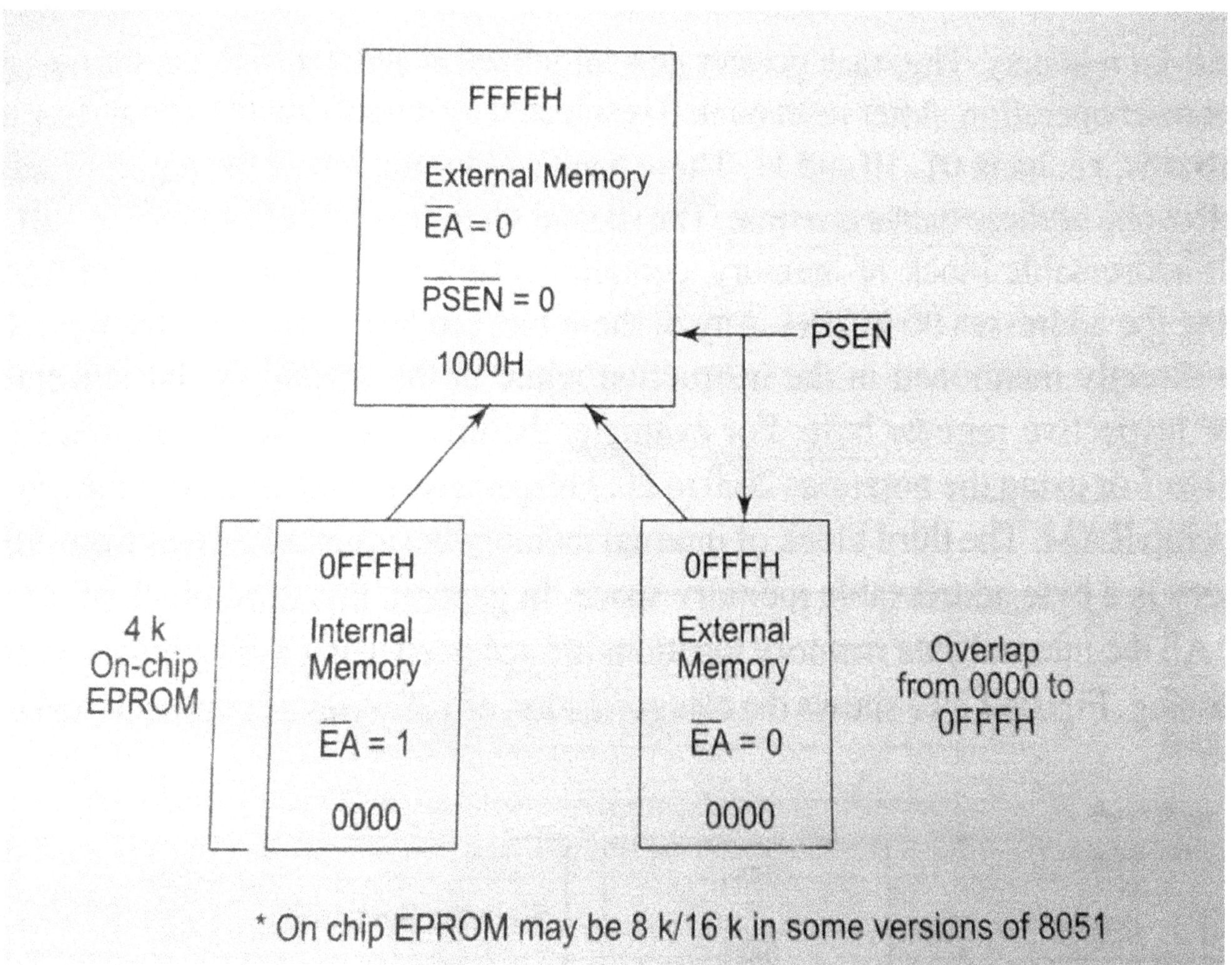

DATA MEMORY

Used to store intermediate results, variables and constants

Data m/y may be read from and written to & implemented using RAM

8051 supports 64kb of external data memory 0000-FFFFH

External data memory **can be accessed under cntrl of DPTR register** which stores address for external data m/y access

8051 generates RD and WR signals during external data m/y access

Internal data m/y consists of **2 parts: RAM block of 128 bytes(00H to 7F)** & set of addresses from 80H to FFH(ie address alloted for **special function registers**)

RAM can be accessed using **direct and indirect mode of addressing**

Special function registers is accessed **only using direct addressing**

In some versions of 8051there are 256 bytes of internal data m/y from 00H to FFH.In **such cases address map of SFR (80H-FFH)will overlap with upper 128 bytes of RAM. Addressing modes differentiate these 2 m/y spaces**

Upper part uses only indirect addressing mode and lower part using indirect and direct addressing.SFR only uses direct memory addressing .Address map of internal RAM and SFR is shown below:-

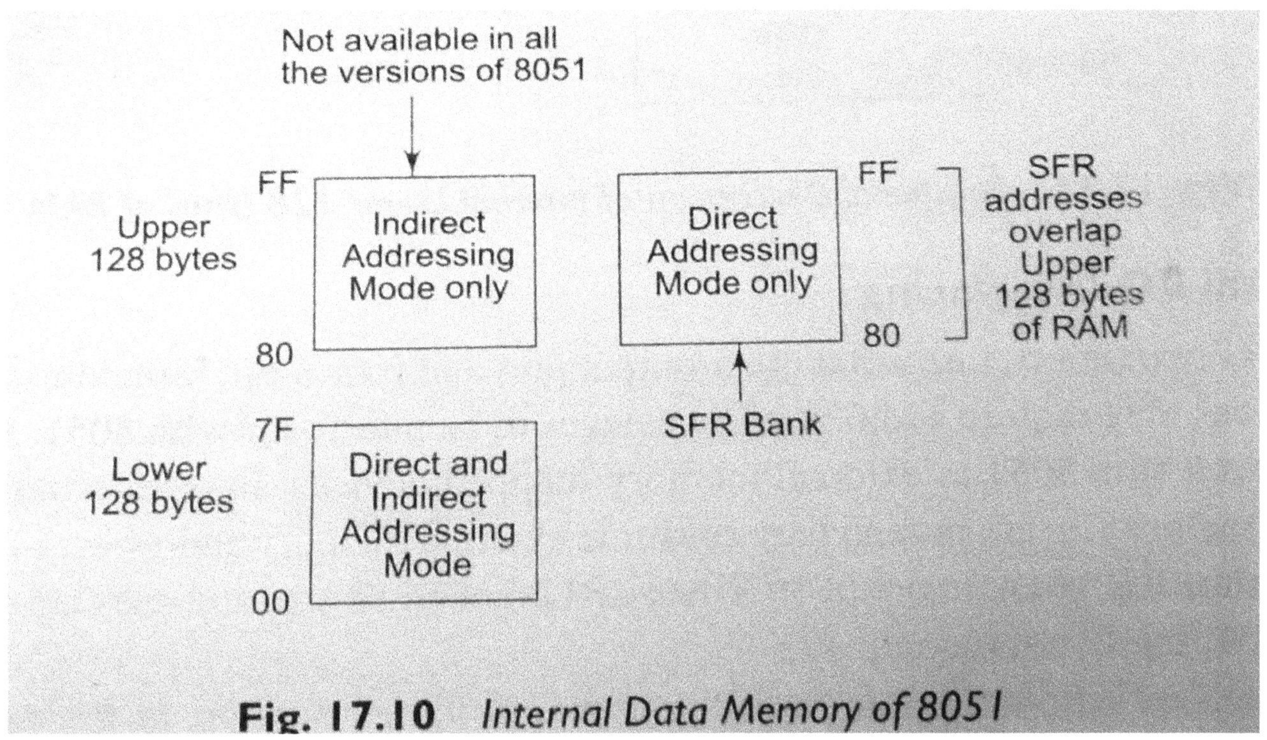

Fig. 17.10 *Internal Data Memory of 8051*

The lower 128 bytes of RAM(00 to 7FH) are organized in **3 sections**

Address block from 00 to 1FH(32 bytes)

This is divided into 4 banks of 8 bit registers(00,01,10,11). Each of these banks contain 8 eight bit registers

Second section contains 16 bytes. 20 H to 2FH. They are bit addressable block of memory. contains 16X8=128 bits. Each of these bits can be addressed using address 00 to 7FH

30-7FH. 80 bytes. Byte addressable memory space. Used as stack memory

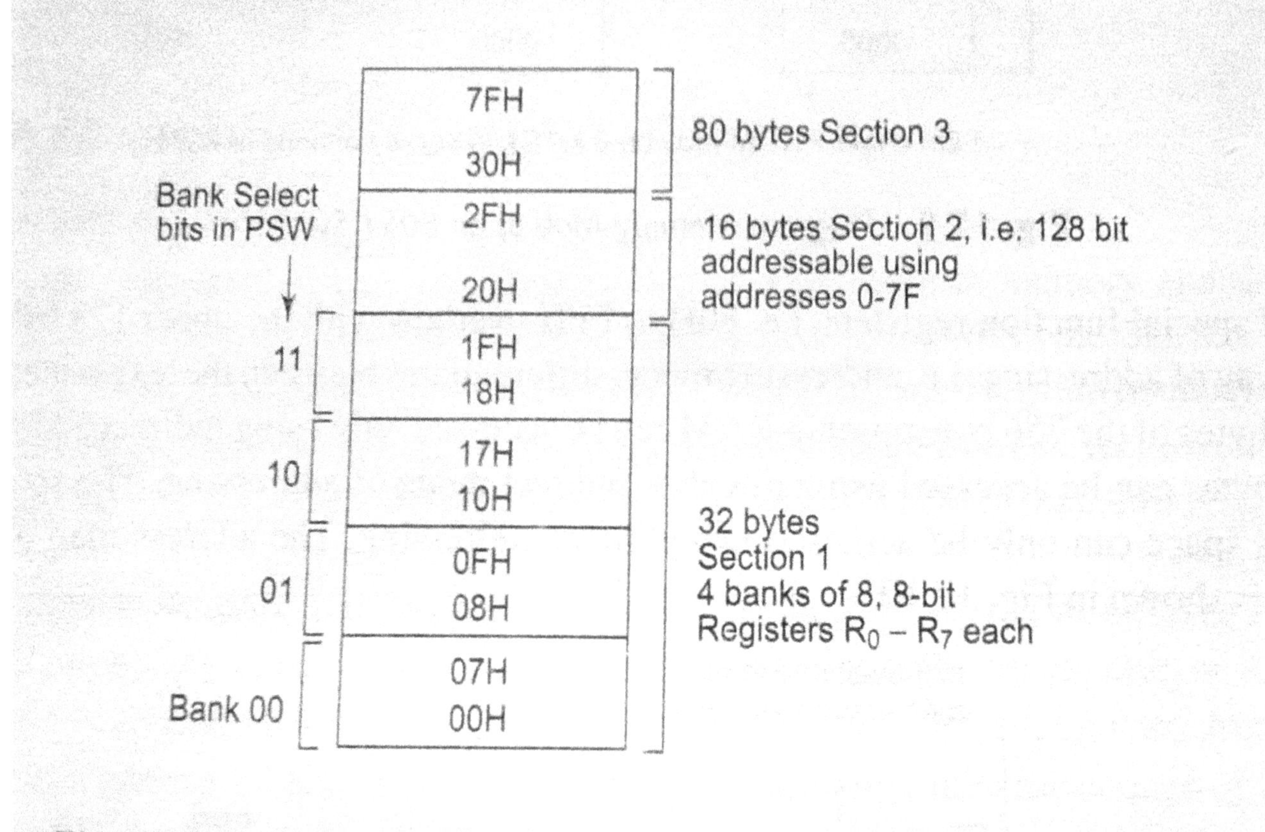

Fig. 17.11 *Functional Description of Internal Lower 128 Bytes of RAM*

Interrupts of 8051

Q.What are the different types of interrupts in 8051?

Q.Describe the interrupt structure of 8051?

Q.Draw the IE and IP register formats of 8051?

Types of Interrupts in 8051 Microcontroller

The 8051 microcontroller can recognize five different events that cause the main program to interrupt from the normal execution. These five sources of interrupts in 8051are:

Timer 0 overflow interrupt- TF0

Timer 1 overflow interrupt- TF1

External hardware interrupt- INT0

External hardware interrupt- INT1

Serial communication interrupt- RI/TI

The Timer and Serial interrupts are **internally generated by the microcontroller,** whereas the external interrupts are generated by **additional interfacing devices or switches** that are externally connected to the microcontroller.

These external interrupts can be edge triggered or level triggered. When an interrupt occurs, the microcontroller executes the interrupt service routine so that memory location corresponds to the interrupt that enables it.

The Interrupt corresponding to the memory location is given in the interrupt vector table below.

Interrupt Number	Interrupt Description	Address
0	EXTERNAL INT 0	0003h
1	TIMER/COUNTER 0	000Bh
2	EXTERNAL INT 1	0013h
3	TIMER/COUNTER 1	001Bh
4	SERIAL PORT	0023h

Interrupt Structure of 8051 Microcontroller

Upon 'RESET' all the interrupts get disabled, and therefore, all these interrupts must be enabled by a software. In all these five interrupts, if anyone or all are activated, this sets the corresponding interrupt.

All these interrupts can be set or cleared by bit in some special function register that is **Interrupt Enabled (IE)**, and this in turn depends on the priority, which is executed by **IP interrupt priority register.**

Interrupt Enable (IE) Register: This register is responsible for enabling and disabling the interrupt. It is a bit addressable register in which EA must be set to one for enabling interrupts. The corresponding bit in this register enables particular interrupt like timer, external and serial inputs. In the below IE register, bit corresponding to 1 activates the interrupt and 0 disables the interrupt

D_7	D_6	D_5	D_4	D_3	D_2	D_1	D_0
EA	–	ET2	ES	ET1	EX1	ET0	EX0

EA	D_7	This disables all interrupts. If EA = 0, no interrupt will be acknowledged. If EA = 1, each interrupt source is individually enabled or disabled by setting or clearing its enable bit.
–	D_6	Not implemented, reserved for future use. User software should not write 1s to reserved bits. These bits may be used in future MCS-51 products to invoke new features. In that case, the reset or inactive value of the new bit will be 0, and its active value will be 1.
ET2	D_5	This enables or disables Timer 2 overflow or capture interrupt (8052 only).
ES	D_4	This enables or disables the serial port interrupt.
ET1	D_3	This enables or disables the Timer 1 overflow interrupt.
EX1	D_2	This enables or disables external Interrupt 1.
ET0	D_1	This enables or disables the Timer 0 overflow interrupt.
EX0	D_0	This enables or disables external Interrupt 0.

Fig. 17.13   *Format of IE Register*

Interrupt Priority Register (IP): It is also possible to change the priority levels of the interrupts by setting or clearing the corresponding bit in the Interrupt priority (IP) register as shown in the figure. This allows the low priority interrupt to interrupt the high-priority interrupt, but prohibits the interruption by another low-priority interrupt. Similarly, the high-priority interrupt cannot be interrupted. If these interrupt priorities are not programmed, the microcontroller executes in predefined manner and its order is INT0, TF0, INT1, TF1, and SI.

D_7	D_6	D_5	D_4	D_3	D_2	D_1	D_0
–	–	PT2	PS	PT1	PX1	PT0	PX0

If the bit is 0, the corresponding interrupt is disabled. If the bit is 1 the corresponding interrupt is enabled.

–	D_7	Not implemented, reserved for future use.*
–	D_6	Not implemented, reserved for future use.*
PT2	D_5	This defines the Timer 2 interrupt priority level (8052 only).
PS	D_4	This defines the Serial Port interrupt priority level.
PT1/PT0	D_3/D_1	This defines the Timer 1/Timer 0 interrupt priority level.
PX1/PX0	D_2/D_0	This defines External $\overline{INT1}/\overline{INT0}$ priority level.

* The software should not write 1s to reserved bits. These bits may be used in future MCS-51 products to invoke new features. In that case, the reset or inactive value of the new bit will be 0, and its active value will be 1.

Fig. 17.14 *Format of IP Register*

TCON Register: In addition to the above two registers, the TCON register specifies the type of external interrupt to the 8051 microcontroller, as shown in the figure. The two external interrupts, whether edge or level triggered, specify by this register by a set, or cleared by appropriate bits in it. And, it is also a bit addressable register.

TCON – Timer Control Register

D7	D6	D5	D4	D3	D2	D1	D0
TF1	TR1	TF0	TR0	IE1	IT1	IE0	IT0

Address: 88H (bit addressable)

TF1 – Timer 1 overflow flag

TR1 – Timer 1 run control bit

TF0 – Timer 0 overflow flag

TR0 – Timer 0 run control bit

IE1 – External interrupt 1 edge flag. Set to 1 when edge detected.

IT1 – Edge control bit for external interrupt 1. 1 = edge, 0 = level

IE0 – External interrupt 0 edge flag. Set to 1 when edge detectd

IT0 – Edge control bit for external interrupt 0. 1 = edge, 0 = level

STACK STRUCTURE OF 8051

Q.Explain the the stack structure of 8051?

The Stack and the Stack Pointer

The stack refers to an area of internal RAM that is used in conjunction with certain opcodes to store and retrieve data quickly. The 8-bit Stack Pointer (SP) register is used by the 8051 to hold an internal RAM address that is called the *top of the stack.* The address held in the SP register is the location in internal RAM where the last byte of data was stored by a stack operation.

When data is to be placed on the stack, the SP increments *before* storing data on the stack so that the stack grows *up* as data is stored. As data is retrieved from the stack, the byte is read from the stack, and then the SP decrements to point to the next available byte of stored data.

Operation of the stack and the SP is shown in Figure 3.6. The SP is set to 07h when the 8051 is reset and can be changed to any internal RAM address by the programmer, using a data move command from Chapter 5.

The stack is limited in height to the size of the internal RAM. The stack has the potential (if the programmer is not careful to limit its growth) to overwrite valuable data in the register banks, bit-addressable RAM, and scratch-pad RAM areas. The programmer is responsible for making sure the stack does not grow beyond predefined bounds!

The stack is normally placed high in internal RAM, by an appropriate choice of the number placed in the SP register, to avoid conflict with the register, bit, and scratch-pad internal RAM areas.

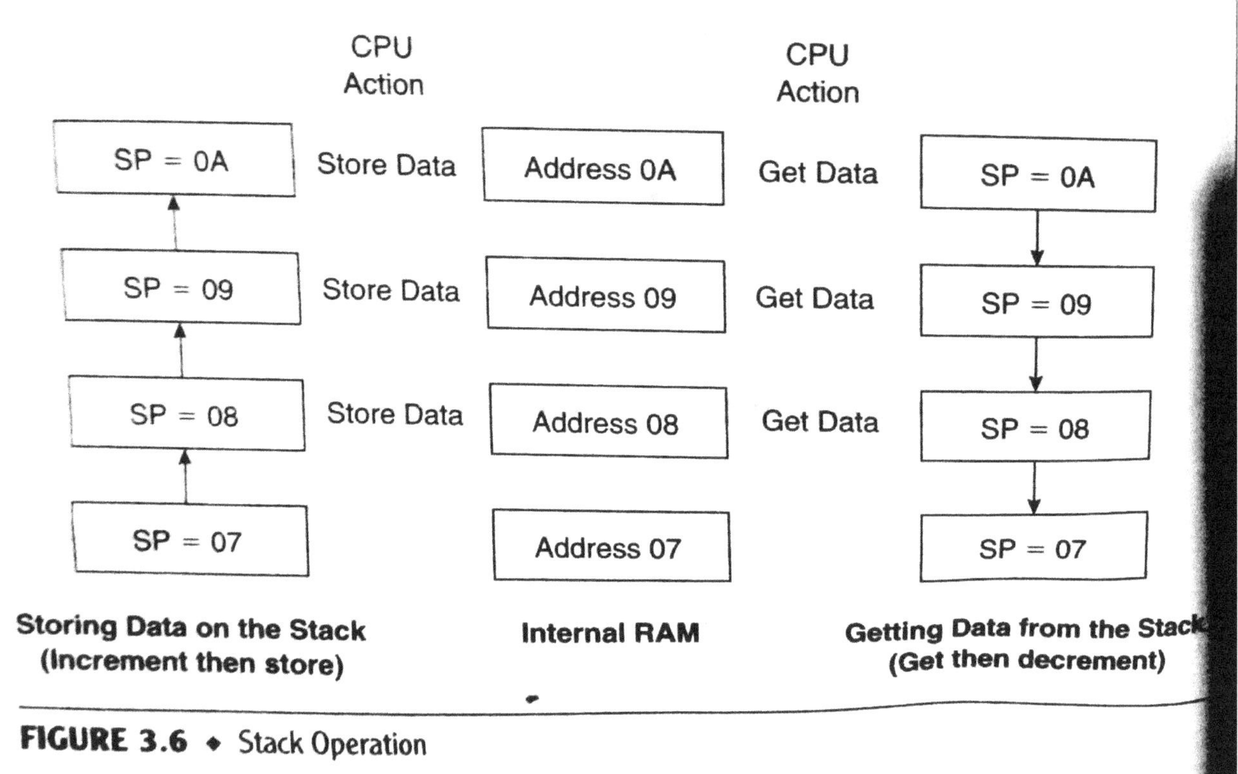

FIGURE 3.6 ◆ Stack Operation

Addressing modes 8051

Q.What are different addressing modes of 8051 microcontrollers?

8051 addressing modes are classified as follows.

Immediate addressing.

Register addressing.

Direct addressing.

Indexed addressing

Indirect addressing.

Relative addressing.

Register specific addressing:

Immediate addressing.

In this addressing mode the data is provided as a part of instruction itself. In other words data immediately follows the instruction.

Eg. MOV A,#30H

ADD A, #83 # Symbol indicates the data is immediate.

Register addressing.

In this addressing mode the register will hold the data. One of the eight general registers (R0 to R7) can be used and specified as the operand.

Eg. MOV A,R0 ADD A,R6

R0 – R7 will be selected from the current selection of register bank. The default register bank will be bank 0.

Direct addressing

There are two ways to access the internal memory. Using direct address and indirect address. Using direct addressing mode we can address the internal memory and SFRs .

In direct addressing, an 8 bit internal data memory address is specified as part of the instruction and hence, it can specify the address only in the range of 00H to FFH. In this addressing mode, data is obtained directly from the memory.

Eg. MOV A,81h

Here 81H is the address of a special function register SP

Indirect addressing

The indirect addressing mode uses a register to hold the actual address and that register that will be used in data movement. Registers R0 and R1 and DPTR are the only registers that can be used as data pointers. Indirect addressing cannot be used to refer to SFR registers.

Both R0 and R1 can hold 8 bit address and DPTR can hold 16 bit address. Eg. MOV A,@R0

ADD A,@R1 MOVX A,@DPTR

Indexed addressing.

Only program memory can be accessed using this addressing mode. In indexed addressing, either the program counter (PC), or the data pointer (DTPR)—is used to hold the base address, and the A is used to hold the offset address. Adding the value of the base address to the value of the offset address forms the effective address. Indexed addressing is used with JMP or MOVC instructions. Look up tables are easily implemented with the help of index addressing.

Eg. MOVC A, @A+DPTR // *copies the contents of memory location pointed by the sum of*

the accumulator A and the DPTR into accumulator A.

MOVC A, @A+PC // *copies the contents of memory location pointed by the sum of the accumulator A and the program counter into accumulator A.*

Relative Addressing.

Relative addressing is used only with conditional jump instructions. The relative address, (offset), is an 8 bit signed number, which is automatically added to the PC to make the address of the next instruction. The 8 bit signed offset value gives an address range of +127 to —128 locations. The jump destination is usually specified using a label and the assembler calculates the jump offset accordingly. The advantage of relative addressing is that the program code is easy to relocate and the address is relative to position in the memory.

Eg. SJMP LOOP1 JC BACK

Register specific addressing:

In some type of instructions,the operand is implicitly specified using one of the registers. Some of the instructions always operate on a specific register. These type of instructions fall under this category.

Eg: RLA ;*this instruction rotates accumulator left*

Classification of the instructions at the instruction set

The instructions of 8051 can be broadly classified under the following headings.

Data transfer instructions

Bolean variable manipulation Instructions(Bit/byte manipulation instructions)

Arithmetic instructions

Logical instructions

Branch instructions /Program flow control instructions

Subroutine CALL And RETURN Instructions

Interrupt flow control instructions

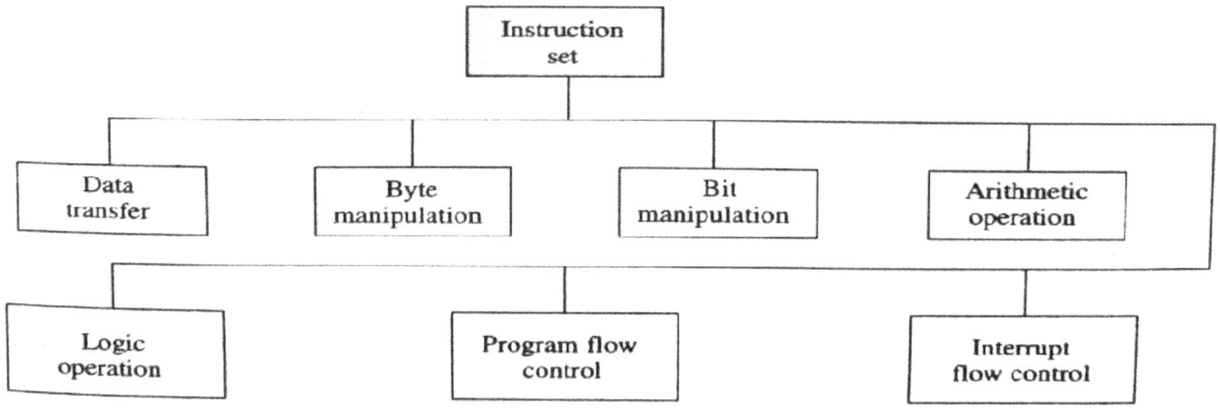

Figure 4.11   Classification of the instructions in the instruction set

Data transfer instructions.

MOV Instructions- Mov,Movc,Movx

In this group, the instructions perform data transfer operations of the following types.

Move the contents of a register Rn to A

MOV A,R2

MOV A,R7

Move the contents of a register A to Rn

MOV R4,A

MOV R1,A

Move an immediate 8 bit data to register A or to Rn or to a memory location(direct or indirect)

MOV A, #45H

MOV R6, #51H

MOV 30H, #44

MOV @R0, #0E8H

MOV DPTR, #0F5A2H

MOV DPTR, #5467H

Move the contents of a memory location to A or A to a memory location using direct and indirect addressing

MOV A, 65H

MOV A, @R0

MOV 45H, A

MOV @R1, A

Move the contents of a memory location to Rn or Rn to a memory location using direct addressing

MOV R3, 65H

MOV 45H, R2

Move the contents of memory location to another memory location using direct and indirect addressing

MOV 47H, 65H

MOV 45H, @R0

Table 4.1 MOV instructions within the registers, internal RAM and SFRs in 8051

Instruction (Mnemonic)	Action	Addressing	Length in Bytes
MOV R_n**, A**	Move R_n[a] into A (Accumulator SFR) Move into R[a] from A	Register	1
MOV A, #data	Move immediate 8-bit data into A (Accumulator SFR)[b]	Immediate	2
MOV R_n**, #data**	Move the immediate data into R_n[b]	Immediate	2
MOV A, direct	Move the byte at the direct address into A (Accumulator SFR)[c]	Direct	2
MOV R_n**, direct**	Move from direct address into R_n[c]	Direct	2
MOV direct, A	Move the byte to the direct address from A (Accumulator SFR)[c]	Direct	2
MOV direct, R_n	Move a byte to the direct address from R[c]	Direct	2
MOV direct, direct	Move the byte to the direct address from the direct address (at the third byte) A[c]	Direct	3
MOV direct, #data	Move the immediate data byte to the direct address from the direct address (at the third byte) A[b]	Immediate	3
MOV A, @R_i	Move into A the byte from the address pointed by R_i[d]	Indirect for source	1
MOV@ R_i**, A**	Move A into the address pointed by R_i[d]	Indirect for destination	1
MOV direct, @R_i	Move into direct address from the address pointed by R_i[d]	Indirect for source	2
MOV @R_i**, direct**	Move from direct address to address pointed by R_i[d]	Direct for source	
MOV @R_i**, #data**	Move data into the address pointed by R_i	Immediate	
MOV DPTR, #data16[e]	Move 16-bit data (second and third bytes) into DPTR	Immediate	

(Con...)

Example 4.15

Write the control bits 0100 0000 (40H) into the TCON.

TCON is an SFR. and it is in the direct-addressable space. TCON address is 88H. Instruction *MOV direct, #data* is there in Table 4.1. Using that the *MOV TCON, #40H* will be the instruction to write into the TCON.

Example 4.16

Load the external memory address pointer DPTR with 0x1000 (1000H). There is an instruction *MOV DPTR, #data16* (Table 4.1). The instruction is, therefore, MOV DPTR, 1000H.

Example 4.17

Load 0x1000 (1000H) in DPTR. Write instructions using the DPL and DPH as the 8-bit operands.

Alternatively for the instruction *MOV DPTR, #0x1000* we can use the fact that DPH and DPL are the SFRs at addresses 83H and 82H, respectively. There is *MOV direct, #data* instruction (Table 4.1). Instructions are as follows:

MOV DPH, #10H and *MOV DPL, #00H* or *MOV 83H, #10H* and *MOV 82H, #00H.*

Figure 4.12(a) shows three steps for instruction MOV @R1, A. This is an indirect addressing mode instruction. First step: R1 is read by the processing unit. Second step: pointed address 30H is found from R1. Third step: A is read and its contents found = 40H and 40H is transferred (copied) to address 30H from A.

Example 4.18

How can a byte be transferred from the address pointed by R0 to the register R2? There is no MOV @ R_i, R_n instruction available.

MOV @R_i, R_n is not an instruction present in 8051 but MOV R_n, A and MOV A, @R_i are available (Table 4.1). Hence, the byte pointed by *R0* can first be moved into *A* and then to *R2*. The instructions are as follows:

MOV A, R0 and *MOV R2, A* to transfer a byte from the address pointed by *R0* to the *R2*.

Move the contents of an external memory to A or A to an external memory address using DPTR or Ri as the pointer.

MOVX A,@R1

MOVX @R0,A

MOVX A,@DPTR

MOVX @DPTR,A

Eg: Using DPTR ,Transter the codes from 1000H and 1001 H to external data memory addresses 1000H and 1001H to show how we copy the code memory in ROM to external RAM?

ANS:

MOV DPTR,1000H; MOV A,#00H, MOVC a,@A+DPTR;MOVX @DPTR,A MOV DPTR,1001H; MOV A,#00H, MOVC a,@A+DPTR;MOVX @DPTR,A

Move the 8 bit contents of program memory to Accumulator

MOVC A, @A+PC

ii. MOVC A, @A+DPTR

Example 4.19

Assuming PC to be 1000H, transfer the code at 1000H to the internal RAM at 70H.

For transferring the codes, the MOVC A, @A + PC is there in Table 4.2. First, we load A with 00H (Table 4.1). Then, we use the MOVC instruction to first get the code into A. From A, we can load it into adderss 70H.

(i) MOV A, #00H; (ii) MOVC A, @A+PC; (iii) MOV 70H, A; to read the code at 1000H into 70H.

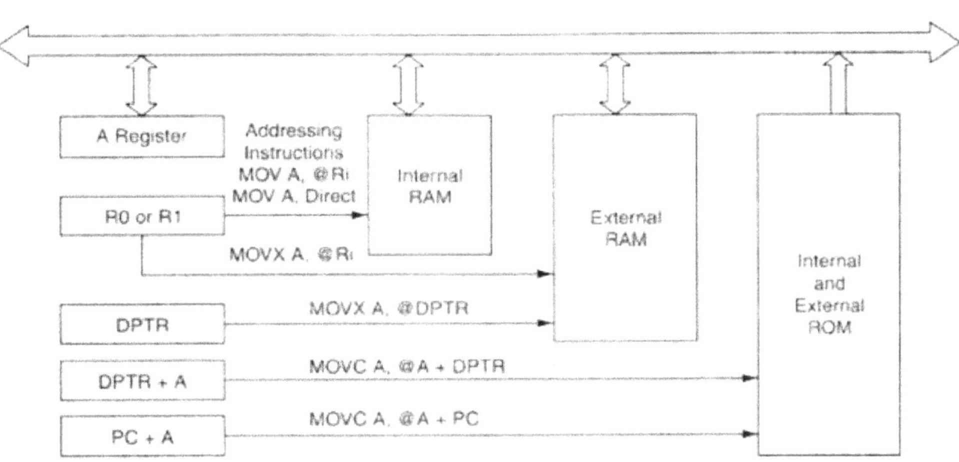

FIG. Addressing Using MOV, MOVX and MOVC

Push and Pop instructions

Push instruction copy the 8 bit data into the stack after incrementing SP.The data are at a direct address. The address is of either an SFR or internal RAM.

POP instruction pops the byte and then decrements SP

```
                    [SP]=07          //CONTENT OF SP IS 07 (DEFAULT VALUE)
MOV R6, #25H        [R6]=25H          //CONTENT OF R6 IS 25H
MOV R1, #12H        [R1]=12H         //CONTENT OF R1 IS 12H
MOV R4, #0F3H       [R4]=F3H         //CONTENT OF R4 IS F3H


PUSH 6              SP=08       [08]=[06]=25H            //CONTENT OF 08 IS 25H
PUSH 1              SP=09       [09]=[01]=12H            //CONTENT OF 09 IS 12H
PUSH 4              SP=0A       [0A]=[04]=F3H            //CONTENT OF 0A IS F3H


POP 6              [06]=[0A]=F3H [SP]=09        //CONTENT OF 06 IS F3H
POP 1              [01]=[09]=12H [SP]=08        //CONTENT OF 01 IS 12H
POP 4              [04]=[08]=25H [SP]=07        //CONTENT OF 04 IS 25H
```

Exchange instructions –XCH, XCHD

Table 4.5   **XCH and XCHD instructions in 8051**

Instruction	Action	Addressing	Length in Bytes	Cycles
XCH A, @R_i	Exchange byte at A with the address pointed by R_i[a]	Indirect	1	2
XCH A, R_n	Exchange byte at A with the register R_n[b]	Register	1	2
XCH A, *direct*	Exchange byte at A with the byte at a direct address	Direct addressing	1	1
XCHD A, @R_i	Exchange lower hex-digits of the bytes at A with the address pointed by R_i[c]	Indirect	1	2

XCH:-The content of source ie., register, direct memory or indirect memory will be exchanged with the contents of destination ie., accumulator.

XCH A,R3

XCH A,@R1

XCH A,54h

XCHD(Exchange digit). Exchange the lower order nibble of Accumulator (A0-A3) with lower order nibble of the internal RAM location which is indirectly addressed by the register.

XCHD A,@R1

XCHD A,@R0

Bolean variable manipulation Instructions(Bit/byte manipulation instructions)

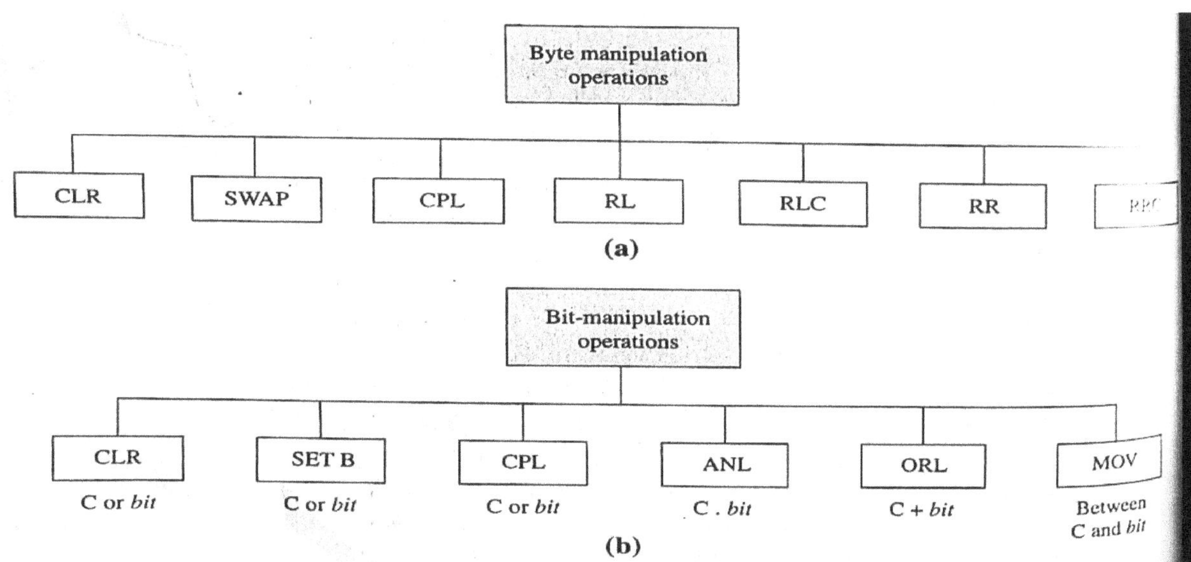

Figure 4.13   (a) Operations in the byte manipulation instructions using *A and* (b) operations in the Boolean variable manipulation (bit manipulation) instruction using *C* or a bit at an address of the bit

Bit manipulation instructions.

8051 has 128 bit addressable memory. Bit addressable SFRs and bit addressable PORT pins. It is possible to perform following bit wise operations for these bit addressable locations.

1. LOGICAL AND
   a. ANL C,BIT(BIT ADDRESS) ; *'Logically And' Carry And Content Of Bit Address, Store Result In Carry*
   b. ANL C, /BIT ; *'Logically And' Carry And Complement Of Content Of Bit Address, Store Result In Carry*

2. LOGICAL OR
   a. ORL C,BIT(BIT ADDRESS) ; *'Logically Or' Carry And Content Of Bit Address, Store Result In Carry*
   b. ORL C, /BIT ; *'Logically Or' Carry And Complement Of Content Of Bit Address, Store Result In Carry*

3. CLR bit
   a. CLR bit ; *Content Of Bit Address Specified Will Be Cleared.*
   b. CLR C ; *Content Of Carry Will Be Cleared.*

4. CPL bit
   a. CPL bit ; *Content Of Bit Address Specified Will Be Complemented.*
   b. CPL C ; *Content Of Carry Will Be Complemented.*

Byte manipulation instructions.

RR A

This instruction is rotate right the accumulator. Its operation is illustrated below. Each bit is shifted one location to the right, with bit 0 going to bit 7.

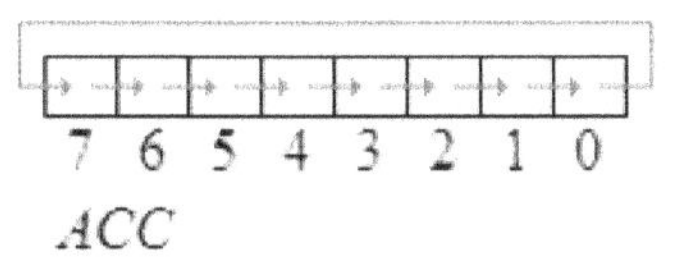

RL A

Rotate left the accumulator. Each bit is shifted one location to the left, with bit 7 going to bit 0

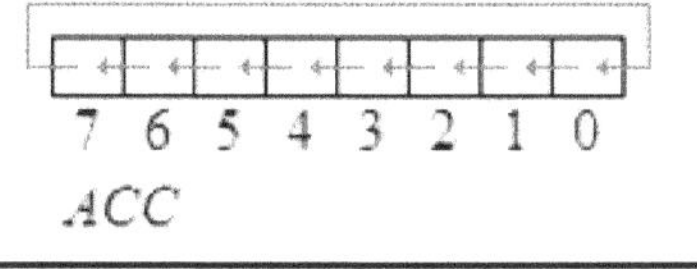

RRC A

Rotate right through the carry. Each bit is shifted one location to the right, with bit 0 going into the carry bit in the PSW, while the carry was at goes into bit 7

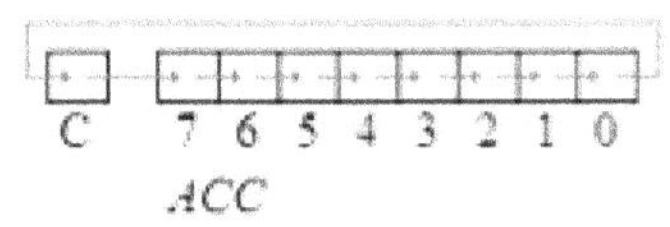

RLC A

Rotate left through the carry. Each bit is shifted one location to the left, with bit 7 going into the carry bit in the PSW, while the carry goes into bit 0.

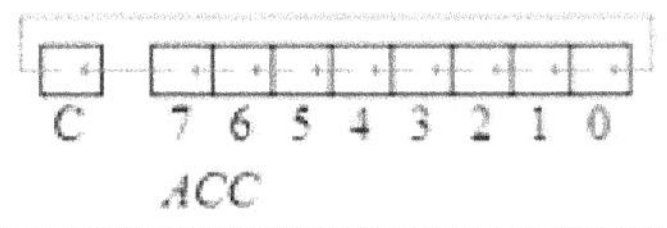

CPL

CPL complements *operand*, leaving the result in *operand*. If *operand* is a single bit then the state of the bit will be reversed. If *operand* is the Accumulator then all the bits in the Accumulator will be reversed.

CPL A, CPL C, CPL bit address

SWAP A – Swap the upper nibble and lower nibble of A (swapping between upper hex digit with the lower hex digit for example 89H will become 98H after swapping.

Eg1 :How do the mode bits of Timers 0 and 1 swapped at TMOD?

```
PUSH 0E0H              //for saving A onto the stack
MOV A,89H              //89H-direct addr of TMOD
SWAP A
MOV 89H,A
POP 0E0H               //Restoring A from Stack
```

Eg 2:what will be the effect of RRC A. Assuming A=02H and C=1?

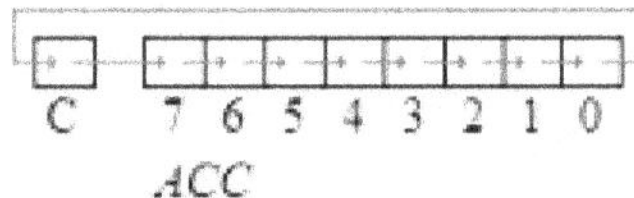

0000 0010 in A becomes
1000 0001

•

Arithmetic instructions

Table 4.8 Arithmetic ADD, SUB, MUL, DIV, INC and DEC instructions in 8051

Instruction	Action	Addressing	Effected flags	Length in Bytes	Cycles
ADD A, R_n	Add R_n into A	Register	C, AC, OV[b]	1	1
ADD A, *direct*	Add the byte at the direct address into A	Direct	C, AC, OV[b]	2	1
ADD A, R_i	Move into the byte from the address pointed by R_i[d]	Indirect	C, AC, OV[b]	1	1
ADD A, #*data*	Add the immediate data byte to A[e]	Immediate	C, AC, OV[b]	2	1
ADDC A, R_n	Add C bit and R_n into A (Accumulator)[a]	Register	C, AC, OV[b]	1	1
ADDC A, *direct*	Add C bit and byte at the direct address into A (Accumulator)[c]	Direct	C, AC, OV[b]	2	1
ADDC A, R_i	Add C bit and the byte from the address pointed by R_c[d]	Indirect	C, AC, OV[b]	1	1
ADDC A, #*data*	Add C bit and immediate data byte to A[e]	Immediate	C, AC, OV[b]	2	1
SBBB A, R_n	Subtract borrow at C bit and R_n into A (Accumulator SFR)[a]	Register	C, AC, OV	1	1
SBBB A, *direct*	Subtract borrow at C bit and byte at the direct address into A (Accumulator SFR)[c]	Direct	C, AC, OV[b]	2	1
SBBB A, R_i	Subtract borrow at C bit and the byte from the address pointed by R_i[d]	Indirect	C, AC, OV[b]	1	1
SBBB A, #*data*	Subtract borrow at C bit and immediate data byte to A[e]	Immediate	C, AC, OV[b]	2	1
INC A	Increment	Register	None	1	1
INC R_n	Increment R_n[a]	Register	None	1	1
INC *direct*	Increment the byte at the direct address[c]	Direct	None	2	1
INC A, R_i	Increment the byte at the direct address[d]	Indirect	None	1	1
INC DPTR	Increment DPTR	Register	None	1	2
DEC A	Decrement A	Register	None	1	1
DEC R_n	Decrement R_n[a]	Register	None	1	1
DEC *direct*	Decrement the byte at the direct address[c]	Direct	None	2	1
DEC A, R_i	Decrement the byte at the ad-dress pointed by R_i[d]	Indirect	None	1	1
MUL AB	Multiply A and B [MSB in B, LSB in A][f]	Register	OV[g]	1	4

Addition –ADD, ADDC

In this group, we have instructions to

Add the contents of A with immediate data with or without carry.

ADD A, #45H

ADDC A, #OB4H

Add the contents of A with register Rn with or without carry.

ADD A, R5

ADDC A, R2

Add the contents of A with contents of memory with or without carry using direct and indirect addressing

ADD A, 51H

ADDC A, 75H

ADD A, @R1

ADDC A, @R0

CY AC and OV flags will be affected by this operation. Subtraction -SBB

In this group, we have instructions to

Subtract the contents of A with immediate data with or without carry.

SUBB A, #45H

SUBB A, #OB4H

Subtract the contents of A with register Rn with or without carry.

SUBB A, R5

SUBB A, R2

Subtract the contents of A with contents of memory with or without carry using direct and indirect addressing

SUBB A, 51H

SUBB A, 75H

SUBB A, @R1

SUBB A, @R0

CY AC and OV flags will be affected by this operation. Multiplication -MUL

MUL AB.:- Can only use register addressing mode.This instruction multiplies two 8 bit unsigned numbers which are stored in A and B register. After multiplication the lower byte of the result will be stored in accumulator and higher byte of result will be stored in B register.

Eg. MOV A,#45H ;*[A]=45H*

MOV B,#0F5H ;*[B]=F5H*

MUL AB ;*[A] x [B] = 45 x F5 = 4209*

;*[A]=09H, [B]=42H*

DIV AB. Can only use register addressing mode This instruction divides the 8 bit unsigned number which is stored in A by the 8 bit unsigned number which is stored in B register. After division the result will be stored in accumulator and remainder will be stored in B register.

Eg. MOV A,#45H ;*[A]=0E8H*

MOV B,#0F5H ;*[B]=1BH*

DIV AB ;*[A] / [B] = E8 /1B = 08 H with remainder 10H*

;*[A] = 08H, [B]=10H*

DA A (Decimal Adjust After Addition).

When two BCD numbers are added, the answer is a non-BCD number. To get the result in BCD, we use DA A instruction after the addition. DA A works as follows.

If lower nibble is greater than 9 or auxiliary carry is 1, 6 is added to lower nibble. If upper nibble is greater than 9 or carry is 1, 6 is added to upper nibble.

Eg 1: MOV A,#23H MOV R1,#55H

ADD A,R1 // [A]=78

DA A // [A]=78 *no changes in the accumulator after da a*

Eg 2: MOV A,#53H MOV R1,#58H

ADD A,R1 // [A]=ABh

DA A // [A]=11, C=1 . ANSWER IS 111. *Accumulator data is changed after DA A*

Increment: *increments the operand by one.*

INC A INC Rn INC DIRECT INC @Ri INC DPTR

INC increments the value of source by 1. If the initial value of register is FFh, incrementing the value will cause it to reset to 0. The Carry Flag is not set when the value "rolls over" from 255 to 0.

In the case of "INC DPTR", the value two-byte unsigned integer value of DPTR is incremented. If the initial value of DPTR is FFFFh, incrementing the value will cause it to reset to 0.

Decrement: *decrements the operand by one.*

DEC A DEC Rn DEC DIRECT DEC @Ri

DEC decrements the value of *source* by 1. If the initial value of is 0, decrementing the value will cause it to reset to FFh. The Carry Flag is not set when the value "rolls over" from 0 to FFh.

Logical Instructions

Table 4.9 ANL, ORL and XRL instructions in 8051

Instruction	Action	Addressing	Length in Bytes	Cycles
ANL A, R_n	AND R_n and A (Accumulator SFR)[a]	Register	1	1
ANL A, *direct*	AND byte at direct address and A[b]	Direct	2	1
ANL $A, @R_i$	AND the byte from the address pointed by R_i[c]	Indirect	1	1
ANL A, #*data*	AND immediate data byte and A[d]	Immediate	2	1
ANL direct, A	AND A and byte at the direct address[b]	Direct	2	1
ANL direct, #data	AND immediate byte and the byte at the direct address[b,d]	Direct	3	2
ORL A, R_n	OR R_n and A[a]	Register	1	1
ORL A, *direct*	OR byte at the direct address and A[b]	Direct	2	1
ORL $A, @R_i$	OR the byte from the address pointed by R_i[c]	Indirect	1	1
ORL A, #*data*	OR immediate data byte and A[d]	Immediate	2	1
ORL direct, A	OR A and the byte at the direct address[b]	Direct	2	1
ORL direct, #data	OR immediate byte and the byte at direct address[b,d]	Direct	3	2
XRL A, R_n	XOR R_n and A[a]	Register	1	1
XRL A, *direct*	XOR byte at the direct address and A	Direct	2	1
XRL $A, @R_i$	XOR the byte from the address pointed by R_i[c]	Indirect	1	1
XRL A, #*data*	XOR immediate data byte and A[d]	Immediate	2	1
XRL direct, A	XOR A and the byte at the direct address[b]	Direct	2	1
XRL direct, #data	XOR immediate byte into the byte at the direct address[b,d]	Direct	3	2
INC A, R_i	Increment the byte at the direct address[d]	Indirect	None	1
INC DPTR	Increment DPTR	Register	None	1
DEC A	Decrement A	Register	None	1
DEC R_n	Decrement R^a_n	Register	None	1
DEC *direct*	Decrement the byte at the direct address[c]	Direct	None	2
DEC A, R_i	Decrement the byte at the ad-dress pointed by R_i[d]	Indirect	None	1
MUL AB	Multiply A and B [MSB in B, LSB in A][f]	Register	OV[g]	1

(Continued)

Logical AND

ANL destination, source:

ANL does a bitwise "AND" operation between *source* and *destination*, leaving the resulting value in *destination*. The value in source is not affected. "AND" instruction logically AND the bits of source and destination.

ANL A,#DATA ANL A, Rn

ANL A,DIRECT ANL A,@Ri

ANL DIRECT,A ANL DIRECT, #DATA

Logical OR

ORL destination, source:

ORL does a bitwise "OR" operation between *source* and *destination*, leaving the resulting value in *destination*. The value in source is not affected. " OR " instruction logically OR the bits of source and destination.

ORL A,#DATA ORL A, Rn

ORL A,DIRECT ORL A,@Ri

ORL DIRECT,A ORL DIRECT, #DATA

Logical Ex-OR

XRL destination, source:

XRL does a bitwise "EX-OR" operation between *source* and *destination*, leaving the resulting value in *destination*. The value in source is not affected. " XRL " instruction logically EX-OR the bits of source and destination.

XRL A,#DATA XRL A,Rn

XRL A,DIRECT XRL A,@Ri

XRL DIRECT,A XRL DIRECT, #DATA

Logical NOT

CPL complements *operand*, leaving the result in *operand*. If *operand* is a single bit then the state of the bit will be reversed. If *operand* is the Accumulator then all the bits in the Accumulator will be reversed.

CPL A, CPL C, CPL bit address

Branch (JUMP) Instructions/program flow control instructions

Delay Cycle Instructions

Long,Absolute,Short Jumps

Conditional short Relative Jumps

Decrement and conditional jump on zero

Jump after Comparison

<u>Delay Cycle Instructions</u>

a) <u>Delay Cycle Instructions</u>

It means no operation, just spent one instruction cycle time

Example 4.46

How can we toggle the bits at Port 2 and again toggle after a delay of 10 μs? (Make the bits = 1s as 0s and 0s as 1s. Delay 10 μs. Again make 1s as 0s and 0s as 1s.)

Refer Example 4.44. Assume that XTAL oscillation frequency = 12 MHz. We introduce the delay of 10 μs using 8 NOPs. Then repeat XOR operation with P2 after the NOPs. Instructions will be as follows:

(i) *XRL 0A0H, #FFH* (XRL with all bits = 1s) (equivalent to XRL P2, #11111111b as *direct* address of P2 is A0H) (ii) to NOP; NOP; NOP; NOP; NOP; NOP; NOP; NOP; (x) *XRL P2, #FFH*.

Eight NOPs for 10 μs because of one instruction cycle time each spent in NOP instructions and XRL P2 takes 2 cycles, there is a 10 instruction cycle time which is spent, thus there is delay of total next address 10 μs.

Table 4.10 Long, absolute and short jump instructions in 8051

Instruction	Action	Addressing	Length in Bytes	Cycles
LJMP addr16	Jump to the next address given by 2 bytes in the instruction (lower address byte first)[a]	Direct 16-bit address	3	2
AJMP addr11	Jump to the next address given by 3 higher bits in the instruction first byte and 8 lower bits in the second byteb (Opcode lower 5 bits are 00001 at the first byte of the instruction)	Direct 11-bit address	2	2
SJMP rel	Jump in the range between −128 and +127 from the address of the next instruction, which would have executed in case of no jump[c]	Direct 8-bit address	2	2
JMP @A + DPTR	Jump in the next address given by an addition of 8-bits of A with 16 bits of DPTR[d]	Indirect 16-bit relative address	1	2

Example 4.47

Jump to a program memory address after 8 kB addresses (2000H addresses) from the location of the next instruction, which is 1000H.

The jump is above 2 kB code space (Table 4.10). We can, therefore, use only the jump long. Now, 1000H + 2000H = 3000H. Therefore, the instruction is as follows: *LJMP 3000H*.

Example 4.49

Jump to a program memory location after 16 locations backwards relative to the DPTR contents. Jump is relative and backward but using DPTR (Table 4.10). We can, therefore, use the JMP @A + DPTR Now −16 decimal = F0H. Therefore, the instructions are as follows:

(i) MOV A, #0F0H

(ii) JMP @A + DPTR

Instruction	Action	Addressing		Length in Bytes	Cycles
XRL direct, #data	XOR immediate byte into the byte at the direct address[b,d] direct address[c]	Direct		3	2
INC A, R,	Increment the byte at the direct address[d]	Indirect	None	1	1
INC DPTR	Increment DPTR	Register	None	1	2
DEC A	Decrement A	Register	None	1	1
DEC R_n	Decrement R[a]_n	Register	None	1	1
DEC direct	Decrement the byte at the direct address[c]	Direct	None	2	1
DEC A, R,	Decrement the byte at the ad-dress pointed by R,[d]	Indirect	None	1	1
MUL AB	Multiply A and B [MSB in B, LSB in A][f]	Register	OV[g]	1	4

Table 4.11   Conditional short relative-jump instructions in 8051

Instruction	Action	Addressing	Length in Bytes	Cycles
JNZ *rel*	Jump to a relative address if A is not zero	Relative (off-set) address	2	2
JZ *rel*	Jump to a relative address if A=0	Relative (off-set) address		
JNC *rel*	Jump to a relative address if C is not 1 (on no carry)	Relative (off-set) address	2	2
JC *rel*	Jump to a relative address if C = 1 (on carry)	Relative (off-set) address	2	2
JB *bit, rel*	Jump to a relative address if addressed bit is 1 (bit set)	Relative (off-set) address	3	2
JNB *bit, rel*	Jump to a relative address if addressed bit is 0 (bit not set)	Relative (off-set) address	3	2
JBC *bit, rel*	Jump to a relative address if addressed bit 1 (bit set) and reset carry (make C = 0) after the jump	Relative (off-set) address	3	2

Table 4.12   Instruction for decrement and then jump in program loops in 8051

Instruction[e]	Action	Addressing	Length in Bytes	Cycles
DJNZ R_n, Rel	Decrement R_n[a] and Jump if R_n is still not zero[b]	Relative (offset) address	2	2
DJNZ *direct, Rel*	Decrement byte at the direct and jump if the byte is still not zero[c]	Relative (offset) address	3	2

Table 4.13 Compare and then conditional jump after comparison in 8051

Instruction	Action	Addressing	Flag Effected[a]	Length in Bytes	Cycles
CJNE A #data, rel	Compare A and immediate data and jump if both are not equal	Relative (offset) address	C	3	2
CJNE R_n, #data, rel	Compare R_n[b], and immediate data and jump if both are not equal	Relative (offset) address	C	3	2
CJNE A, direct, rel	Compare the bytes at A and direct[c] and jump if both are not equal	Relative (offset) address	C	3	2
CJNE @R_i, #data, rel	Compare the byte[b] from the address pointed by R_i[d] and immediate data and jump if both are not equal	Relative (offset) address	C	3	2

Subroutine CALL And RETURN Instructions

Subroutines are handled by CALL and RET instructions

There are two types of CALL instructions

LCALL address(16 bit)

This is long call instruction which unconditionally calls the subroutine located at the indicated 16 bit address. This is a 3 byte instruction. The LCALL instruction works as follows.

During execution of LCALL, [PC] = [PC]+3; (if address where LCALL resides is say, 0x3254; during execution of this instruction [PC] = 3254h + 3h = 3257h

[SP]=[SP]+1; (if SP contains default value 07, then SP increments and [SP]=08

[[SP]] = [PC7-0]; (lower byte of PC content ie., 57 will be stored in memory location 08.

[SP]=[SP]+1; (SP increments again and [SP]=09)

[[SP]] = [PC15-8]; (higher byte of PC content ie., 32 will be stored in memory location 09.

With these the address (0x3254) which was in PC is stored in stack.

[PC]= address (16 bit); the new address of subroutine is loaded to PC. No flags are affected.

ACALL address(11 bit)

This is absolute call instruction which unconditionally calls the subroutine located at the indicated 11 bit address. This is a 2 byte instruction. The SCALL instruction works as follows.

During execution of SCALL, [PC] = [PC]+2; (if address where LCALL resides is say, 0x8549; during execution of this instruction [PC] = 8549h + 2h = 854Bh

[SP]=[SP]+1; (if SP contains default value 07, then SP increments and [SP]=08

[[SP]] = [PC7-0]; (lower byte of PC content ie., 4B will be stored in memory location 08.

[SP]=[SP]+1; (SP increments again and [SP]=09)

[[SP]] = [PC15-8]; (higher byte of PC content ie., 85 will be stored in memory location 09.

With these the address (0x854B) which was in PC is stored in stack.

[PC10-0]= address (11 bit); the new address of subroutine is loaded to PC. No flags are affected.

RET instruction

RET instruction pops top two contents from the stack and load it to PC.

[PC15-8] = [[SP]] ;content of current top of the stack will be moved to higher byte of PC.

[SP]=[SP]-1; (SP decrements)

[PC7-0] = [[SP]] ;content of bottom of the stack will be moved to lower byte of PC.

[SP]=[SP]-1; (SP decrements again)

POP the current stack top to the PC.

POP the current stack top to PSW.

Interrupt flow control instructions (RETI Instruction) ISR will always ends with RETI instruction. The execution of RETI instruction results in the following.

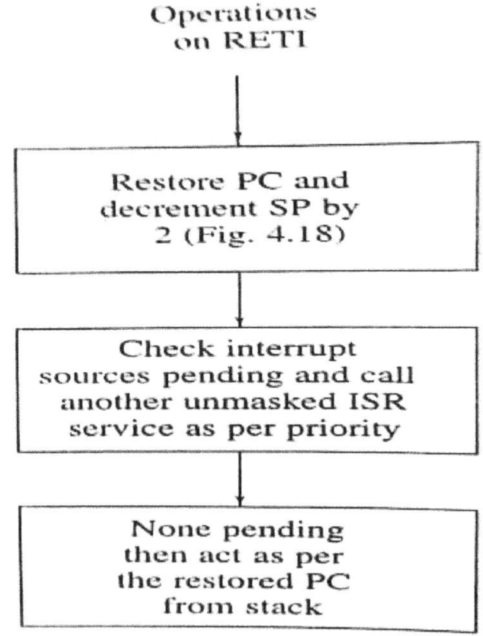

Figure 4.19   Steps on return instruction at the end of an ISR

Write a program to add the values of locations 50H and 51H and store the result in locations in 52h and 53H.

ORG 0000H ; Set program counter 0000H

MOV A,50H ; Load the contents of Memory location 50H into A ADD ADD A,51H ; Add the contents of memory 51H with CONTENTS A MOV 52H,A ; Save the LS byte of the result in 52H

MOV A, #00 ; Load 00H into A

ADDC A, #00 ; Add the immediate data and carry to A

MOV 53H,A ; Save the MS byte of the result in location 53h END

Write a program to store data FFH into RAM memory locations 50H to 58H using direct addressing mode

ORG 0000H ; Set program counter 0000H

MOV A, #0FFH ; Load FFH into A

MOV 50H, A ; Store contents of A in location 50H

MOV 51H, A ; Store contents of A in location 5IH

MOV 52H, A ; Store contents of A in location 52H

MOV 53H, A ; Store contents of A in location 53H

MOV 54H, A ; Store contents of A in location 54H

MOV 55H, A ; Store contents of A in location 55H

MOV 56H, A ; Store contents of A in location 56H

MOV 57H, A ; Store contents of A in location 57H

MOV 58H, A ; Store contents of A in location 58H

END

Write a program to subtract a 16 bit number stored at locations 51H-52H from 55H-56H and store the result in locations 40H and 41H. Assume that the least significant byte of data or the result is stored in low address. If the result is positive, then store 00H, else store 01H in 42H.

ORG 0000H ; Set program counter 0000H

MOV A, 55H ; Load the contents of memory location 55 into A CLR C ; Clear the borrow flag

SUBB A,51H ; Sub the contents of memory 51H from contents of A MOV 40H, A ; Save the LSByte of the result in location 40H

MOV A, 56H ; Load the contents of memory location 56H into A

SUBB A, 52H ; Subtract the content of memory 52H from the content A MOV 41H, ; Save the MSbyte of the result in location 415.

MOV A, #00 ; Load 005 into A

ADDC A, #00 ; Add the immediate data and the carry flag to A MOV 42H, A ; If result is positive, store00H, else store 0lH in 42H END

Write a program to add two 16 bit numbers stored at locations 51H-52H and 55H-56H and store the result in locations 40H, 41H and 42H. Assume that the least significant byte of data and the result is stored in low address and the most significant byte of data or the result is stored in high address.

ORG 0000H ; Set program counter 0000H

MOV A,51H ; Load the contents of memory location 51H into A ADD A,55H ; Add the contents of 55H with contents of A

MOV 40H,A ; Save the LS byte of the result in location 40H MOV A,52H ; Load the contents of 52H into A

ADDC A,56H ; Add the contents of 56H and CY flag with A MOV 41H,A ; Save the second byte of the result in 41H MOV A,#00 ; Load 00H into A

ADDC A,#00 ; Add the immediate data 00H and CY to A MOV 42H,A ; Save the MS byte of the result in location 42H END

Write a program to store data FFH into RAM memory locations 50H to 58H using indirect addressing mode.

ORG 0000H ; Set program counter 0000H

MOV A, #0FFH ; Load FFH into A

MOV RO, #50H ; Load pointer, R0-50H

MOV R5, #08H ; Load counter, R5-08H

Start:MOV @RO, A ; Copy contents of A to RAM pointed by R0 INC RO ; Increment pointer

DJNZ R5, start ; Repeat until R5 is zero END

Write a program to add two Binary Coded Decimal (BCD) numbers stored at locations 60H and 61H and store the result in BCD at memory locations 52H and 53H. Assume that the least significant byte of the result is stored in low address.

ORG 0000H ; Set program counter 00004

MOV A,60H ; Load the contents of memory location 6.0.H into A

ADD A,61H ; Add the contents of memory location 61H with contents of A DA A ; Decimal adjustment of the sum in A

MOV 52H, A ; Save the least significant byte of the result in location 52H MOV A,#00 ; Load 00H into .A

ADDC A,#00H ; Add the immediate data and the contents of carry flag to A MOV 53H,A ; Save the most significant byte of the result in location 53:, END

Write a program to clear 10 RAM locations starting at RAM address 1000H.

ORG 0000H ;Set program counter 0000H MOV DPTR, #1000H ;Copy address 1000H to DPTR CLR A ;Clear *A*

MOV R6, #0AH ;Load 0AH to R6

again: MOVX @DPTR,A ;Clear RAM location pointed by DPTR

INC DPTR ;Increment DPTR

DJNZ R6, again ;Loop until counter R6=0 END

Write a program to compute 1 + 2 + 3 + N (say N=15) and save the sum at70H

ORG 0000H ; Set program counter 0000H N EQU 15

MOV R0,#00 ; Clear R0

CLR A ; Clear A

again: INC R0 ; Increment R0

ADD A, R0 ; Add the contents of R0 with A CJNE R0,#N,again ; Loop until counter, R0, N

MOV 70H,A ; Save the result in location 70H END

Write a program to multiply two 8 bit numbers stored at locations 70H and 71H and store the result at memory locations 52H and 53H. Assume that the least significant byte of the result is stored in low address.

ORG 0000H ; Set program counter 00 OH

MOV A, 70H ; Load the contents of memory location 70h into A MOV B, 71H ; Load the contents of memory location 71H into B MUL AB ; Perform multiplication

MOV 52H,A ; Save the least significant byte of the result in location 52H MOV 53H,B ; Save the most significant byte of the result in location 53

END

Ten 8 bit numbers are stored in internal data memory from location 5oH. Write a program to increment the data.

Assume that ten 8 bit numbers are stored in internal data memory from location 50H, hence R0 or R1 must be used as a pointer.

The program is as follows. ORG 0000H

MOV R0,#50H MOV R3,#0AH

Loopl: INC @R0 INC RO

DJNZ R3, loopl END END

Write a program to find the average of five 8 bit numbers. Store the result in H. (Assume that after adding five 8 bit numbers, the result is 8 bit only).

ORG 0000H MOV 40H,#05H MOV 41H,#55H MOV 42H,#06H MOV 43H,#1AH MOV 44H,#09H MOV R0,#40H MOV R5,#05H MOV B,R5

CLR A

Loop: ADD A,@RO

INC RO

DJNZ R5,Loop DIV AB

MOV 55H,A END

Write a program to find the cube of an 8 bit number program is as follows

ORG 0000H MOV R1,#N MOV A,R1 MOV B,R1

MUL AB //SQUARE IS COMPUTED MOV R2, B

MOV B, R1 MUL AB MOV 50,A MOV 51,B MOV A,R2 MOV B, R1 MUL AB ADD A, 51H MOV 51H, A MOV 52H, B

MOV A, # 00H ADDC A, 52H

MOV 52H, A //CUBE IS STORED IN 52H,51H,50H END

Write a program to exchange the lower nibble of data present in external memory 6000H and 6001H

ORG 0000H ; Set program counter 00h MOV DPTR, #6000H ; Copy address 6000H to DPTR

MOVX A, @DPTR ; Copy contents of 60008 to A MOV R0, #45H ; Load pointer, R0=45H

MOV @RO, A ; Copy cont of A to RAM pointed by 80

INC DPL ; Increment pointer

MOVX A, @DPTR ; Copy contents of 60018 to A

XCHD A, @R0 ; Exchange lower nibble of A with RAM pointed by RO MOVX @DPTR, A ; Copy contents of A to 60018

DEC DPL ; Decrement pointer

MOV A, @R0 ; Copy cont of RAM pointed by R0 to A MOVX @DPTR, A ; Copy cont of A to RAM pointed by DPTR END

Write a program to count the number of 1's and o's of 8 bit data stored in location 6000H.

ORG 0000H

; Set program counter 0000H

MOV DPTR, #6000h

; Copy address 6000H to DPTR

MOVX A, @DPTR

; Copy number to A

MOV R0,#08

; Copy 08 in RO

MOV R2,#00

; Copy 00 in R2

MOV R3,#00

; Copy 00 in R3

CLR C

; Clear carry flag

BACK:

RLC A

; Rotate A through carry flag

JC NEXT ; If CF = 1, branch to next

INC R2 ; If CF = 0, increment R2 AJMP NEXT2

NEXT: INC R3 ; If CF = 1, increment R3 NEXT2: DJNZ RO,BACK ; Repeat until RO is zero END

Write a program to shift a 24 bit number stored at 57H-55H to the left logically four places. Assume that the least significant byte of data is stored in lower address.

ORG 0000H ; Set program counter 0000h

MOV R1,#04 ; Set up loop count to 4

again: MOV A,55H ; Place the least significant byte of data in A CLR C ; Clear tne carry flag

RLC A ; Rotate contents of A (55h) left through carry MOV 55H,A

MOV A,56H

RLC A ; Rotate contents of A (56H) left through carry MOV 56H,A

MOV A,57H

RLC A ; Rotate contents of A (57H) left through carry MOV 57H,A

DJNZ R1,again ; Repeat until R1 is zero END

Two 8 bit numbers are stored in location 1000h and 1001h of external data memory. Write a program to find the GCD of the numbers and store the result in 2000h.

ALGORITHM

Step 1 :Initialize external data memory with data and DPTR with address Step 2 :Load A and TEMP with the operands

Step 3 :Are the two operands equal? If yes, go to step 9 Step 4 :Is (A) greater than (TEMP) ? If yes, go to step 6

Step 5 :Exchange (A) with (TEMP) such that A contains the bigger number Step 6 :Perform division operation (contents of A with contents of TEMP) Step 7 :If the remainder is zero, go to step 9

Step 8 :Move the remainder into A and go to step 4

Step 9 :Save the contents 'of TEMP in memory and terminate the program

ORG 0000H ; Set program counter 0000H TEMP EQU 70H

TEMPI EQU 71H

MOV DPTR, #1000H ; Copy address 100011 to DPTR MOVX A, @DPTR ; Copy First number to A

MOV TEMP, A ; Copy First number to temp INC DPTR MOVX A, @DPTR ; Copy Second number to A

LOOPS: CJNE A, TEMP, LOOP1 ; (A) /= (TEMP) branch to LOOP1 AJMP LOOP2 ; (A) = (TEMP) branch to L00P2

LOOP1: JNC LOOP3 ; (A) > (TEMP) branch to LOOP3 NOV TEMPI, A ; (A) < (TEMP) exchange (A) with (TEMP)
MOV A, TEMP

MOV TEMP, TEMPI LOOP3: MOV B, TEMP

DIV AB ; Divide (A) by (TEMP) MOV A, B ; Move remainder to A

CJNE A,#00, LOOPS ; (A)/=00 branch to LOOPS LOOP2: MOV A, TEMP

MOV DPTR, #2000H

MOVX @DPTR, A ; Store the result in 2000H

END

<u>Peripheral chips for Timing Control (8254/8253)</u>

Q.What is 8254?

Q.Draw the internal architecture of 8254? Q.Draw the pin configuration of 8254?

Q.Describe different modes of 8254?

Intel 8253 - Programmable Interval Timer

8253 facilitates the generation of accurate time delays.When 8253 is used as a timing and delay generation peripheral , the microprocessor becomes free from the tasks related to the counting process and can execute the programs in memory, while the timer device may perform the counting tasks.this minimizes the software overhead on the microprocessor

The Intel 8253 and 8254 are Programmable Interval Timers (PTIs) designed for microprocessors to perform timing and counting functions using three 16-bit registers. Each counter has 2 input pins, i.e. Clock & Gate, and 1 pin for "OUT" output. To operate a counter, a 16-bit count is loaded in its register. On command, it begins to decrement the count until it reaches 0, then it generates a pulse that can be used to interrupt the CPU.

Difference between 8253 and 8254

The following table differentiates the features of 8253 and 8254 –

8253	8254
Its operating frequency is 0 - 2.6 MHz	Its operating frequency is 0 - 10 MHz
It uses N-MOS technology	It uses H-MOS technology
Read-Back command is not available	Read-Back command is available
Reads and writes of the same counter cannot be interleaved.	Reads and writes of the same counter can be interleaved.

Features of 8253 / 54

The most prominent features of 8253/54 are as follows –

- It has three independent 16-bit down counters.
- It can handle inputs from DC to 10 MHz.
- These three counters can be programmed for either binary or BCD count.
- It is compatible with almost all microprocessors.
- 8254 has a powerful command called READ BACK command, which allows the user to check the count value, the programmed mode, the current mode, and the current status of the counter.

-

8254 Architecture

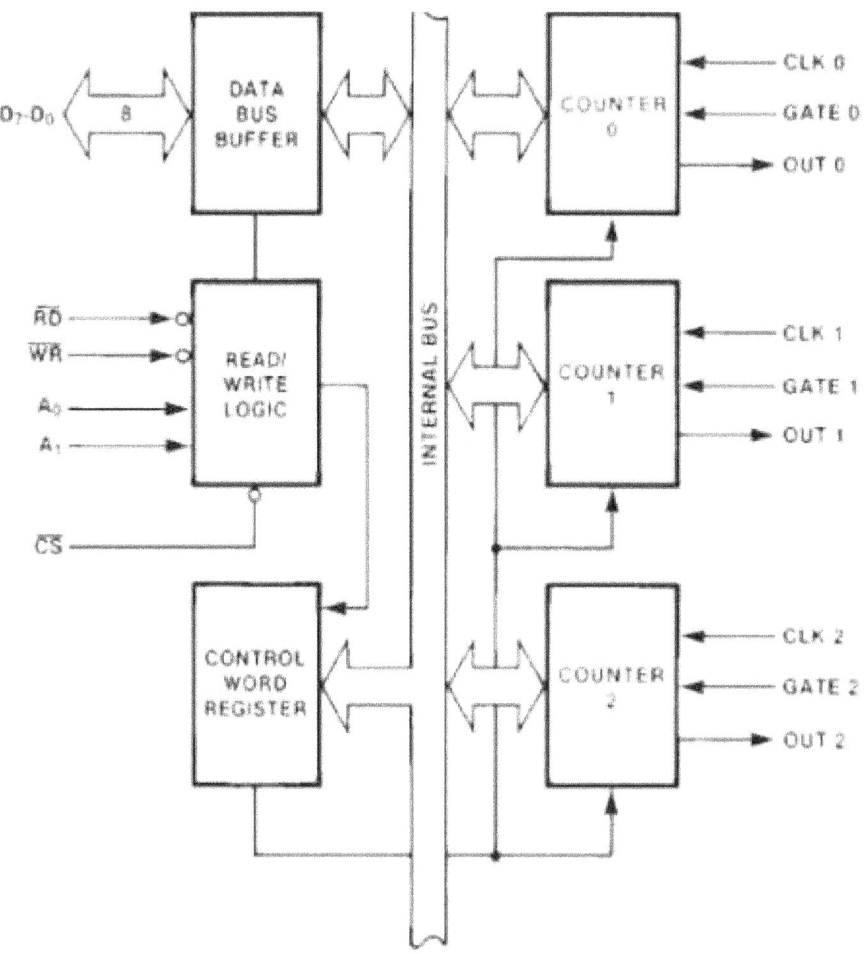

In the above figure, there are three counters, a data bus buffer, Read/Write control logic, and a control register. Each counter has two input signals - CLOCK & GATE, and one output signal - OUT.

Counters

8253 has three independent 16-bit down counters. Each counter consists of a single, 16 bit-down counter, which can be operated in either binary or BCD. Its input and output is configured by the selection of modes stored in the control word register. The programmer can read the contents of any of the three counters without disturbing the actual count in process.

ie the speciality of 8253 counter is that they can be easily read online without disturbing the clock input to the counter. This facility is called as **"On the fly" reading of counters**, and is invoked using a mode control word.

Data Bus Buffer

It is a tri-state, bi-directional, 8-bit buffer, which is used to interface the 8253/54 to the system data bus. It has three basic functions –

Programming the modes of 8253/54.

Loading the count registers.

Reading the count values.

Read/Write Logic

It includes 5 signals, i.e. RD, WR, CS, and the address lines A0 & A1. In the peripheral I/O mode, the RD and WR signals are connected to IOR and IOW, respectively. In the memorymapped I/O mode, these are connected to MEMR and MEMW.

Address lines A0 & A1 of the CPU are connected to lines A0 and A1 of the 8253/54, and CS is tied to a decoded address. The control word register and counters are selected according to the signals on lines A0 & A1.Table below shows this:-

A_1	A_0	RD	WR	CS	Result
0	0	1	0	0	Write Counter 0
0	1	1	0	0	Write Counter 1
1	0	1	0	0	Write Counter 2
1	1	1	0	0	Write Control Word
0	0	0	1	0	Read Counter 0
0	1	0	1	0	Read Counter 1
1	0	0	1	0	Read Counter 2
1	1	0	1	0	No operation
X	X	1	1	0	No operation
X	X	X	X	1	No operation

Control Word Register

•

This register is selected when A0, A1 are at logic 1. It then accepts the information from the data bus buffer and stores it in a register. The information stored in this register ie the control word ,controls the operation MODE of each counter, selection of Hexadecimal or BCD counting , either a read or write operation and the loading of each count register. The control word register can only be written to into, but no read operation is possible. The control word format is shown below:

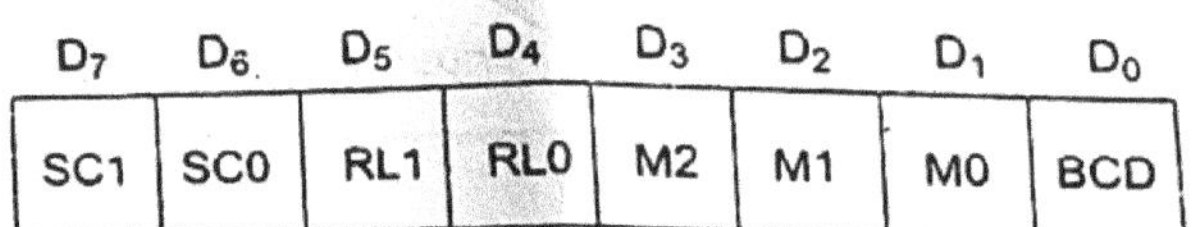

SC₁	SC₀	OPERATION
0	0	Select Counter 0
0	1	Select Counter 1
1	0	Select Counter 2
1	1	Illegal

SC-Select Counter Bit Definitions

RL₁	RL₀	OPERATION
0	0	Latch Counter for 'ON THE FLY' reading
0	1	Read/Load Least Significant Byte only
1	0	Read/Load MSB only
1	1	Read/Load LSB first then MSB

RL-Read/Load Bit Definitions

M₂	M₁	M₀	Selected Mode
0	0	0	Mode 0
0	0	1	Mode 1
x	1	0	Mode 2
x	1	1	Mode 3
1	0	0	Mode 4
1	0	1	Mode 5

M₂M₁M₀ Mode Select Bit Definitions

BCD	Operation
0	Hexadecimal Count
1	BCD Count

HEX/BCD Bit Definition

Fig. 6.2 *Control Word Format and Bit Definitions*

Counter 0, Counter 1, Counter 2

These three functional blocks are identical in operation. Each counter consists of a single

16 bit, pre-settable DOWN counter. The counter can operate in either binary or BCD and its input, gate and output are configured by the selection of modes stored in the control word register. The counters are totally independent. The counter can be read by a simple READ operation for event count applications.

<u>Modes of operations of 8253</u>

While using 8253/54 we must write the control word to initialize the counter to be used.

For every counter we use, the control word must be written and select the counter and set it up.8253/54 can operate in six different modes. The modes of operation are explained below.

Mode 0 (Interrupt on Terminal Count)

The output of the counter will be initially low after the mode set operation. After the count is loaded into the selected counter register the output will remain low and the counter will count. When terminal count is reached, the output will go high and remain high until the selected count register is reloaded with the mode or a new count is loaded.

Mode 1 (Programmable one shot)

In this mode, the out signal is initially high. When the GATE is triggered, the OUT goes low, and when count reaches 0, the OUT goes high again. Thus a one shot signal is generated due to the signal on the GATE.

Mode 2 (Rate Generator)

It is a divide by N counter.

In this mode If,N is the clock period at a given interval, count value is loaded as N and then after N pulses, the output becomes low only for one clock cycle.

The Count N is reloaded and again the output becomes high and remains so for N clock cycles

Mode 3 (Square-wave Generator)

Operation somewhat similar to mode 2.

When the count loaded is even,then for half of the count,the output remains high, and for the remaining half it remains low.

When the count loaded is odd, the first clock pulse decrements it by one resulting in an even count value.then the output remains high for half of the new count and goes low for the remaining half

Mode 4 (Software Triggered Strobe)

After the mode is set, the output goes high.

When a count is loaded, counting down starts.

On terminal count, the output goes low for one clock cycle and then it again goes high.

This low pulse can be used as a strobe , while interfacing the microprocessor with other peripherals.

The count must be reloaded for more strobe signals.

Mode 5 (Hardware - Triggered Strobe)

This mode is similar to mode 4, except the strobe is hardware triggered with a signal on the GATE signal.

Read-Back Command

The read-back command in the 8254 allows the user to read the count and the status of

the counters (This command is not available in 8253). When the read-back command is selected in the control word (SC1 SC0 - 11) each of the counters specified is latched and then the count and/ or the status may be read for each counter latched.

The command is written in the control register and the count of the specified counter(s) can be latched if COUNT (bit D5) is 0. A counter or a combination of counters is specified by making the respective CNT bits (D1, D2 and D3) high. The read-back command format is shown below.

D_7	D_6	D_5	D_4	D_3	D_2	D_1	D_0
1	1	$\overline{\text{COUNT}}$	$\overline{\text{STATUS}}$	CNT2	CNT1	CNT0	0

D0 = 0 (Reserved for future expansion)

CNT0, CNT1, CNT2 are counter select bits.

The STATUS of the counters can be read if D4 bit (STATUS) of Read-back command is 0.

The Read-back command eliminates the need of writing separate counter latch commands for different counters.

www.ingramcontent.com/pod-product-compliance
Lightning Source LLC
Chambersburg PA
CBHW040206110726
48005CB00019B/2915